Praise for *How Boards Work*

"*How Boards Work* is exactly what any prospective—or sitting—board member needs to understand the true rigors and realities of board life. Having seen it all, Dambisa Moyo offers valuable guidance on how boards can best focus their time and energy while grappling with social, governance, and environmental issues."

—ARIANNA HUFFINGTON,
founder and CEO, Thrive Global,
and former Uber board member

"*How Boards Work* offers a thorough and nuanced take on the ever-evolving role of corporate boards today. Dambisa Moyo provides a candid assessment of the challenges and opportunities that directors face and wisely warns of the dangers of stasis. The book is not only a must-read for the most tenured and experienced board members, but it also provides critical context to those who one day hope to have a seat at the table. CEOs and corporate leaders everywhere would also be wise to pick up this book."

—MELLODY HOBSON,
co-CEO, Ariel Investments; chair of the board of
directors, Starbucks; board member, JP Morgan;
former board chair, Dreamworks;
and former board member, Estee Lauder

"This highly engaging book will rightly attract those interested not just in good corporate governance but also the well-functioning of market-based economies. Drawing on her direct involvements on several boards of companies facing difficult decisions, as well as her global economic expertise, Dr. Moyo has written an indispensable guide to how boards function, malfunction, and, most importantly, should operate better. In not shying away from arguing for more assertive boards to overcome costly corporate failures and malaise, she sets out an action-oriented agenda for improving governance—to deal better with long-standing challenges, including better globalization and management of our environment, and to meet mounting new ones in a post-pandemic world. Simply put, this is a must-read for those who realize that, anchored by a more diverse mindset and modernized governance structures, companies can and must play a more important role in helping society overcome too many years of low, unequal, and non-sustainable growth, as well as proliferating mistrust and spreading marginalization."

—MOHAMED A. EL-ERIAN,
president of Queens' College, Cambridge University;
board member, Under Armour; and author of
The Only Game in Town and *When Markets Collide*

"Boards have incredible power to impact how companies and their stakeholders meet the challenges of the modern age. But boards are complex and living organisms that require more than just getting smart people in a room. Dr. Moyo's book, informed by real-world experience in negotiating complex situations, should be a must-read for any board that wants to excel and have an impact today."

—DAN LOEB,
founder and CEO, Thirdpoint,
and former Sotheby's board member

HOW
BOARDS
WORK

HOW BOARDS WORK

And How They Can
Work Better in a Chaotic World

DAMBISA MOYO

BASIC BOOKS

New York

Basic Books
Hachette Book Group
1290 Avenue of the Americas, New York, NY 10104
www.basicbooks.com

Printed in the United States of America

First Edition: May 2021

Published by Basic Books, an imprint of Perseus Books, LLC, a subsidiary of Hachette Book Group, Inc. The Basic Books name and logo is a trademark of the Hachette Book Group.

The Hachette Speakers Bureau provides a wide range of authors for speaking events. To find out more, go to www.hachettespeakersbureau.com or call (866) 376-6591.

The publisher is not responsible for websites (or their content) that are not owned by the publisher.

Print book interior design by Jeff Williams.

Library of Congress Cataloging-in-Publication Data

Names: Moyo, Dambisa, author.
Title: How boards work: and how they can work better in a chaotic world / Dambisa Moyo.
Description: First edition. | New York: Basic Books, 2021. | Includes bibliographical references and index.
Identifiers: LCCN 2020057073 | ISBN 9781541619425 (hardcover) | ISBN 9781541619418 (ebook)
Subjects: LCSH: Boards of directors. | Directors of corporations. | Corporate governance.
Classification: LCC HD2745 .M69 2021 | DDC 658.4/22—dc23
LC record available at https://lccn.loc.gov/2020057073

ISBNs: 978-1-5416-1942-5 (hardcover), 978-1-5416-1941-8 (e-book)

LSC-W

Printing 1, 2021

To current management and employees,
so they know what their boards do

To investors, so they appreciate boards' limits
and possibilities

To policymakers and regulators, so they are
more aware of the trade-offs that boards face

To current board members, to help guide
their reform agenda

To future board members, to help them
grasp the board role

To the general public, so they better understand
why successful boards and well-governed corporations
are critical for society at large

Contents

Preface

I TOOK A SEAT ON MY FIRST LARGE CORPORATE BOARD OVER A DECADE AGO. In the years since, I have had the privilege of being intimately involved in corporate decision-making in an era of fascinating transformations around the world. From the early days of my professional career, I have been intrigued by the perspective provided by a board's high corporate perch and its decision-making power.

As it turned out, corporate boards deal with issues that are ideally suited to my own academic and professional experience, including business, economics, finance, and geopolitics. The companies I have served span a wide range of sectors: banking, consumer goods, technology, oil and gas, media, and mining. Each company is worth multiple billions of dollars, most employ a workforce numbering in the tens of thousands, and many serve hundreds of thousands of customers around the globe. Every one of these companies relies on a dozen or so people, sitting at a boardroom table, to oversee a vast and varied enterprise.

In my time serving on corporate boards, I have witnessed and helped respond to some of the most extreme and testing situations in the corporate world, including

» the death of a chairman of the board while he was in office;

» multiple CEO successions, and hiring and firing of chief executives;

» buying and selling companies, including the sale of a global corporation for $100 billion, the largest global mergers and acquisitions transaction in 2016;

» enormous regulatory fines stemming from a crack-down on corporate behavior;

» activist shareholders seeking to disrupt the company strategy;

» the unique challenges of having an insider—a large, dominant, usually family member—shareholder on the board;

» expropriation of company assets by host governments; and

» massive corporate restructuring prompted by a share-price collapse.

In short, I have been through virtually everything, save a corporate bankruptcy. Yet the boardroom is not all fire and brimstone. Many companies—and indeed most of the companies I have been involved with—have maneuvered through an unstable decade without significant incident. They have increased their stock-market value, invested in innovation and their communities, and rewarded their shareholders with financial returns, despite difficult times. All have had to navigate an array of complicated global events and trends—from the 2008 financial crisis, to Brexit, to changing views around social issues, to the 2020 pandemic, as well as the specific challenges that individual companies face. Through it all, I have seen the important role that boards play in guiding corporations. I have seen what works and what does not. I have seen why boards must change to better suit the times, and specifically why they must become more assertive. For me, more than a decade of serving on corporate boards has been an opportunity to learn about the vagaries of global business, as well as to contribute to the running of many great corporations.

It is common knowledge that any corporation's survival depends on the day-to-day leadership of its senior executives. Further from the spotlight, but just as essential, the board of directors sits at the helm of a corporation, making decisions that can lead to its success—or failure.

An Unconventional Candidate

I was thirty-nine years old when I joined the board of a large, publicly traded corporation for the first time. I was a young face at the table of SABMiller's board, but it was not just my age that set me apart—it was also my race and gender. As a young, Black woman (from Africa to boot), my ascent into the corporate boardroom was unconventional in many respects. Among these was the fact that I did not come through the C-suite— the traditional route and selection test for candidates to a board position.

For as long as I can remember, I have been fascinated by how the disparate pieces of a jigsaw puzzle come together to form a clear, coherent picture. In much the same way, what appeals to me about being on a board is helping a company's different business units—each with their own goals and aspirations—pull together toward a unified vision of the corporation. When contributing to board discussions, I draw on my academic and business experience, which has tended to weave together data and trends—economic, political, and social—to form a composite view of how the world economy is evolving and its effect on individual nations and global corporations.

I had been interested in serving on a corporate board for many years before I landed my first board seat. I was eager to contribute my perspective to important discussions about corporate strategy, succession, and culture—and I was especially keen to help shape the future of business. Yet as I began to pursue this ambition, meeting with numerous search firms and headhunters, it became clear that I was just one face in the crowd of people seeking board seats—many of whom had a great deal more experience running businesses.

What finally set me apart was my writing. In 2009, I published a book on the failure of international development policy that became a best seller, and I subsequently published several books that captured many of the defining dynamics of the world emerging from the 2008 financial crisis—from skepticism about market capitalism, to the disruption of geopolitics, to the rise of China and other emerging markets. In particular, my work has analyzed a number of long-term threats to the world economy: technology and the risk of a jobless underclass, demographic shifts in the quantity and quality of the workforce, worsening income inequality, natural resource scarcity and climate change concerns, unsustainable debts, and marked declines in global productivity. Ultimately, my work helps me form judgments on how best to deploy a corporation's labor force and allocate its capital.

Writing these books more clearly defined for me, as well as for those recruiting, what value I could bring to the boardroom. Given my background and expertise, many of the boards I initially served on had significant emerging-markets footprints and international business interests. My books helped me stand out as someone who had real contributions to make in the boardroom, which was especially important because of the perception that boards are only seeking to enhance their diversity by appointing women, minorities, and people with diverse political views or country backgrounds.

This is not a superficial concern. If they are to succeed, companies really do need to cultivate a diversity of ideas. Boards composed predominantly of people with the same kind of background risk engaging in groupthink, as a wealth of evidence has shown. Factors such as race and gender can give valuable insights that provide boards with a more complete and inclusive perspective, but candidates need to bring more than their identity to the table. After all, the worst situation a person can find themselves in is having their ideas discounted because they are viewed as being in the boardroom only because of their race or gender. Ultimately, to warrant a seat, a prospective board member must offer relevant expertise and experience. To reframe this in a crude way, someone interested in gaining a place on a corporate board must ask themselves: Who from the management team would call me for advice, and when and why?

Diversity is just one of the many major issues facing boards today. I conceived this book, and wrote most of it, well before the coronavirus pandemic of 2020. But the first months of the pandemic only reinforced my conclusions about the importance of functional, decisive, and wisely run boards. The coronavirus may have amplified the challenges facing today's global companies, but I believe now more than ever in the positive role these corporations—and their boards—can play in society.

Businesses are reckoning with a period of shocks, tremendous uncertainty, and heightened complexity that is testing whether corporations, and indeed capitalism itself, will survive. The damage caused by the 2020 global pandemic—both in economic terms and in the cost to human health—has intensified a debate about corporate power that was already underway. Today, popular opinion is turning against large corporations, and political, social, and cultural landscapes are shifting at a rapid clip. Boards go about their work acutely aware of the stakes of their decisions. Failure could imperil the health of the global economy and, with it, jobs, prosperity, human progress, and the "American way of life" that not only Americans but people around the world have long pursued. No one organization, government, or individual can provide stability amid the turbulence. But the 2020 global pandemic has revealed that corporations have an important and central role to play in navigating global disruption.

In all times, but especially in times of turmoil, corporate boards have a responsibility as custodians not just of a single organization, but of our economic well-being as a whole. The prosperity of society relies on corporate boards succeeding. If corporations are to succeed, change is imperative. This book lays out an array of reforms proposed to create strong, independent, diverse, technologically savvy, and socially responsible boards. The unique challenges of the twenty-first century demand nothing less. Championing a modernized approach to governance, this book specifies what it will take for boards to successfully oversee the enterprises of the future. The size, scope, and scale of today's global corporations—combined with the powerful impact they have on people's daily lives—underscore the importance of these changes. Boards can and must transform their thinking to meet the moment and rebuild trust in corporations.

This book is an insider's account drawing on over ten years of corporate board experience to reveal the inner workings, tensions, and shortcomings of today's boards. I aim to demystify for current executives and employees exactly what it is their boards do, educate investors about boards' ability to effect meaningful change—both the limits and opportunities—help policymakers and regulators better understand the trade-offs and conflicting priorities that boards face, and guide the next generation of prospective board members. For current board members, my hope is to underscore the complex task of reform that is before them. I also hope that this book can help the general public better understand why successful boards and well-governed corporations are so important for society at large. At a time when corporations and their boards of directors are under greater public scrutiny than ever—not just from politicians and regulators, but from workers, customers, and communities—I hope this book can open up boardroom life to the world beyond the Wall Street analysts, MBAs, and corporate insiders who typically focus on these matters.

This is the book that I would have found invaluable when I took up my first board role. It covers not only the basics—what boards really do, how they are structured, and how strategies are set—but also the truly tough questions: how difficult decisions are made, what the major challenges will be in the coming years, and how boards can adapt to survive in a world of rapid social, economic, political, and technological change.

I came to my first board with a great deal to learn. One of my first lessons was that a board member's responsibility extends beyond approving or interrogating big organizational proposals. More than anything else, the job is about showing good judgment in the face of difficult problems. Exercising that sort of discretion, above all, means being open-minded and accepting that there are no off-the-shelf solutions. Processes, regulations, and legal guardrails help organizations of scale operate effectively, but they can leave gray areas—where the board makes the judgment calls. The situations where the board can make the greatest difference are those that hinge on members' ability to think beyond the strictures of conventional wisdom.

While this book does not address the specific roles and responsibilities of all fiduciary or governing bodies—be they the board of governors of a school, university, or hospital; the board of trustees of a museum; or the board of a nonprofit—this exploration of corporate boards allows for a comparison of governance practices. From board structures to decision-making processes, this book's insights are instructive for those sitting atop a variety of organizations.

The boardroom can be a tough place, fraught with disagreements and difficult questions that need urgent answers. But board members can transcend conflict so long as they are united on the basics: that the challenges corporations face are existential, that fundamental change is inescapable in a rapidly shifting business landscape, and that organizations can only survive by leaving behind business as usual.

—**DM**, May 2021

Introduction

SCARCELY A MONTH GOES BY, IT SEEMS, WITHOUT SOME SORT OF CORPO-rate scandal appearing in the business pages. Problems ranging from inept leadership, to sexual harassment, to operational failures, to outright financial fraud and embezzlement are engulfing large institutions. And there is a credible sense that the frequency of corporate mishaps and malfeasance in the years following the 2008 financial crash has far surpassed that of the previous decade.

This backdrop has galvanized a growing sense that global businesses are self-interested, corrupt, and do not work for much of society. The anti-corporate spirit has inspired employee revolts and environmental activism, and it has even influenced movements such as Black Lives Matter and #MeToo, the latter of which is estimated to have ousted over four hundred high-profile executives within an eighteen-month period.

The last two decades of business history are littered with examples of challenged and even disgraced companies. Boeing, Enron, General Electric, Kmart, PG&E, Theranos, the Weinstein

Company, WeWork, and WorldCom are just a handful of the many corporations left in ill repute, their financial value decimated and the reputations of their leaders indelibly stained. In fact, this phenomenon extends beyond individual companies. Whole industries have been severely damaged, including the US auto industry, banking, and technology in the dot-com crash.

Of course, there are stark differences between the criminal acts that led to the downfall of Enron, Theranos, and World-Com and the managerial ineptitude seen in most other cases. But even so, what many corporate scandals have in common is that they do not rest on the shoulders of management alone. Often, boards also bear a measure of responsibility.

Most large global companies share a common leadership structure. The most senior key executives, often called the C-suite, include the chief executive officer (CEO), chief financial officer (CFO), and chief operating officer (COO). The C-suite is ultimately accountable to roughly a dozen people known as the board of directors. The board is charged with helping to oversee and shepherd the organization toward future success. When companies struggle or fail, workers, investors, and the general public are often left wondering what management and the board might have done differently.

Each round of unflattering headlines about corporations and their leaders prompts a set of reasonable questions: What exactly are these boards doing? Why are employees who commit misdeeds allowed to leave with large compensation packages? And when businesses collapse without notice, with far-reaching consequences for jobs, the economy, and communities, is it not reasonable to assume that the board of directors has abdicated its duties?

There is no shortage of opprobrium leveled at corporations these days. It comes from all sides—from politicians, pundits, employees, investors, customers, and society at large—and some of it is wholly justified. Yet for every company attracting headlines for the wrong reasons, there are numerous others quietly thriving as their boards and management strive to do the right thing.

We take for granted that many companies deliver innumerable goods and services every day with minimal variance. Think about a drug company that can produce a million doses of penicillin without error. We only occasionally hear (let alone celebrate) such corporate success stories. One can only imagine that we would certainly notice a difference if we lived in a world where boards and corporations were more consistently and uniformly effective.

Given all the anti-corporate sentiment, it is worth saying explicitly what once would have been an article of faith: strong and successful corporations are in the best interest of society. Indeed, the centrality of corporations to human progress cannot be overstated.

For one thing, large corporations underpin the economy. According to *Fortune*, in 2019, the five hundred largest US corporations represented two-thirds of the country's GDP: $13.7 trillion in revenues, $1.1 trillion in profits, and $22.6 trillion in market value. They employed nearly thirty million people worldwide. In Europe, stock market value was 78 percent of nominal GDP in December 2017.

By helping to create economic growth, corporations contribute to the betterment of society in many ways. First and foremost, they create jobs, contributing to workers' livelihoods and counteracting poverty. They also provide a tax base that contributes to the fiscal health of governments. In 2018, the US government took in $208 billion in direct corporate income tax. However, even this substantial figure does not take into account the considerable indirect income taxes paid by the employees of those corporations or the sales taxes generated by their goods and services.

Furthermore, corporations drive innovation through their investments in research and development (R&D). The annual *Fast Company* list of the "World's 50 Most Innovative Companies" underscores that corporations are at the cutting edge of transforming how we communicate, travel, cure disease, and combat illiteracy. Corporations also act as partners to governments in administering education, health care, pensions, and infrastructure. They are increasingly serving as agents of change, pushing for reforms and innovation in areas previously thought to be solely the purview of government—from environmental change to diversity and inclusion across the workforce. Finally, corporations make invaluable contributions to human progress, joining with government to respond to global crises like the 2020 pandemic. Leading pharmaceutical companies were at the forefront of the development of a vaccine and treatments against the coronavirus, producers and suppliers mobilized to keep essential goods moving toward society's most vulnerable, and formerly obscure industrial companies took center stage as providers of necessary equipment such as face masks, respirators, and ventilators.

So the fates of corporations and society as a whole are closely linked. Just as corporate success lifts society, corporate failure has the potential to sap its vitality. Given the importance of corporations to our daily lives, GDP, government tax revenues, and technological innovation, it's easy to see why corporate failures place economic and societal stability at risk. The growth of anti-corporate sentiment in recent years has even led some to hope for such an outcome—there are those who would cheer the destruction of the corporate landscape as we know it. Of course, they overlook the devastating consequences of such a scenario: the economy would contract, investment in innovation would plummet, millions of jobs would be lost, pension and health-care benefits would evaporate, and living standards would collapse worldwide.

The 2020 global pandemic and economic shutdown has offered an unnerving idea of what economic carnage might look like in terms of spiking unemployment and plummeting growth prospects, especially in the most affected sectors of travel, tourism, and retail. Recent memory provides plenty of examples of the fallout of individual corporate failure. Kmart's bankruptcy and restructuring in 2002–2003 led to over sixty thousand job losses. The collapse of Lehman Brothers at the start of the financial crisis in 2008 destroyed nearly $700 billion and paralyzed the financial system. That crisis writ large had a devastating effect across the whole economy. A huge number of families defaulted on their mortgages and had their homes repossessed, with disastrous consequences for communities. According to the US Government Accountability Office, the combined cost of the 2008 financial crisis—in terms of lost economic output and wealth lost by US homeowners—was more than $20 trillion.

For all these reasons and more, the world needs strong corporations governed by strong boards. Rather than dismantle corporations—which would cause immeasurable harm to our lives and societies—we should focus our energies on reforming them. This should start with corporate boards.

A New Era of Uncertainty

The very notion of what an effective board looks like has shifted over the years. At a most basic level, board members consider themselves successful if they leave the company more prosperous and functional than they found it. At the very least, they should strive to maintain the company as a thriving concern. If a company must be sold, the board should endeavor to secure a premium value and not sell it for scrap; the board should certainly avoid filing for bankruptcy.

Leaving a good legacy is becoming harder, however, as the corporate board's oversight role becomes ever more challenging and baseline notions about shareholder value and social responsibility shift with the changing times. Twenty-first-century companies are buffeted by unprecedented economic headwinds. Particularly after the onset of the coronavirus pandemic, the global economy is facing a deep and protracted recession, adding to already slowing long-term economic growth trends. Furthermore, de-globalization—in the form of new trade tariffs, capital controls, and increased barriers to immigration—threatens to harm global commerce and limit investment flows and the movement of labor, thereby worsening an already dire economic outlook.

As many nations abandon their strict commitment to the values of liberal democracy and market capitalism, it is becoming increasingly difficult for corporations to operate effectively. This new era of economic and geopolitical uncertainty brings with it a shortage of skills and talent; two-thirds of America's workforce has a high school diploma or less. Global corporations also face a fast-changing competitive landscape that includes a new generation of rivals aggressively harnessing cutting-edge technologies that tap into the hearts and minds of modern consumers. Furthermore, global companies no longer compete solely among themselves but contend with increasingly fierce challenges from strong local and regional companies, especially in the world's largest developing markets.

Though we may instinctively regard the CEO as the leader most responsible for grappling with these challenges, corporate boards exist to help senior management. These new and extremely complex problems are forcing boards and corporate leaders to reexamine the strength of their businesses through a new lens. In fact, the changing times have made boards more indispensable than ever. But unless boards can change with the times, and become more assertive, the companies they guide will struggle to keep up.

To the average person, the board's job might seem unclear or even superfluous. Among the wider public there is a simmering suspicion that the work of a corporate director is not unduly demanding—that boards meet only a handful of times a year to offer high-level words of advice to management, taking on little personal risk in the process. Board members, in other words, are seen as having all upside—prestige, board fees, and shares in the company—and very little downside. After all, in the public arena at least, the buck stops with the CEO. Another school of thought looks with suspicion on the entire enterprise of board governance. These observers believe that a company's board of directors only becomes relevant when the company runs into trouble, and that the very structure belongs to a bygone era.

I wholly disagree. Individual board members take on enormous personal and financial risk by serving at the helm of companies on which they can have a relatively limited impact. For example, board members can be sued for the decisions they make on behalf of the company, and their individual reputations can be lost as a result of a decision that was made in good faith but that led a company toward trouble. This is leaving aside the important work that boards do on a regular basis, quarter to quarter, determining company strategy, selecting the CEO, and guiding the corporate culture. I suspect that many of the misconceptions about boards stem from a lack of understanding about their actual role. Addressing MBA students in top business schools, I have often asked the question "What does a board do?" only to be met with blank stares. Even employees rarely grasp the scope of their corporate board's work. In the eyes of many, it might seem that board members stealthily come and go without leaving any visible sign of their efforts. To understand why boards exist in the first place, it may be helpful to consider the history of how they developed.

A Brief History of Boards

In *The Historical and Political Origins of the Corporate Board of Directors*, Franklin Gevurtz explains that boards first emerged in the seventeenth century, and that many of their features have been the same ever since.

The 1694 charter of the Bank of England introduced the term "director" for members of its first board, which contained twenty-four members. According to Gevurtz, this charter served as a model for how the earliest American corporations would organize their own boards. More than a century later, New York's 1811 Act Relative to Incorporations for Manufacturing Purposes allowed companies to form themselves rather than be incorporated through legislation. The law established what we would recognize today as a modern board structure, giving boards the responsibility to oversee "the stock, property and concerns" of their companies. In terms of board structure and responsibilities, the Bank of England's charter set guidelines on directors' tenure, including the number of terms they could serve. The 1811 New York act specified that board members had to be annually elected by shareholders. Later, the East India Company created possibly the first charter that gave the board the responsibility of hiring and firing the most senior executive of the company (then known as the governor).

"Governance" is a key concept for understanding the difference between a board and a CEO. In his book *Principles*, renowned hedge fund founder Ray Dalio defines governance as an oversight system that removes people and processes when they are not working well. It is a system of checks and balances on power, designed to ensure that the interests of the community always supersede the interests of any individual or faction. Dalio writes, "Because power will rule, power must be put in the hands of capable people in key roles who have the right values, do their jobs well, and will check and balance the power of others." At the highest levels of the corporation, these capable people form the board. The essential difference between a board and a CEO is that a board is fundamentally a structure of governance, while the CEO is a day-to-day leader.

Within boards themselves, there is an important distinction between executive directors and nonexecutive directors (NEDs). Executive directors (including the CEO) are full-time employees of the company, responsible for finance, operations, and the implementation of strategy. NEDs are not employees and are engaged on a contractual basis and paid a flat fee for their services.

Beyond this basic distinction, however, governance structures can vary from country to country. For example, corporate boards in the United States and the United Kingdom are based on what is called a unitary board approach, meaning that the company's executive and nonexecutive directors serve together on a single board. Under this model, NEDs also hold private sessions among themselves where they can express their unfiltered views on how the company is progressing and the performance of the CEO. The lead independent director will then pass on feedback to the CEO.

In Germany and other countries in continental Europe, corporate boards are typically governed in a two-tiered structure, consisting of a supervisory board and an operating board, where the former generally oversees the latter. In Germany, up to 40 percent of the operating board can be composed of the company's employees.

Shareholders of some large American companies—for example, at Walmart, Microsoft, and Google—are advancing proposals to select board members from rank-and-file employees, echoing the German board structure. In a similar vein, a bill sponsored by US senator Elizabeth Warren in 2018 proposed that employees elect as many as 40 percent of board members.

For the most part, corporate boards—wherever they may be—share commonly accepted standards of operation. At a minimum, board members have attendance requirements and are expected to serve on committees responsible for matters such as audits, executive and staff compensation, nominations, and governance. Furthermore, most corporations have some form of articles of association: a governing document that includes guidelines to ensure that the board is neither too small nor too big, and neither too old nor too young.

It is important to emphasize that these conventions are not hard-and-fast rules; rather, they are guidelines and points of ongoing debate. Standards can vary from company to company and they can change over time. The average size of boards and the typical age at which directors retire are two examples. In the past, boards were often larger. It was not unusual for them to comprise fifteen members or more, but today there is a wide consensus that a number closer to twelve is ideal. As the average life expectancy has lengthened, many companies are extending the retirement age for board members from around seventy to seventy-five years old.

Board Basics—Structure and Role

Boards generally have three main committees: nominations and governance, audit, and compensation. These standing committees are a permanent feature within the board structure, and each generally requires three nonexecutive board members to form a quorum. Most boards also have a fourth committee, which oversees other areas such as risk, finance, or corporate social responsibility (CSR), if these topics are not already covered by one of the three main committees.

As its name implies, the nominations and governance committee has two main responsibilities. The nominations side consists of overseeing the process of identifying, vetting, and nominating potential new board members. As part of that process, the nom-gov committee (as it is commonly abbreviated) evaluates the needs of the company and board at particular times and seeks to recruit individuals with requisite skills and experiences.

In some companies, the role of the nom-gov committee extends to overseeing the CEO succession process and broader recruitment into the C-suite. To this end, the chairman of the board will almost invariably sit on this committee. On the governance side, the nom-gov committee serves as the custodian of the board's code of ethics, deciding how the company sets its tone from the top and providing ongoing oversight of the broader company culture.

The audit committee is responsible for ensuring the company's adherence to accounting rules, which includes signing off on the company books and financial records before they are made public. This committee focuses on the effectiveness of the company's controls and makes sure the company is operating in line with the operational, financial, and economic rules and regulations.

As a rule of thumb, the audit committee is backward-looking, whereas a board risk committee tends to be forward-looking, seeking to mitigate the multitude of risks facing the company. In cases where regulators insist that a company perform stress tests to measure its ability to withstand different shocks (as is common for banks and insurance companies), this task tends to fall under the purview of the risk committee. In some cases, companies choose to have a single committee that covers both audit and risk functions.

The compensation committee is tasked with approving the compensation of the corporation's executives as well as managing pay policy across the staff. This committee makes recommendations to the full board, which then decides among allocating profits to shareholders (through dividends or share buybacks), reinvesting in the company, paying down existing debts, and remunerating staff via bonus payments and salaries. Very often, the committee relies on outside counsel to monitor their executive compensation and track if it is in line with peer companies and industry standards.

Today, at a time of widening income inequality in many countries, the board compensation committee is increasingly influenced by public policy surrounding issues such as gender pay equity and gaps between the highest and lowest paid within a company. This has led some companies to explicitly outline fair pay agendas, which will be examined in greater depth in this book.

Corporate social responsibility committees are a relatively new feature of some boards. By and large, the CSR committee mandate is to address environmental and social concerns. As we will see in the next chapter, this can be a challenging and constantly evolving set of responsibilities.

Having served on each type of committee over the previous decade, I can attest that they are critically important to the functioning of the board. Some boards are so dependent on their committees that a great deal of the board's work is done at the committee level. This allows the full board to focus its energies on more substantive decisions and to deal with the unexpected, rather than the routine.

At least on the surface, most boards are structured as described above. A cursory look across many company annual reports reveals numerous similarities in what different corporations say their boards do. These views are echoed by industry associations—such as the National Association of Corporate Directors in the United States or the Institute of Directors in the United Kingdom—that codify the tasks of the board and set out best business practices. It is not uncommon, however, to find that board structures can vary in their details, and that most of today's corporations have developed their own idiosyncratic views as to what the board's role should be and how it should function.

My experience suggests, and I believe most board directors would agree, that today's boards are tasked with three things: shaping the company strategy, selecting leaders (in particular the CEO), and safeguarding the company's culture, ethics, and values. The first three chapters of this book explore each of these tasks in detail, while the final two chapters look at the landscape today's boards are facing and the changes they need to make to flourish in a chaotic world.

We begin, in Chapter 1, with the board's responsibility for long-term planning and the strategic direction of the company. In looking at how boards navigate this responsibility, we get a better sense of how they think and a deeper understanding of the traits that determine their success or failure. Chapter 1 highlights the complexity of this role, as strategic decisions require balancing short-term pressures with longer-term considerations. It looks at boards' choices when allocating capital in the face of considerable regulatory shifts, economic headwinds, and political obstacles, as well as a rapidly changing marketplace where their customers, clients, and employees become more diverse.

Chapter 2 describes the board's work of picking both the CEO and new board members. This chapter examines what the board looks for when selecting the CEO, how it monitors the CEO's performance, how it assesses pay and punishments, and when it might decide to let an underperforming CEO go. The board task of picking the CEO is critical, as it entrusts one individual with the leadership of the whole organization. With regard to turnover in the boardroom itself, Chapter 2 surveys pressures on board structure including term limits, age limits, and the challenge of a combined chair-CEO role. Key board responsibilities include the succession and selection of the board chair, the lead independent director, and the chairs of different committees.

In my decade of sitting on corporate boards, I have seen how the meaning of "culture" has varied from company to company and shifted over time. Chapter 3 centers on this ever-changing facet of the board's role. In recent years, the board's responsibility for overseeing company culture has come to encompass issues such as fair pay, diversity and inclusion, environmental concerns, and even social and cultural matters such as gun control. This sort of responsibility is rapidly becoming a central part of the board's duties, expanding its role beyond simply minding the financial bottom line and toward embracing good corporate citizenship efforts in areas such as education and health. Increasingly, a board is tasked with ensuring that its organization represents and reflects the fact that its customers, clients, and regulators are changing.

A range of headwinds have arisen to make board responsibilities more complicated and the board's role more complex. In the coming years, boards will face the challenges of providing oversight amid exponential technological change; rising activism by ever more powerful investors; mounting geopolitical risks that are trending toward insularity, protectionism, and de-globalization; and a war for global talent. Chapter 4 explores each of these critical issues and how short-term thinking alters boardroom decision-making on strategy and investment. It examines how myopia can exacerbate many of the risks that boards face, which can further hamper their choices.

Finally, Chapter 5 presents specific proposals for reforming corporate boards so that they can better govern twenty-first-century corporations and more effectively tackle the deep, complex problems these companies face. First, boards should be given more say in devising the company strategy. Second, when hiring a CEO, greater emphasis should be placed on candidates' moral compass and values. And third, committees dealing specifically with ethics should become a standard element of the board structure.

The twenty-first-century corporation is nothing if not globally expansive, operationally complex, and culturally evolving. Despite the headlines about corporate scandals and brazen failures of leadership, for many companies the proverbial trains continue to run on time as they have for decades or even centuries. Customers, by and large, continue to get the goods and services they need in a safe way, employees get paid on time, and—through it all, across countries, languages, time zones, and cultures—the pieces of the puzzle somehow fit together.

At the same time, calls for corporations to do more to support society grow louder and louder. Boards stand accused of being tone-deaf, behind the curve, and even patently corrupt. It is perhaps not surprising that the trend line of the Edelman Trust Barometer—an annual survey of trust in different institutions—for businesses has pointed downward for over a decade.

How Boards Work is not a tell-all or a whistle-blowing book—after all, as a board member and fiduciary, I am bound by confidentiality. Rather, it draws on my direct experience to assess how boards function and how they can do better. It shows how even a group of talented, qualified, intelligent people can get things wrong. And, ultimately, it challenges boards to use their power wisely.

CHAPTER 1

Setting the Company Strategy

THE OLDEST COMPANY ON WHOSE BOARD I HAVE SERVED HAS EXISTED AS an independent corporation for more than three centuries. Founded in 1690 on Lombard Street in London, Barclays has survived industrialization, two world wars, the Great Depression, decolonization, oil-price shocks, and the 2008 financial crisis. It has outlived whole nations and political regimes.

Barclays is certainly not the only company that has survived over one hundred years and endured a great deal of historical change. Other companies on whose boards I have served date back to the 1800s, such as the US oil major Chevron, which has been trading for over 140 years. There are American companies from even earlier still operating today: Cigna, the global health-service corporation, began in 1792, and banking giant JPMorgan Chase started in 1799. Toothpaste maker Colgate, financial giant Citigroup, and clothing atelier Brooks Brothers all opened their doors in the 1800s, each passing their two-hundredth-year anniversary. In the UK, the Royal Mail, a listed mail and courier company, dates back to 1516, Lloyds Bank opened its doors in 1765, the pharmacy

Boots started in 1849, and the clothes maker Burberry began in 1856.

These companies have stood the test of time by developing strategies that allow them to fight another day. Behind each of these strategies has been a group of people meeting year after year to map out the company's destiny and determine how to achieve it. This group—the board—helps the company seek opportunities and confront challenges head-on. To my mind, the task of setting company strategy is the most important role of the board, key to determining the company's ultimate success or failure.

For a company as long-lived as Barclays, it may now appear that survival was assured from the start. But in business, progress is never linear and success is never inevitable. Even the most successful companies suffer ups and downs along the way—and odds are that at several points in their long histories, their independence and even survival were cast into doubt. Indeed, only sixty of the companies that made the first Fortune 500 list in 1955 were still operating independently in 2017. This chapter explains how strategic decisions about a company's future get made and what sort of questions boards should focus on as they chart a company's course.

A Director's Duties

Boards don't (and can't) get every strategic decision right, and board members are acutely aware of the permanent costs of getting one wrong. In the United States, the duties of a board director are enshrined in state law as well as in federal securities law, and they include obligations known as the duty of care and the duty of loyalty.

The duty of care says that directors must be sufficiently informed before making a decision and that board members may reasonably rely on information, opinions, and reports provided by officers of the company or outside experts. The duty of loyalty requires board members to act in good faith and in a manner that they reasonably believe is in the best interest of the company and its stockholders. This requires them to advise other board members of any conflicts of interest they might have and prohibits them from taking personal advantage (for themselves or another corporation) of an opportunity that belongs to the company. It also obligates board members to keep corporate information confidential.

In the United States, these responsibilities are codified in law as the business judgment rule, which requires board members to act on an informed basis, in good faith, and in the honest belief that the actions they take are in the best interest of the company. (Boards are generally also governed by their own code of ethics that parallels the duty of care and duty of loyalty.) Crucially, the business judgment rule offers board members protections so that their actions will be justified as long as they can be attributed to any rational business purpose—even if those decisions later turn out to have a negative effect on the company. What this means is that beyond the collective responsibility of the board, each individual board director must ensure that they are consistently making strategic decisions in the company's interest based on the available information.

At the helm of the board, and by extension serving as leader of the company, is the board chairman. In many companies around the world, the chairman is a nonexecutive director, though there are exceptions where the chairman is an executive director. In the UK, the chairman role is commonly separate from the CEO to provide an additional layer of checks and balances over the CEO and corporate executives. Meanwhile, for about two-thirds of US companies, the chairman position is filled by the CEO.

More and more, investors in US corporations are calling for the chairman-CEO role to be split. However, proxy agencies—such as Institutional Shareholder Services (ISS) and Glass Lewis, which vote on behalf of shareholders at meetings of listed or quoted companies—still overwhelmingly back the joint chairman-CEO model.

One obvious hurdle related to the combined chairman-CEO role is that the CEO can be fired by the very board they are expected to lead. While this arrangement may seem complicated, my sense is that these boards generally end up with a strong lead director, as they would with a split chairman-CEO. Having a senior, independent director in place provides the necessary checks and balances when the chair and CEO roles are combined.

The chairman sets the tone of engagement for the board, smooths out misunderstandings, referees relationships among board members, and acts as a liaison between the board and management. Ultimately, the chairman is responsible for ensuring the board stays true to its mandate. They also set the agenda for each meeting and decide how much time should be devoted to different topics.

Board meetings are a significant undertaking, lasting half a day in many cases and occurring four to five times per year. Bringing twelve board directors to corporate headquarters often requires flying them in from across the country or around the world. It is imperative, therefore, that board members are knowledgeable about the major issues facing the company. They receive their schedules and relevant materials well in advance of these meetings, allowing them to make the most of their limited time together.

Board chairs are subjected to the same rigorous vetting and annual reviews as other board members. They can be unceremoniously forced out, with all the nastiness of a political coup, because of shortcomings at the board level or failings by the executive management as a collective. One example of this occurred on October 12, 2016, when John Stumpf, the chairman and CEO of Wells Fargo, announced that he would be retiring, effective immediately, in the wake of a significant scandal involving the creation of fake customer accounts that provoked pressure from the public and lawmakers.

Boards and management are regularly charged with solving complex problems while equipped with incomplete information and facing enormous uncertainty. After all, the board-approved strategy will ideally withstand not just an ordinary economic downturn but also a significant crisis of unknown size and duration. The 2020 global pandemic is an example of such a crisis.

One can imagine being on the board of Boeing, the US aircraft maker, in March 2019, as it was dealing with the fallout from two fatal crashes of their new 737 MAX 8 aircraft within the span of five months. These crashes led to the entire line of planes being grounded and precipitated a 20 percent decline in Boeing's stock price. The causes and consequences of the crashes were shrouded in uncertainty, so the board was largely seen as impotent and unable to shape the company's narrative. For a time, it seemed inevitable that the company's path forward would be defined by government regulation, customer fear, or unchecked speculation on social media. In such cases, the board and the company must act decisively to reset the strategy, urgently demonstrating that the board is in control and the company can recover from a dire situation.

The bottom line is that external shocks are inevitable. It is a board member's responsibility to remain vigilant, assessing whether and to what degree such shocks will affect the business.

How Strategy Is Done

For the most part, boards meet once a year for two to three days to discuss, interrogate, and challenge the strategic plan proposed by management. This proposal typically consists of a short-term plan (STP) covering the next twelve months, a medium-term plan (MTP) for the coming three to five years, and the perennial question of what the company aims to achieve over the long term.

The end goal of these strategy sessions is to approve and endorse the company's direction, while revising the company's STP and MTP where necessary. For a simple example of how these plans interact, imagine that a company's long-term strategic goal is to become the number one producer of widgets in China. The STP might be to deploy a marketing strategy that will ensure that more Chinese consumers become familiar with the brand. The MTP might be to build a factory and distribution network. Only by building off the short- and medium-term plans can the company achieve its ultimate goal.

The most effective strategic plans generally combine the very broad and the very specific. On a broad level, the company needs to define its mission before management and the board decide on the specific metrics of operational and financial performance. This strategic mission serves as a compass as the company codifies the bounds of its ambition. For example, a company must decide: Is it seeking to become the dominant leader by market share in a country, a region, or globally? Or is it aiming to be a market-leading brand, known globally for its quality—a top-flight luxury good as opposed to mass-market?

On a more practical level, the management team takes primary responsibility for strategy. This means that the CEO pitches and convinces the board of the strategic direction that the management team wants to take. But it is not a forgone conclusion that the board will accept management's proposals. In these strategy sessions, the board directors and management test assumptions and debate the company's plans for the future.

As a result, the board, along with management, is accountable for any strategic initiative it approves. The governance structure is meant to allow for—and even encourage—frequent disagreement between the board and management (and within them as well). In effect, this means that the board structure can only work if there is trust between the two groups.

In general, strategy sessions tend to be guided by discussions of trends expected in the coming decades, such as disruptive technological shifts. Because the strategy meetings are time constrained, it is essential that they are planned in a way that allows board members to drill down on the points most salient to the success of the business, avoiding detours into topics and details that distract from the core goal.

In essence, boards are always fighting the temptation to focus on immediate issues rather than longer-term strategic decisions. For example, even at a planned strategy session, the board members might end up devoting their energy to an urgent regulatory issue, rather than holding a strategic debate about the role of China and technology in the competitive landscape.

Regular board meetings provide the chance to delve deeper into the specifics of strategic plans. These meetings, outside the annual strategy session, occur at least quarterly and serve as essential checkpoints, offering an opportunity for the board to monitor the company's performance and ensure that management is effectively carrying out the agreed-upon plans.

While management operates the company on a day-to-day basis, it is the board's responsibility to look on from forty thousand feet. At its meetings, the board asks questions about whether the leadership is innovating enough, hiring the right people, and building the best management team, and whether the company is growing its customer base and beating the competition according to the latest plan. The board must remain open-minded about revisiting the strategic plan to determine if it is still keeping the company on track, or if new plans and new targets are in order. Board meetings are also an opportunity for the board to abide by its regulatory obligations, which often include releasing the company's results to the public.

Boards regularly use their meetings to take stock of how the climate in which a company operates is changing. Typically, these meetings are shaped by an assessment of the macro environment—economic and geopolitical—as well as the micro environment.

Macro Factors

The macro factors that the board considers include the global economic and political outlook, the business environment, and shifts in regulations. These in turn drive changes in consumer preferences, the development of new technologies, and changes to public policy that can substantially affect the company's top and bottom lines. In cases when these shifts are extreme, the board may be pushed to consider whether its business plan, or even business model, is in need of revision.

Discussion of these factors is usually prompted when management presents a narrative about how larger changes in the world economy are affecting the business. Armed with this information, management and the board are in a stronger position to recognize, anticipate, and act on market trends and shifts. These decisions can materially affect the company's financial success—for example, using a new technology to develop cheaper and better substitutes that can win over consumers.

Among the factors that the board scrutinizes are classic macroeconomic variables, such as changing interest rates, inflation, and economic growth forecasts. At a quarterly meeting, management will set the stage and present the current state of affairs to the board, as well as various projections and competing scenarios as to how the shifts might affect business. Management might opine, for example, on upcoming interest-rate hikes that could increase the company's cost of operation, inflationary pressures that threaten to raise the costs of wages and production, and economic growth improvements that could improve the trajectory of the company's revenue.

One illustration of how macroeconomic shifts can create threats, opportunities, and crucial decision points can be seen in boards' responses to the historically low interest rates that have persisted in the United States and Europe since the 2008 global financial crisis. These low rates have forced boards to decide whether they should borrow cheaply to invest in growing the business through innovation or entering new markets. However, given the unusual economic circumstances that companies have faced in this period—including the dim prospects for global growth and unsustainable levels of government borrowing—boards were obliged to think long and hard about the wisdom of borrowing so aggressively, knowing full well that their corporations could soon face higher tax bills from overstretched governments.

Another example is the onset of the global coronavirus pandemic in March 2020, which forced corporate boards to consider both the immediate impact and the longer-term implications of the ensuing shutdown. In the short term, many corporate boards opted to simplify decision-making processes to improve the company's ability to react to the rapidly changing situation. Boards also had to assess the company's ability to pay its debts and access capital for its operations and investments. Beyond these immediate questions, boards had to consider their company's longer-term viability and even survival. In the midst of the crisis, for example, many airlines and cruise operators faced a fundamental threat as the stock market doubted that demand for travel services would swiftly rebound. Some boards were prompted to overhaul their company's business models, considering major changes to their strategy and weighing whether certain operational changes, like having employees work from home, should be made permanent.

Another macro factor that boards consider is what a company's competitors are doing as they fight for market share and margin. At a time when technology is lowering the barriers to entry for many industries, companies and their boards must be cognizant of new forms of competition. One example is the threat that online shopping has posed for traditional retail stores. Several decades ago, corporations like Nestlé, Unilever, Procter & Gamble, and Walmart considered their competition to be other large, global firms in their sectors. Today they are competing with emerging brands at home and in developing-market countries such as India and China. Twenty years ago, Walmart competed with brick-and-mortar retail chains like Costco, Target, and Kroger. But in the past decade Amazon has emerged as a formidable retail force, becoming America's third-largest retailer overall. Today, competition in this sector is increasingly coming from operators such as China's Alibaba and JD.com, India's Flipkart, Europe's Delivery Hero, and South Africa's Naspers—all of which are quickly extending their reach.

Boards have to monitor and respond to a constantly changing regulatory landscape. Global corporations could face regulations that challenge anticompetitive or monopolistic behavior. They also face rule changes that create or remove barriers to entry. For example, tighter rules on data protection might lead to higher costs and require new expertise.

Perhaps unsurprisingly, boards tend to focus on specific regulation that immediately affects their business. The 2010 Dodd-Frank overhaul of financial regulation, which came in response to the 2008 crisis, encouraged—and in some cases even forced—bank boards to change their strategic plans and business models. Many banks had to shrink their balance sheets, reduce the amount of overall risk they took, and even close proprietary trading desks, which had contributed significantly to profits in the boom years.

The deluge of regulation on banks in the wake of the financial crisis was, of course, a unique situation. In more normal conditions, management should be able to anticipate new laws and regulations—in some cases even before they appear on the legislative agenda—because policymakers often run a consultative process with companies and industry representatives. When a specific regulatory decree looms, it is up to the company's board to oversee preparations. Members must weigh how the new rules will affect the company's bottom line, or if they will have any effect at all. Because corporate decision-making is so heavily influenced by anticipated regulatory shifts, it is imperative that boards and management stay connected to policymakers. To that end, it is often worthwhile to staff the board with members who have previously worked in policymaking and government. Boards need directors who have a deep understanding of how government decisions and public policy choices are made, as well as connections with lawmakers.

But even with the guidance of such experts, the fallout of broader geopolitical shifts can be impossible to predict. Brexit is just one example. Since the 2016 referendum, the business sector has had to operate with a very uncertain sense of the timeline for implementation and what the ultimate regulatory outcomes will be—including the new tax, trade, and investment regime—now that the UK is no longer part of the European Union. Nevertheless, boards have had to make judgments on how to manage and mitigate the risks associated with it.

The changes associated with Brexit are not the only regulatory shifts looming over the future. The ongoing geopolitical contest between China and the United States has already led to new trade regulations and tariffs, and it is likely to produce regulatory changes in areas such as intellectual property, biotechnology, national security (aerospace and defense), and finance. For boards, these changes are no simple matter—any regulatory change born out of geopolitical shifts means additional work will be needed to realign the corporation's operations and reassess its profitability.

Looking ahead, boards and corporate leaders will need to consider how governments will manage their growing deficits and debts. According to a forecast by the Congressional Budget Office, the United States will face increasing challenges over the next decade due to rapidly expanding health-care and social security entitlement obligations. The US deficit, which as of this writing is projected to hit $1 trillion in 2020, is forecast to reach $1.3 trillion in 2030. US public debt, meanwhile, is expected to rise from 81 percent of GDP in 2020 to 98 percent in 2030—its highest level since 1946. In the wake of COVID-19, advanced economies were revising their debt-to-GDP ratios to surpass 100 percent in 2020. In this scenario, it seems inevitable that US political leadership in the coming years, Democrat or Republican, will have to seriously consider raising taxes on corporations. The smartest boards are already looking at the implications of such a scenario for their businesses.

Another example of challenges stemming from government can be seen with energy and mining companies. When these companies make multibillion-dollar investments, they sometimes enter into direct contracts with governments on specific and well-defined terms regarding taxes, employment, royalties, and capital controls. However, as history has shown, governments have been known to renege on these agreements after a company has invested, demanding better terms and, in extremis, seizing company assets. This can force the board and management to reassess and even write off large amounts of investment. In essence, companies that operate internationally must always bear in mind that their investments can sometimes take a stark turn for the worse, and those risks must be analyzed and mitigated as much as possible.

The shifting nature of public policy means that boards find themselves operating in a world of policy inconsistency, where policymakers seem to always be reversing earlier decisions, even without a change in the political regime.

Micro Factors

Micro factors, such as internal data, provide boards with a valuable sense of the company's financials and operations over time. This information helps the board to assess where the company is succeeding and where it is struggling or failing. It allows the board to test management's assumptions and forecasts—to scrutinize how effectively management allocates capital, how productively the company invests it, and whether the returns generated exceed the cost of operating the business. All these functions guide the board in managing the company's assets. The board's strategic decision-making is generally guided by four kinds of micro factors: revenue, capital allocation, use of resources, and returns.

Revenue Recognition

The board reviews the company's financial and operating performance, gauging it against previous years as well as against management's expectations, forecasts, and plans for how the company should perform. Specifically, the board is charged with probing whether management's revenue and profit forecasts are in line with the forecasts set at the start of the business year. Of course, as part of this exercise, the board regularly reviews whether management's plans are realistic and sustainable. For many companies, a comparison of forecasts with actual production numbers can offer a good starting point, revealing how closely the company's revenue growth is tracking nominal GDP and the country's industrial production index. This type of analysis merges the macroeconomic factors detailed above with microeconomic factors to produce a granular assessment of a company's financial outlook.

Using this information, the board determines whether the company is overly revenue reliant in its pursuit of profits. "Revenue reliant" is a way of describing a company that is overdependent on the revenues of a particular business line or unit, which may mean that the company is too exposed to a particular customer segment or trend. If the company is overly dependent on a country or business line that is showing signs of slowing down, or else perhaps underexposed to one that is showing signs of stronger growth, the board must act accordingly.

But testing the strength of revenue assumptions is not enough. Revenue is the company's top line, but it isn't everything. Boards should also help oversee other metrics, such as earnings, revenues less expenses, and cash-flow statements. The cash-flow statement is an especially vital part of understanding the health of the company. It provides essential information about the sources and uses of the cash coming into and going out of the company, be they investments, spending, or returns to shareholders.

The board must check and challenge management's revenue and profit assumptions. If members sense an overdependence on revenue from a key product or business line, it is important for them to push back and give the management team an opportunity to reassess company forecasts and even rework the corporate strategy. If the board fails to spot a risk or push back, the company could miss its revenue forecasts, lose ground to competition, and possibly have its overall performance derailed.

Take the example of the board of an airline that has commanded a market-leading position flying passengers between North America and Europe. Management presents the board with forecasts that rely on further growth in the transatlantic passenger business. The revenues from this business line had steadily accumulated over ten years, but signs are emerging that the market has been flattening. Meanwhile, there are new possibilities for growth across Asian hubs and international freight. A board must be alert to such changes and be ready to intervene. This means questioning growth assumptions in the core business, asking where growth will come from in the future, and exploring the potential for expansion. For an airline, this might mean more aggressively targeting freight on existing routes or new markets. Whatever the case, it is up to the board to monitor, challenge, and disrupt the status quo.

The board might even initiate an investigation into the full health of the business, which would include a review of the all-important relationship between costs and revenues, ensuring that costs are fully under control in the face of flattening or falling revenues in a key business. In normal times, an airline's cost-management efforts would include capping new hires and capital expenditure, as well as putting any plans to expand the fleet on hold. Under extreme conditions—when revenues fall precipitously, as they did during the 2020 coronavirus pandemic—airlines have been forced to take more draconian measures such as furloughing employees, slashing capital expenditures, and cutting dividends and share buybacks. Making these sorts of judgment calls is precisely where boards add value: they can present management with a reality check, ask the right questions at the right time, and examine the details to determine where trouble may lie.

Yet the C-suite leaders are not the only ones susceptible to blind spots. Boards, too, can suffer from complacency, especially when the company performs well over multiple years. A business unit with high growth in its profit and revenue numbers for four years running will likely be seen as on track for a fifth bumper year. But boards and management should never assume that performance will persist, or that a successful business will remain successful.

To be truly successful, boards must contend with business life-cycle considerations. Among the most high profile of today's early stage businesses are technology start-ups—companies that have become notorious for fast revenue growth fueled by heavy investments with the promise of later profits. For many investors, it makes sense for start-ups to spend capital now for the chance to reap huge rewards in the future, but that is not the case for most well-established and mature businesses. The risk is that the allure of a fast-growing product or business line might cloud the judgment of the board and management. But the board members must remain clear-eyed as they interrogate the longevity and strength of market trends, since their job is not as much to reap short-term profits as to position the company for growth over the long term.

Underlying these discussions of strategy and the pursuit of growth is a central question for boards: Where should the company allocate its capital for the best outcome in the years ahead?

Allocating Capital

In *The Outsiders*, William Thorndike argues that capital allocation, above all else, is the most important predictor of a company's success. He reveals that those companies that consistently outperform their peers and stock-market benchmarks are the ones with a CEO whose sole job is to define and test the company strategy, allocating capital in pursuit of success.

Capital allocation is the task of determining where each dollar is spent—operations, investment, debt reduction, or redistribution to shareholders—with the goal of continuing to sustain and grow the enterprise. In many respects, capital allocation is the art of balancing and prioritization. To do it well, company leadership must decide whether investing a dollar in project A will be more valuable than investing it in project B.

When the management team presents its strategic plan to the board, it is essentially answering the question: What should the company do with each marginal dollar? Management sets out a plan of where to invest and expand in terms of geography, product, customer base, and expertise. The board must then assess whether the management team is deploying its capital and resources in the best possible way. It is a relationship that revolves around capital allocation, with management setting out and executing a plan, and the board asking questions and conducting analysis to determine whether the plan is sound. For the most part, boards approve capital expenditures and budgets annually, but the company spending is tracked and reviewed at nearly every board meeting.

This oversight of capital allocation can be the source of much consternation and depends on board members' judgment about the best use of the company's marginal dollar. The board has essentially three options: reinvestment, payments to share-holders, and buying or selling assets. Reinvestment entails ear-marking capital for greater growth, such as promoting higher revenue growth or market share, enhancing the operational efficiencies, or instituting newer and faster technologies. Of course, this can also include cutting costs.

Marginal dollars could also be spent in a way that affects shareholders and share prices. This could mean giving money back to shareholders via dividends or share buybacks, or by reducing debt, which can improve the company's share price. A great deal of thought and consideration goes into each of these options, because a company's shareholder base usually includes a range of investors with differing motivations, needs, and wants. For example, in 2016–2017 the dividend-to-payout ratio for US banks was more than 100 percent, and this placed pressure on boards and management teams across the banking sector to match the payouts of their competitors. Some share-holders value money today over investment for tomorrow. But picking one option over the other depends on a range of fac-tors: Can the dividend be sustained? How do you manage the expectations of a shareholder buyback program? How much debt can you pay down? Inherent in the board's responsibility is the understanding that all decisions should put the share-holders first. As we will explore in greater detail in Chapter 3, boards and companies are facing mounting pressure to widen their focus beyond their financial shareholders to include the community as well, which further complicates deliberations over the best use of the company's capital.

A third option for the board to consider is the acquisition and sale of assets, which should be part of the regular process of reviewing and upgrading the company's asset portfolio. The board must see, first, if all assets are generating value and, second, if the assets on the balance sheet are helping the company achieve its long-term strategic aims. In my decade of serving on boards, there have been numerous occasions when companies have had to dispose of noncore assets that were no longer the best use of resources—be they capital, labor, or management's time and attention.

Upgrading a company's portfolio is a complex task. Numerous studies have shown that even the most transformational mergers and acquisitions (M&A) plans sometimes fail to enhance value for shareholders. A 2004 study by the global consulting firm McKinsey of 160 M&A transactions found that almost 70 percent failed to achieve the projected revenue synergies, and only about 60 percent delivered the planned cost synergies.

Why does this happen? One reason is that management teams sometimes overestimate the profit outlook for the combined company. The whole ordeal frequently ends up being a more complicated and drawn-out exercise than expected and, in many cases, ends up costing several times the original estimate. Synergies that should enhance value when two companies come together can also seem rosier in the abstract than in practice. The idea, of course, is that the combined entity will be worth more than the sum of its parts. But companies can overstate the revenue growth that the combined company will generate, and they tend to overestimate savings generated by eliminating areas of overlap.

Worse still, some acquisitions destroy value and leave the merged company severely weakened. One of the most famed examples of a failed merger was the $165 billion combination of AOL and Time Warner in 2000. Two years later, AOL Time

Warner reported a loss of $99 billion—including a $46 billion write-down of the value of AOL. This was attributed, at least in part, to a clash of corporate cultures between old media (Time Warner) and new media (AOL), which impeded the ability of management to successfully integrate the two companies.

More recent mergers have run into similar problems. In 2011, the US technology company Hewlett-Packard (HP) acquired UK software company Autonomy for just under $12 billion. Within a year, HP had written off $8.8 billion of Autonomy's value. A legal case ensued, in which HP claimed that Autonomy had engaged in accounting improprieties, misrepresented itself, and failed to make proper disclosures. In 2017, HP sold the remaining Autonomy assets for an undisclosed amount as part of a broader deal. Of course, an extreme version of selling off company assets would be selling the company in its entirety. This nuclear option does happen, and it's a scenario we will address later in the chapter.

Fundamentally, boards and management must work together to make sure that they are not overpaying for assets and companies they acquire. By the same token, they must also ensure that they are never underselling assets in their own portfolio. Here, again, regular portfolio assessments are where the board's judgment can help keep the company's strategic direction on track.

Use of Resources

In addition to correctly allocating capital, boards must make sure that management is efficiently using the resources at its disposal, which include labor and capital. A number of metrics can capture this. The cost-income ratio, for instance, is a good gauge of how many employees a company needs to generate a unit of income. Often used in the financial sector, it is a useful cross-industry comparator, allowing for an easy assessment of which companies are most efficient.

Inventory turnover is another metric that offers a measure of capital efficiency. This reveals the number of times inventory is sold or used in a period of time. A higher number can raise concerns that the company is holding too much inventory and not selling enough.

The best boards spend a good deal of time thinking about ways to improve their company's efficiency. If a business's productivity is stalling, the board must consider importing and using outside technology, standardizing existing processes, or achieving more output with the same or fewer assets. Although the responsibility for efficient operations rests squarely on management's shoulders, boards must take it upon themselves to probe for greater efficiency and improvements over time and against competitors.

Generating Returns

The board's fourth goal is to assess how much money the company is getting back compared to the amount put in. When boards undertake this task, perhaps the most common strategy is to consider the returns generated against the capital employed. But there are, in fact, a variety of different ways to track this, and companies will adapt their approach depending on the particular demands of their industry. The board of a bank or a financial services company might look at return on equity (ROE). For an oil field or a mine, a board might instead examine returns on assets or return on invested capital (ROIC).

Each of these measures is intended to capture how well the company uses its money to generate earnings and returns. ROE shows how well a company uses investments to generate earnings growth, while ROIC reflects how well a company is using its invested money to generate returns. These ratios offer boards and management a variety of ways to track performance, compare different business units, and measure the company's progress against that of its competitors and peers. All this information helps form the basis for future capital allocation.

One exercise I took part in involved management ranking each of the company's more than fifty business units from highest to lowest return on capital. The return on capital was compared against the cost of capital, which was how much the company pays to finance the business unit (both the cost of debt and the cost of equity). Management was able to assess which business units were generating returns higher than the company's cost of capital and which were falling behind. Those that generated higher returns were, simply put, generating value, while those that were falling behind were eroding value.

Of course, boards should never blindly follow a numerical template. These ratios are extremely valuable, but they are only a first approximation of how well a business is using its money to generate returns. Boards must use them in conjunction with their sound judgment and their understanding of the longer-term considerations facing the company.

At times, the board may opt to override the data. There might be cyclical or strategic reasons to give an underperforming business some leeway. For example, a superficial response to a business unit's returns falling below the cost of capital might be to restructure or even close the unit. However, a more in-depth review may reveal that the business is merely going through a cyclical dip and could be expected to return to profit. The automobile industry provides a good example of this. In devising the company strategy, the board must determine whether an observed dip in car sales reflects a temporary, cyclical shift in customer demand—say, due to a brief economic recession—or a more structural, permanent change in the car sector.

Customer tastes moving from gas-fueled cars to alternatives is a shift where the underlying demand for cars stays the same, so the decision could be to invest in electric-car production. However, the board must also consider a more threatening path, whereby a dip in auto sales reflects a fundamental decline in demand for car ownership, signaling that people may be more inclined to stop owning individual cars and instead use car-sharing schemes such as Uber or Lyft. The board's analysis on this matter has real material value. As of May 2020, Uber's market value of $60 billion was greater than that of General Motors and Ford combined, suggesting that investors may indeed see a more fundamental shift away from traditional car ownership.

In making these judgments, the board and its management must combine a working knowledge of the business with data-driven analysis of company performance to judge the cyclicality of the different business units. Taking this information into account, board members must also discern whether a business unit is of long-term strategic value to ensure that the company remains profitable through economic cycles.

For example, universal banking is a business model where banks maintain both retail and corporate clients, allowing them to make profits through periods of both high and low interest rates. In periods of high rates, individuals tend to borrow less, taking out fewer loans and mortgages and spending less on credit cards. The retail arm suffers as a result. However, high rates tend to produce higher M&A activity, as stronger companies acquire weaker ones, to the benefit of investment banks. Likewise, during periods of low rates, retail banks tend to make up for investment banks' weaker returns. Looking at either unit's return ratios without a sense of overall strategy can provide only an incomplete picture.

The ability to assess a seemingly faltering business unit using these ratios is essential for a properly functioning company. For example, a bank might accept lower performance in its corporate-lending division from time to time because that business underpins relationships that lead to higher-margin activities, such as advising on mergers and acquisitions. A 2016 study by the consultancy Oliver Wyman showed that while many European businesses were not profitable as stand-alone units, they were nevertheless necessary components of global financial institutions. The report made the case that any genuinely global banking service must have a European footprint, in order to support international corporations that need advice globally.

It is natural to focus on areas that appear problematic—that is, business units where returns are below the cost of capital—but an effective board should be just as cautious regarding those businesses that are doing uncharacteristically well. Early in my board career, I was cautioned by an external auditor not to fall into this trap. The auditor stressed that business units generating outsize returns multiple times the cost of capital should be scrutinized just as aggressively as ones that were underperforming.

When a business unit earns above-average returns over long periods of time, a charitable conclusion might be that it has discovered a competitive advantage that sets it apart. Nevertheless, it is the board's duty to probe deeper and determine whether high performance is masking underlying risks. It may be that a business unit is actually generating high returns through illegal or unethical behavior. Even if the business unit's actions are legal, the board should bear in mind that regulators are especially likely to crack down on and investigate any business where they see evidence of monopolistic behavior, such as excess returns.

As a matter of due diligence, board members should seek assurances from management that any returns generated do not breach legal or ethical boundaries. Furthermore, seemingly high-performing businesses should remain on the board's radar. Tempting as it is to give these business units a pass, the reality is that their excess returns are highly susceptible to disruption, whether through new regulations or greater competition.

All these caveats aside, return ratios remain an extremely valuable tool. They help boards and investors calibrate performance across industries (enabling them to compare, say, pharmaceuticals to banking to airlines), across competitors, and across business units within the same company. Yet investors must accept that returns analysis is not an end unto itself. Boards are regularly obliged to make judgment calls about whether to buy or sell a company based on broader context and evidence. When contemplating such decisions—where the fate of a company hangs in the balance—the art of the board's job must override the science. Inevitably, these nuances are often beyond the grasp of Wall Street analysts, investors, and stakeholders.

It is not uncommon for a disconnect to emerge between the decisions boards make and the preferences of outside investors. For example, outside investors might agitate for a company to sell a business unit that they interpret, on the basis of public financial filings, to be underperforming. But they might not understand the extent to which this unit supports other parts of the company, perhaps by offering access to a key client base. From the perspective of the company's leadership, meanwhile, it is perfectly clear that the business unit's value in a sale would be compromised, because, for example, it depends on support from the corporate hub or a central R&D function. The bottom line is that the board must wield a deep understanding of the business in addition to keeping up with the metrics and how exactly the company makes money. For example, in magazine publishing this means understanding just how much a company's revenues stem from advertising rather than subscriptions and how to respond as this balance changes.

This level of understanding enables the board to stand back when the company is on the right course, to defend the management team from outsiders when the metrics suggest weakness but the strategy is sound, and to assert itself should the company find itself faltering.

What Could Go Wrong?

The mechanics of "doing strategy" that we see here are vitally important, but they can take us a long way from the board's core responsibility, which is to approve a strategy that enables the company to operate as a going concern, capable of generating positive returns.

Year after year, boards go through the exercise of setting the company strategy, as if by clockwork. The rapid proliferation of a disruptive technology or the negative effects of a new wave of regulation can require a reevaluation of that strategy and, in the extreme, threaten the existence of the company. Even the most rigorous strategic review does not completely insulate a board from unforeseen shocks. Some board members might go so far as to argue that no board can focus on strategy if the company is fighting to survive—survival becomes the strategy.

A board-approved strategy can stop working. Companies can be outmaneuvered by regulators, investors, other stakeholders, or merely the impact of unexpected change. In some cases, this may lead to a company declaring bankruptcy or being acquired. When this happens, investors are right to question the decision-making and judgment of both management and the board.

Company failures come in different shapes and sizes. Some companies fall into decline because they could not keep up with rapid changes in technology, market innovation, and customer preferences. Nokia and BlackBerry are well-known examples of companies that once led their field but did not adapt to changing technology and ended up failing and being acquired. The two companies dominated the market in mobile handsets before losing their luster as smartphones, especially Apple's iPhone, emerged. In the end, both companies opted for a change in management, and then in ownership.

Of course, neither company's board intended these outcomes when setting strategy. As custodians of a business, board members generally come to the boardroom with the purpose of keeping a company independent, profitable, and afloat. In 2011, Nokia's then CEO Stephen Elop famously issued a call for his employees to get off the "burning platform" and make drastic changes in order to survive. But the board judged that the company was no longer able to compete on its own and accepted a bid to be acquired by Microsoft. Research in Motion, the owner of BlackBerry, was acquired by a consortium of financial investors who have kept the company as a private entity trading under the BlackBerry name—albeit greatly reduced in size. From a peak of $19.9 billion in sales in 2011, BlackBerry fell to $932 million in 2018. The proliferation of the iPhone transformed the landscape for Nokia and BlackBerry, just as Airbnb has taken traditional hotels to task and Lyft and Uber have disrupted the transportation and car industries. It is impossible to know what actually transpires in the boardrooms of failing businesses, but later analyses often point toward slow reactions to changes in consumer trends and the competitive landscape, leaving a company to operate under flawed assumptions.

Even when disruptive trends are identified, companies can still fail by poorly executing their responses. Kodak famously filed for bankruptcy in 2012 after falling behind competitors in the switch to digital cameras, despite the fact that the company had created its first digital camera in 1975. Even as the Kodak board and leadership were aware of the changes in technology and the need to innovate, the company was unable to execute new plans and products in a timely manner.

Many board crises are slow. They settle in over a long period of time, gradually eating away at the value of the company but seemingly going unnoticed, often until it's too late. Boards must remain alert to these creeping threats: technological obsolescence, the loss of competitiveness, deteriorating competence and quality of management, and inattention to organizational culture and values. These gradual crises can lead to the ultimate slow-motion car crash, which may or may not be fatal.

One such disaster occurred in 2018 to General Electric, the US conglomerate with global footprints in aviation, health care, transportation, and power. The legacy of the great inventor Thomas Edison, GE faced an existential crisis—which remains largely unresolved—and has seen a spectacular erosion of its value, from a market capitalization of $700 billion to $70 billion.

Founded in 1892, GE was America's largest company until it was overtaken by Microsoft in 1999, and it remained America's largest manufacturer by market cap until 2017. In 2018, though, the company experienced such a precipitous fall that it lost its place in the Dow index ranking of the largest public corporations in the United States, after more than one hundred years as a member. This slump was caused by a confluence of three problems: GE Capital, the company's financial services division, never fully recovered from the financial crisis; GE's $11 billion acquisition of the French power group Alstom delivered disappointing returns; and the power division, a long-term key contributor to group profits, failed to meet its targets.

Even when a company is buffeted by share-price gyrations, strategic stumbles need not be fatal. I witnessed this firsthand when I served on the board of Barrick Gold Corporation, the largest gold producer in the world. Natural-resource companies are inherently (and notoriously) exposed to violent swings in their share price because they have little direct control over the market-determined price of the commodity they produce, whether it is gold, copper, oil, or agricultural commodities. In other words, they are price takers, exposed to volatility in the market-determined price of their key product. During my tenure on the board, the company's share price swung from a high of $53 to a low of under $7 in the course of just four years.

In 2011, as Barrick's stock value absorbed the blow of a collapsing gold price and the company's revenues declined precipitously, a large part of the board's role was keeping the company afloat. The board had to delicately balance the immediate need for cuts in operations, capital expenditure, and production with the long-term goals of maintaining growth, profits, and market share.

Scaling back costs, closing operations, and reducing dividend payments are standard measures for boards facing tough times. However, a company cannot cut its way to growth, and deep cuts combined with a low share price can quickly turn a company into an acquisition target. Barrick's fortunes rebounded after the board oversaw dividend cuts, asset sales, and a careful scaling back of its operations. Helped along by a rebound in the price of gold, these actions by the board contributed significantly to the company's recovery.

Many companies trundle along, quarter after quarter, without major incident, until crises emerge. Sometimes these are the result of outside shocks; in other instances, they are the product of flawed strategy. Nevertheless, when they finally hit, they can be disruptive to the employee base and overwhelm management's time and energy. At these moments, it is the board's responsibility to make the hard decisions needed to keep the company alive, restabilize it, and reset its strategy for the future. No board should assume their company has a right to survive. Although some old corporations are still going strong, and for good reason, age alone is no guarantee of continued survival.

After all, corporate history is littered with examples of once-thriving companies that disappeared—subsumed into other companies or destroyed. Examples include Compaq, the 1990s PC maker acquired by HP in 2002; PaineWebber, a successful US broker established in the 1880s that was swallowed by the Swiss giant UBS in 2003; and Enron, the energy company that declared bankruptcy in 2001. No matter the size or sector, every company is vulnerable.

What's more, the rate at which companies merge or disappear from the public market is increasing. According to a 2016 report from the strategy consultancy Innosight entitled *Corporate Longevity: Turbulence Ahead for Large Organizations*, corporations in the S&P 500 in 1965 stayed in the index for an average of thirty-three years. By 1990, the average tenure had contracted to twenty years, and it is now forecast to shrink to just fourteen years by 2026. At the current churn rate, about half of today's S&P 500 firms will be replaced over the next ten years.

While there are examples of companies that are one hundred years old or more, they are in a small minority. As John Elkann of Fiat remarked, "If you look at companies that have lasted more than one hundred years, it is forty-five companies for one million." Perhaps more pointedly, Amazon founder Jeff Bezos made the sobering prediction that his company will not make it to one hundred: "Amazon is not too big to fail," he declared. "In fact, I predict one day Amazon will fail. Amazon will go bankrupt. If you look at large companies, their life spans tend to be thirty-plus years, not a hundred-plus years."

This trend in large part reflects growing consolidation. The result is an oligopoly, where a handful of companies (for example, airlines, banks, energy companies, pharmaceuticals, mining conglomerates) dominate their sectors on either a national or global scale. In such situations, there is a risk that companies will collude to set prices and thereby avoid being subject to market forces. Furthermore, the speed in the rise and consolidation of modern technology companies—in many ways the epitome of creative destruction—is adding to the number of companies that stall and simply disappear. According to the April 2014 McKinsey article "Grow Fast or Die Slow," which studied nearly three thousand companies, only 28 percent reached $100 million in annual revenues, 3 percent achieved $1 billion in annual sales, and just 0.6 percent grew beyond $4 billion.

Companies can disappear as a result of strategic miscalculation, but they can also cease to exist because the board has made a rational judgment that the company and its shareholders will gain more value by merging than by retaining independence. Indeed, in principle, any board should be prepared to face the end of its company's life.

Selling the Company: Strategic Trade-Offs

In 2016, while I served on the board of the global brewer SABMiller, the company was acquired by its chief competitor for just over $100 billion. It was deemed the largest M&A transaction of the year, and selling the company certainly had not been part of the board's plans.

The board's approved strategic plan had been to pursue organic growth. This was a departure from the strategy the company had successfully pursued for the preceding two decades, which had relied on a number of key acquisitions that had catapulted SABMiller from number one hundred, when it first listed on the FTSE 100 in 1999, into the top twenty in the index by market capitalization in 2014. At its height, the company was the second-largest brewer in the world.

When direct rival Anheuser-Busch (AB) InBev made its initial approach in 2016, SABMiller was, by most metrics, the definition of a thriving company in complete control of its own destiny. The board and management had convinced themselves that a takeover approach was unlikely, and that the best strategy for the company was to continue as an independent concern with its tried-and-true strategy, as it had for decades. This strategy, however, had assumed that it would be impossible for SABMiller to be taken over by a rival because of the company's size and the seemingly insurmountable costs that a takeover would require. AB InBev would have to issue the biggest bond ever in the capital markets to swallow SABMiller.

Another deterrent was the likelihood that anti-trust regulators would block the deal because the two companies had sizable and overlapping operations in major markets such as China, the United States, and Brazil. Furthermore, the board agreed with SABMiller management that a merger would be unappealing as the business models of the two companies were polar opposites. While SABMiller was focused on organic growth and building the brands in its existing portfolio, AB InBev had been pursuing financial returns through cost cutting and financial engineering.

When the SABMiller board received a bid for the company from AB InBev, it was forced to make a life-or-death decision: Should the company remain independent? Clearly AB InBev was willing to pay a substantial price and meet the challenge of financing the takeover by issuing the largest corporate bond at that time, around $40 billion. AB InBev's board and management were also willing to navigate a range of regulatory challenges in jurisdictions around the world, including selling assets to satisfy anti-trust scrutiny and more generally obtaining approval from governments concerned about retaining investments and jobs.

SABMiller's board faced the ultimate strategic question: Do we sell the company?

Before contemplating whether the price is right, any board faced with a takeover has to consider a number of questions that could derail the transaction. These include what it would mean for the company's employees, how it would affect the communities in which the company operates, what the environmental consequences could be, and whether the deal could be halted by regulators and policymakers.

Many deals, in fact, are blocked on the basis that a foreign investor poses a risk to national security. In the United States, this regulation is carried out by the Committee on Foreign Investment in the United States (CFIUS), a government agency with the power to review investments by foreign entities and reject any deemed to threaten US national security. Many other countries have designated strategic sectors—such as energy, banking, and media and telecommunications—where foreign ownership is restricted or even barred. Moreover, even if governments prefer to avoid such an explicit approach, they can tacitly signal their opposition in other ways.

As with any other M&A deal, the SABMiller transaction prompted a great deal of debate, discussion, and natural disagreement—not only between the board and management, but also within the board itself—over whether to sell the company and, perhaps most crucially, at what price. Negotiations on price can span many months as boards calibrate the value of the bid and assess if the offer is in a reasonable range.

Once approached with an acquisition bid, the board spends an enormous amount of time studying the business, revising revenue projections, and ascribing appropriate discount rates against the backdrop of any known risks—essentially making the decision whether to sell based on the best information available. The board's primary goal is to determine the company's fair market value so as to judge what an acceptable bid might be. As part of the exercise, management has a duty to show the board how long it would take for the company to match the value of the bid independently and on its own steam. If management forecasts indicate that the company is unlikely to reach the value of the bid for several years, a board will naturally be more inclined to accept it. After all, shareholders will judge the board and management on the returns the company garners.

Boards need to be on high alert, as unexpected shocks can alter the terms of a deal. Even the most judicious board has to contend with surprises that can materially alter the terms of a deal, and it must therefore be flexible throughout the process. Amid the final stages of the negotiations of the SABMiller deal, the UK voted to leave the EU—a result that confounded nearly all polls and expert predictions. Critically, this led the British pound to fall sharply against the US dollar. With SABMiller listed in London and its shares priced in sterling, the value of the bid declined, forcing SABMiller's board to reprice, renegotiate, and revise the terms of the deal. In the aftermath of the referendum, the board was able to mitigate the risks and successfully secure an increased price.

Corporate takeovers are, in a manner of speaking, a tug-of-war between two boards. The acquiring board has a duty to probe whether its company is overpaying for assets and whether planned synergies are achievable. Meanwhile, the target board must manage a delicate balance: neither selling too soon in the life cycle of the company for too little, nor holding out and missing a sale opportunity before the value of the company begins to erode. In February 2008, for example, Microsoft made a takeover bid to buy Yahoo for $44.6 billion—a bid that Yahoo's board and management rejected on the grounds that it substantially undervalued the company. Nine years later, in 2017, Verizon Communications acquired most of Yahoo's core internet business for just $4.48 billion—a mere 10 percent of the price offered by Microsoft.

This is complicated stuff, and boards' reputations—both collectively and as individual members—are tied to getting it right. Even the best intentions and the most assiduous efforts will be of little help if they get it wrong. The only way for boards to avoid mistakes is to insist that they are receiving the best possible information. However, what constitutes the best information and how to get it can be extremely difficult questions.

The Data Minefield

Board decision-making is hard. Board members are trusted to make crucial decisions based on an assessment of all available data and every conceivable perspective. And yet the environment in which a board operates is fluid. A decision that may appear totally logical and defensible today could seem questionable tomorrow, after new data and trends come to light.

Imagine, for example, that you are serving on the board of a retail company as the internet took off in the mid-1990s. It would seem entirely reasonable to sign off on a brick-and-mortar expansion, opening up a wave of new retail stores, as you are obviously unaware that within the next twenty years online sales would account for 40 percent of sector revenue. Of course, the pivot to online would never have been an all-or-nothing decision. At that point, you would have been aware of e-commerce, but you might easily have discounted the possibility that online channels would thoroughly undermine the business. It would have been hard to foresee to what extent a major new player, Amazon, would disrupt the sales and distribution channel.

Or imagine being on the board of a bank in the years building up to the 2008 financial crisis, overseeing the company's expansion into the mortgage market. It would have been hard in the early 2000s for the board to see the extent to which a mortgage-investing strategy would fail: not only sinking the bank's profitability but threatening its very existence and harming the broader economy. At the time, numerous boards approved the investment in subprime mortgages, lured by the outsize profits available. Any dissenting views would have been hard to defend when management and board members had data showing the sheer scale of profits on offer from the strategy.

Imagine, also a decade ago, you served on the board of a large tech company making multibillion-dollar investments in China to capitalize on its rapid economic growth and newly emerging consumer class. You surely would not have been able to foresee how much the state would back local competitors and pass privacy laws to make foreign companies less competitive and less profitable. Foreign boards worry that their companies have had limited success growing market share and revenue in China. To be sure, international companies may have benefitted from the low costs of production in the country. Still, these cost gains may not assuage board members and shareholders who had greater expectations for top-line revenue and profit growth, rather than just cost benefits.

When things go awry, outsiders all too easily assume that boards are out of touch, behind the curve, or just plain naive, if not outright stupid. In my experience, boards can certainly make mistakes, but for the most part these interpretations are wrong. Boards face impediments to perfect decision-making, so making the right call amid a lot of uncertainty is not foolproof.

When dealing with major strategic decisions that require deep and fundamental changes to organizations—say, to the business model or a reorientation of product lines—boards face two potential dangers: receiving incomplete or poor data, and management failing to execute a board-approved plan.

In the first case, the board makes decisions based on incorrect data or data that present an incomplete picture. As a result, the board may deploy resources to the wrong parts of the business (for example, to business lines that have already peaked and are starting to decline), or fail to allocate sufficient resources to other areas with potential for earnings growth.

In January 2002, the US retailer Kmart filed for Chapter 11 bankruptcy protection. In the months leading up to this fateful event, Kmart had seen record customer-satisfaction scores alongside healthy sales of $32 billion. But, as it turned out, the high scores were mostly reflective of positive responses from Kmart's lower-spending clientele—the overall numbers masked a growing disaffection among higher-spending customers, who were vital for boosting the company's revenues. Because there was no mechanism for relaying the satisfaction of high-spending customers specifically, management and the board remained ignorant of that enormously important data point. In essence, more disaggregated data would likely have revealed this underlying anomaly and better guided an appropriate response, perhaps even helping to avert bankruptcy.

Whereas Kmart's board and management can reasonably be accused of having imperfect information, boards of other companies might have a more complete data picture but still struggle to use that information effectively. For example, technology companies are regularly challenged on whether strong growth in data usage inures the boardroom to repeated low revenue and low profit numbers. In this context, "eyeballs"—such as followers and engagement on a social media platform—can serve as a false currency in board discussions. Again, the risk here is that the board can make misguided strategic decisions based on this interpretation of the data and therefore misallocate financial and human capital.

Such a risk is not restricted to technology companies. Many Western companies have invested heavily in China and point to market-share gains rather than financial profitability as evidence of success. Here, too, boards face the criticism of being overly seduced by the idea of selling their products to China's hundreds of millions of potential customers, even in the face of financial losses and without evidence that the story might turn. The questions for the boards of these companies are: How long can they sustain this? And should they instead pursue more profitable ventures elsewhere?

The second trap is the failure of management to execute on a board-approved plan. Even if the board has access to the highest-quality information showing what the company needs to change, there is still no guarantee that management will be able to effectively carry out the plan. Just as management's role is to implement the strategy as agreed by the board, the board's role is to monitor management's progress and intervene if necessary. If a company does not deliver on its articulated strategy and ultimately fails as a result, the board is also on the hook—in that sense responsible and accountable—for the company's performance, as evidenced by the many companies that have refreshed their boards after falling on hard times. In 2017, for example, half of GE's board left in the wake of the company's significant financial and operational challenges.

A classic issue faced by innumerable boards and management teams is cannibalization. This refers to the idea that existing business lines are managed by employees who resist change. These business lines consume a significant proportion of a company's financial and human capital and soak up senior management's time. Cannibalization starves new business units of capital, labor, and management expertise, hurting the company's chances of moving toward a new and more innovative strategy. In essence, it is a tension between the vested interest of the traditional core business and the as-yet-unproven venture.

From the board and senior management's perspective, the immediate concern is the possibility of killing the company's golden goose by shifting capital and human resources away from the existing (and often profitable) line. A related fear is that the new venture, if successful, could further undermine the traditional business by inadvertently competing against it for the company's finite resources. What makes this situation particularly complicated is that the existing businesses are often viable, making money and performing well. However, forecasts may indicate that they could face profit declines and may not be strategically viable in the long term.

Imagine a company making money from traditional sales in physical stores. The company's board might recognize that it needs to transition and sell more online. But even once the board accepts the change it sees coming, it could face resistance from the traditional employee base and thereby struggle to channel resources away from its stores. Perhaps it chooses to invest in refreshing the stores instead of providing the online venture with the capital and strategic focus it needs to succeed. One solution to combat cannibalization is ring-fencing, or granting the new business its own financial and managerial lines that are clearly delineated from the existing mother ship. This approach defuses the competition for resources, thereby giving the new venture the opportunity to flourish. Western Union, for example, set up WU.com as a separate entity headquartered in Silicon Valley. This ensured that the new division would benefit from economies of scale and the local talent pool, while also remaining free from the established thinking, entrenched processes, and possible constraints of the larger company. When it comes to managing potential cannibalization, there is no hard evidence that one approach is better than another. This means boards have to assess their own company's risk appetite before making a choice on whether to procced with or without ring-fencing.

Winning in All Environments

This chapter has centered on the board's key responsibility of devising the company's strategy. Beyond the normal challenges of incomplete data producing a bad strategy and poor execution undoing a good strategy, boards face an increasingly hostile environment for setting strategy in the first place. As such, there is a distinction between these normal challenges that will probably always exist and the broader uncertainties that loom, including geopolitical turmoil, economic stresses, and changing customer preferences. It is impossible to overstate the escalating risks that boards will face in the coming years, as detailed in Chapter 4.

What will distinguish the most successful companies' performance is the ability of their boards and management to constantly identify, quantify, and mitigate these risks. There will be important trade-offs for boards to assess as they determine the company's strategy. To achieve the best outcomes possible, companies will need to regularly update the risk tools, data, and models upon which the board's strategic decisions rely.

Boards are asked to make and endorse critical, win-lose strategic decisions about the companies they serve in an environment of limited knowledge and while facing a fundamental unpredictability of future events. This frame, called Knightian uncertainty after the University of Chicago economist Frank Knight, underscores the central challenge of strategy setting for a board: risk can be measured and managed, but uncertainty is unquantifiable and thus much harder to mitigate.

A number of critical risks determine the corporate winners and losers of the future. These risks include short-termism, fast-evolving technology, and rising protectionism. The best boards are continuously striving to put in place a strategy that survives come hell or high water—a strategy that does more than just generate profits but carries the company through the very worst market conditions, winning in all environments. As we will see in the next chapter, executing this strategy requires the very best leadership—not only from the board, but also from the CEO. This is why leadership selection is such a critical task for the board.

CHAPTER 2

Hiring (and Firing)
the CEO—and the Board

CEO SUCCESSION—THE HIRING (AND FIRING, WHEN IT IS WARRANTED) OF the company chief executive—is one of the key responsibilities of the board. Just as important is refreshing the board's own membership, recruiting those who will oversee the corporation smoothly and competently through the years. The selection of leadership is the one function over which the board has complete control and where management does not set the terms of debate, furnish key information, or drive the process. Some might argue that it is the most important board task of all.

Considering the rapidly changing economic, geopolitical, and business environment, the board's responsibility to install effective leadership is more pressing than ever. The tasks of setting and implementing strategy and allocating capital to the right investments are inherently difficult in this era of flux. Corporations increasingly require nimble CEOs who are open to changing a company's business model as circumstances dictate.

When the board picks a CEO, it entrusts a single person with forming a leadership team to model the tone and work ethic that will pervade the organization. Moreover, the CEO and other leadership must deliver on the strategic plans that the board has approved. For this reason, it is important for the board to scrutinize candidates carefully and be leery of the potential blind spots and weaknesses of the CEO and the team the CEO assembles. For example, the board should be wary of the dominant CEO who surrounds themselves with weaker executives in order to avoid having an obvious internal successor in place. This kind of CEO may be less open to challenges from their executive colleagues and the board itself.

As the leader of the executive team, the CEO is responsible for the day-to-day management of the organization. As such, the CEO is nearly always an executive director on the board as well. The board checks, challenges, and supports the CEO, all while making sure that the management team executes on the agreed strategy within the specified time frame. Given that the CEO is responsible for the company's operational performance and financial results, they are first in front of the firing line when a company underperforms. When the time comes, it is up to the board to put a CEO in place—and sometimes to put them out of a job.

The process of hiring a CEO is often an incredibly involved, multiyear task. Though boards for the most part get it right, it can also go horribly wrong. For instance, a great deal of turnover in the CEO position can be hugely disruptive to the organization. I once served on the board of a company that had four CEOs over a six-year period! Each new CEO brings a change in management style that can affect the company's culture. They also bring a fresh approach to the company's strategy, which fundamentally alters the company's direction. Frequent CEO turnover, therefore, can be destabilizing and confusing to employees. It also raises the question of what missteps the board was making in its CEO selection process.

To make an ideal pick, the board needs to interview numerous candidates and conduct a thorough vetting of their management, operations, and financial experience. Although at least one of my boards used psychometric tests as an additional assessment tool, most aspects of the CEO search process are quite prosaic. The vast majority of CEO selection processes follow a simple checklist:

» Has the CEO successfully managed many employees?

» Have they increased the market share or revenues of a business?

» Have they cut costs in a manner not inimical to the ongoing fortunes of a company?

» Do they have a past record of effectively carrying out a strategy? International experience? An ability to navigate bad times? Sufficient leadership to inspire employees? A facility for engaging externally with Wall Street analysts and other stakeholders? The capacity to embody the values of the company?

Boards must also decide whether they will seek a CEO from within the company's ranks. Often boards find internal candidates appealing, partly because they have usually seen the person up close at work, and they can expect the candidate to be familiar with the company's culture. There is also a good chance that an internal candidate's existing facility with the organizational workings will expedite the process and make the transition more efficient. Of course, the company's circumstances may also lead the board to look externally. When a company is in a growth phase or facing an urgent need to consolidate or restructure, the board might be wise to seek an outside candidate with prior experience in turning a company around—someone who would be well positioned to offer a fresh perspective on shaping strategy.

All these questions are necessary, but they are not by themselves sufficient to select a quality CEO. In a world of greater transparency and an ever-growing emphasis on ethics and behavior, it is essential to look beyond a candidate's ability to generate profits. The board must also assess the moral and ethical compass of prospective CEOs to determine if they can truly serve as the company's emissary.

Just as hiring a CEO is a mainstay responsibility of the board, when things go awry and the CEO must be let go, it falls to the board to make the final call. The reasons to terminate a CEO are numerous and varied: they can include ethical infringements, the perceptions of society (fair or unfair), or a simple lack of performance. In some cases, the dismissal of a CEO involves a pretty straightforward ethical failure, such as fraudulent accounting, harassment and discrimination, or health-and-safety breaches. The CEO and members of the wider management teams in the collapses of Enron (2001), Parmalat (2003), and Worldcom (2002) are standout examples. When such an issue comes to light, an outside entity—such as an ombudsman, a governmental regulatory body, or even a court—will rule on the culpability of the company as a whole and the CEO in particular. In such cases, board members are regularly updated, but they are largely bystanders. In other, less clear-cut instances of CEO failure, the board may be called upon to act as the proverbial judge, jury, and executioner.

During my own board tenures, these more nuanced ethical questions have only rarely arisen, and the underlying issues tended to be incredibly complex and difficult to resolve. The right decision, in such circumstances, is often far from obvious. For example, in 2019 the Swiss bank Credit Suisse was embroiled in a public scandal in which the CEO was accused of orchestrating a campaign to spy on a senior employee who had agreed to join an archrival. According to media reports, the CEO was concerned that the employee was preparing to hire away some of his colleagues after joining the competitor. Before long, it was alleged that the CEO had hired a private investigator, and the sensationalist media coverage that followed made the issue impossible to ignore. The Credit Suisse board faced enormous pressure to investigate the CEO. The challenge was that even though the CEO's actions appeared unethical, they were not technically illegal. The board undertook an investigation, which ultimately led to the resignation of the company's COO and later the CEO as well.

In recent years, events like these have become more public than ever. We are increasingly seeing regulators, politicians, and media figures opine on corporate matters that fly in the face of ethics and morality, even when a CEO has not committed a crime. The increasing power of both traditional and social media has created an environment in which these actions can take on outsize importance, forcing the board to act. In November 2018, for example, Jeff Fairburn, chief executive of the UK housebuilder Persimmon, faced a public outcry about his pay. Politicians and the media criticized a £110 million (approximately $140 million) bonus the board had awarded him for the company's strong performance. Critics argued that this result was largely a result of a government-led house-building scheme, rather than any specific initiative the CEO had undertaken. Even after the board reduced the bonus to £75 million, the public pressure on Fairburn did not abate, and he stepped down four months later.

Ethical conundrums and public outcries aside, the vast majority of CEOs who are removed are ousted for more conventional performance issues. These can include deviations from the agreed company strategy, weak managerial skills that erode organizational morale, missed financial targets, or simply an intolerable decline in performance, quarter after quarter. In these circumstances, termination should not come as a surprise to the CEO. Because the board is responsible for hiring the CEO in the first place, and unseating a CEO is never taken lightly, boards regularly offer feedback to the CEO, specifying where performance is weak and suggesting remedies. Nevertheless, when a board's interventions are simply unable to address an underlying systemic issue, the board may have to make the difficult decision to let the CEO go.

This is a weighty decision that will invariably have ripple effects throughout the organization. After all, installing a new CEO creates its own growing pains, including new staff and the need to build credibility with employees, external stakeholders, and the board. As the board considers the fate of a CEO, it should reflect on the question of trust. Ultimately, firing becomes necessary when the board's trust in the CEO breaks down and the board loses faith in their ability to deliver results, their moral or ethical judgment, their leadership, or their capacity to drive organizational transformations.

The relationship between the board and the CEO, and indeed the wider executive committee, is a complicated one, but at its core is the need for trust. On the one hand, it is a relationship founded on collaboration and openness, but on the other, it is hierarchical, as the board has a supervisory role judging the executive's performance. In this oversight role, all information flows to the board through the leadership, so it is almost impossible for directors to know anything beyond what management wants them to know. This means that the board is asked to blindly trust the information management provides. This asymmetry in information means that the board's judgment is only as good as the facts that it has. Some would say that this places the board at a distinct disadvantage, and that the board should have its own set of independent advisors. But such an arrangement would almost certainly harm the working relationship between the board and management by casting them in adversarial roles.

But the issue of trust goes beyond the information that the board is getting. The board must also trust how the CEO is running the company and executing the strategy. This can be especially difficult when it becomes clear that the strategy, rather than the CEO, is the problem.

Finding Where the Problem Lies

In the previous chapter, we considered the board's responsibility for overseeing and endorsing a company's strategy with imperfect information. More quality information is always better than less in helping the board to form its best judgments on the questions it faces. In this regard, board members should be assertive. They should be curious and probing when it comes to areas where they lack clarity. But at the same time, the board should remain constructive by supporting the management team and allowing it to take the lead in setting priorities for the future.

When a company is underperforming, boards are often tempted to look for fault in the CEO even if the problem lies elsewhere. Boards are wedded to the company's strategy—they approved it—so they can be disinclined to see their own missteps. They are more inclined to see problems with the CEO than problems underlying their industry. But if an industry's economics are flawed, some have argued, it almost does not matter who the CEO is. Warren Buffett, the famed US investor, has remarked: "When a management with a reputation for brilliance tackles a business with a reputation for bad economics, it is the reputation of the business that remains intact."

As such, boards must resist the temptation to assume that a company's woes are attributable to the CEO, rather than a result of poor strategic choices in which they, too, played a role. Any serious consideration of replacing a CEO must also include a hard look at the larger industry. The board's job here is to determine if the business environment has so materially changed that the company cannot compete and achieve sufficient sustainable returns that clear the cost of capital.

Of course, the board must also avoid blindness in the other direction. Board directors should take care not to be so seduced by a CEO's stellar past performance that they cannot objectively judge the executive's performance when the business regime changes substantially. A CEO who excels in a period of growth has different priorities than a CEO guiding their company through a recession. In an environment of declining sales, margin compression, shrinking market share, persistently slow growth, and poor stock performance, the question of whether the CEO is working must be considered, but the board-approved strategy also requires careful examination.

Business cycles can be discussed using an analogy of war and peace: a poor business environment is likened to wartime while a period of growth is like peacetime. Ben Horowitz, co-founder of the Silicon Valley venture capital firm Andreessen Horowitz, contrasted the attributes of wartime and peacetime CEOs in a 2011 article. In his view, peacetime CEOs have the luxury of focusing on expanding market share and can set big, ambitious goals, reflecting a high-risk appetite. Wartime CEOs, on the other hand, must avoid taking on significant new risk. They have to focus on defending their position and executing a survival plan. While a peacetime CEO will recruit in large scale and beef up the company stores of social, intellectual, human, and financial capital, a wartime CEO will likely have to prepare the organization for mass layoffs. Board members must therefore remain alert to where their company lies on the spectrum of war and peace as they evaluate a CEO's performance.

Another distinction between wartime and peacetime CEOs is their relative adherence to company culture. It is generally accepted today that peacetime CEOs value clear and transparent protocols as essential ingredients for success. These protocols (company rules, controls, and processes) are, in essence, the codification of a company's culture. However, when the company's survival is on the line, a wartime CEO might find it necessary to violate these protocols, opting for expedience over adherence to the cultural values and choosing to compromise or even jettison the company values.

Another risk during harsh economic periods is that wartime CEOs will choose to ignore or be intolerant of dissenting points of view and avoid building consensus, instead acting unilaterally in an attempt to stabilize the company. In this case, the board must be more vigilant and assertive in monitoring its CEO. Similarly, a board must remain alert to a peacetime CEO who, overtaken by the euphoria of burgeoning markets and improving economic conditions, may recklessly overinvest, overcommitting the company's resources in pursuit of returns and profits that never materialize and thereby placing the company on a precarious path. Like Horowitz—who by his own account has served as both a peacetime and wartime CEO—I am inclined to believe that it is a very rare individual who can execute both these roles effectively.

Even during the best of times, CEO succession is difficult. Recruiting the ideal CEO means finding someone with a range of skills, a deep knowledge of organizational management, and an unflappable temperament. As businesses become more complex and more global, candidates with the necessary combination of broad and deep knowledge become ever more rare. Meanwhile, as the economic environment gets choppier and more unpredictable, the need for care, consideration, and assertiveness on the board's part is even more essential.

Board Structure and Membership

Though board members are not in the business of deliberately making executives' lives difficult, their interactions with the CEO and other executives can be fraught with tension. A surefire way to minimize tensions and maintain a constructive working relationship between the board and senior executives is to clarify the structure of the board and the duties of its members.

Hiring and firing CEOs is just one part of the board's task. Another essential part is recruiting and hiring its own future membership. In each case, boards must deal with the challenges of making these selections well and of effectively organizing the leadership personnel. After all, who is chosen for CEO and for board membership will define the company's future success or failure. There is, of course, natural attrition and change in the boardroom because of term limits mandated by many countries. Still, boards must regularly check that they possess the skills, knowledge, and experience needed to fulfill their duties.

Board structure is not static. It can and does change, even if at a glacial pace, shaped by a range of factors. Assessments of the ideal board size, the type of board committees, term limits, and age limits have changed over time. The same is true of more involved questions about annual board assessments, annual election of board members by shareholders, and rules on board attendance. Other issues up for debate include whether board members should own their company's stock, board compensation more generally, the number of boards on which a director is allowed to serve, the ideal ratio of independent to nonindependent board members, and whether or not the roles of the board chairman and CEO should be merged. Board rules must also dictate whether, how, and when activist investors, company founders, or employee representatives should have a seat on the board.

Even as these arguments rage on, there are certain rules and guidelines in place to set the conventions of the board's structure, mostly to ensure its independence. According to a 2018 survey by recruitment firm Spencer Stuart, 71 percent of S&P 500 boards have a mandatory retirement age, the most common of which is seventy-two years. In my experience, guidelines can often be more valuable and more successful than ironclad rules. At the same time, however, boards need a flexible structure to best match their company's circumstances. Rules that dictate how long any individual can serve or that prescribe a compulsory retirement age can end up working against the best interests of the organization.

I have witnessed several occasions when board members who were adding valuable experience and knowledge were, unfortunately, forced to leave because of their age or because of a term limit. In one case, a seasoned former CEO reached his term limit in the middle of an operational crisis, precisely at the time when his experience would have been of greatest value.

Board size is, perhaps, the least contentious matter on this list. Most boards I have served on have had between twelve and fourteen members at any given time. This number generally works well because it provides adequate staff for the board's three main committees: nominations and governance, audit, and compensation. A *Harvard Business Review* study argues that the ideal board size is twelve directors: large enough to provide sufficient resources to cover the committees' work (as most board members sit on at least two committees) and to meet the board's obligations, but not so big as to encourage free riding. It is essential, after all, that all voices are heard and opinions shared and debated. Not least because boards generally rely on consensus generated by vigorous debate, rather than a majority vote by board members. On rare occasions when consensus is not achieved, there is a risk that a board member can choose to abstain from a decision or even leave the board altogether.

Term limits restrict the length of time or number of terms a board member is allowed to serve. While there are no hard-

and-fast rules specifying a term limit in the United States, the UK's term limits tend to be relatively strict. Board members are allowed to serve three three-year terms, or a maximum of nine years. After that, board members are no longer considered independent enough to carry out their role. Exceptions can be made, but in such rare cases the board is required to "comply or explain" the decision to allow directors to extend their board stay.

The main critique of such a strict approach is that it erodes the board's institutional memory. This can be truly problematic if the company faces unplanned attrition or a mass exodus of board members at the same time as planned departures required by law, or if a newly minted board has to deal with preexisting, complex legal and regulatory issues before they are able to gain a full understanding of them. Even though boards keep scrupulous records of their activities, the personal know-how and context that is lost to stringent term limits can be costly.

Statutory term limits are less common among US boards. Instead, more emphasis is placed on annual evaluations of individual directors' performance and contributions. This approach assumes that a director's effectiveness should be the most important factor in determining whether and for how long they stay in their position. Arbitrary limits, on the other hand, imply that boards automatically become ineffective after a certain amount of time.

Beyond term limits, it has become a more regular occurrence for some proxy agencies and shareholders to advocate for age limits on board members. Many corporations have set this limit between seventy-three and seventy-five years old, but both this number and the average age of board members overall have inched higher as people live and work longer. Based on the proxy statement for the annual meeting of shareholders filed with the Securities and Exchange Commission (SEC), as of May 2019, the board of Warren Buffett's Berkshire Hathaway has an average director age of 72.6 years old, with three board members in their nineties. Still, few would find this state of affairs objectionable—and even if some shareholders do, they are frequently willing to overlook it, considering the company's legendary and consistent success over such a long period of time.

The presence of older board members can at times serve to counteract and complement management teams populated by younger executives. In an effort to "have adults in the room," many technology start-up companies, as well as more established ones, choose older board members who have experience with the long-term ups and downs of running companies and who have engaged with or even served as regulators. Still, a tension arises between this perceived wisdom of older board members and the underlying assumption of age limits: directors who have retired from executive roles may struggle to remain current with refreshed thinking and ideas—a grave weakness in an era of rapid innovation and technological change.

Age limits can be seen as an opportunity to usher younger talent into the board, even with the risk that younger candidates might have limited or narrow experience. To the extent that many corporate boards have traditionally been less diverse in their makeup, age limits can be a way of populating boardrooms with talent that is more diverse in terms of gender, race, and background. More fundamentally, as technology talent tends to skew young, the quest for technology expertise will likely force boards to confront some of their embedded requirements, such as traditional operational experience, corporate tenures, and minimum age.

Corporate boards are periodically subjected to formalized board assessments. These reviews are generally administered by search firms or consultants, and they provide an opportunity for directors to review not only the overall performance of the board but also its committees and individual directors. It is also a vital chance to pressure-test that the board structure and the chairman are working. A 2018 report on effective board evaluation by the *Harvard Law School Forum on Corporate Governance* found that the vast majority of Fortune 100 corporate boards, 93 percent, undergo some form of evaluation.

Board assessments are a barometer of the inner workings of the board team as well as the collaboration between the board and management. On a few occasions over the course of my board career, the assessment revealed discord both among board members and between the board and management—none of which had been previously apparent. In this regard, assessments are extremely useful in helping ensure that the board effectively carries out its duties and maintains a constructive engagement with the management and leadership team.

Importantly, board reviews mean that a director's performance is given greater weight than term or age limits. These assessments evaluate the board's stewardship of the company as well as its ability to meet its mandated goals on strategy, CEO selection, and culture. They also take into account peer feedback on the contributions of each individual director. This approach provides a more complete picture, which the board can use to help identify which members should stay and which should be let go.

Though there is a public perception that board seats are secure, board reviews can, and do, result in turnover when directors underperform, are ill-prepared, or fail to make any significant contribution. In this regard, ongoing board education and peer feedback on how board members are adding value are critical for the success of both the individual directors and the board as a whole.

Regardless of how effective a board is, performance reviews can improve directors' work by highlighting opportunities for improvement. They often include a full board evaluation, individual self-assessments, and peer reviews. In a *Harvard Business Review* article, "What Makes Great Boards Great," Jeffrey Sonnenfeld identified a range of benefits that board evaluations offer. For instance, a comprehensive board review can help members better oversee the development of the company strategy, verify the board's access to information, and ensure that the levels of candor, energy, and engagement are high. Meanwhile, through individual self-assessments, directors can reflect on how to optimize their time, skills, knowledge of the company and sector, and general preparedness. The peer review highlights the roles individual directors play in discussions, their interpersonal styles, their initiative, and their links to critical stakeholders.

Sonnenfeld goes on to rightly conclude that "if a board is to truly fulfill its mission—to monitor performance, advise the CEO, and provide connections with a broader world—it must become a robust team—one whose members know how to ferret out the truth, challenge one another, and even have a good fight now and then." His point is essentially that it is harmful to boards—and ultimately to the corporations that they serve—if they do not receive feedback on their own performance.

There is also the matter of board member independence. Board members are, for the most part, independent, serving in a fiduciary capacity on behalf of financial shareholders. According to the *Wall Street Journal*, 66 percent of all board members in the United States are independent, as are 72 percent of all board members of S&P 500 companies. This comports to the standards and requirements of stock market exchanges such as the NASDAQ and New York Stock Exchange, which require that "a majority of the board of directors of a listed company be 'independent.'"

Increasingly, boards are adopting a corporate oversight approach that takes into account other stakeholders. Even so, traditionally, independent board members are elected to serve the interests of a company's shareholders and, apart from the board-sitting fees they earn, do not have a monetary or other material relationship with the company.

Although a board's articles specifying the duty of loyalty go some way toward policing conflicts of interest, there remain other questions around directors' independence. For instance, there is the question of whether board members should hold stock in the companies they serve. I have been on boards where members were required to hold company stock and others where we were not.

Those who support board members owning company stock argue that it better aligns directors' interests with those of the company, employees, and other shareholders—in other words, board members should have proverbial skin in the game. In response, many corporations now compensate board members at least partly in company stock, and in some cases, directors must buy stock in the company with their own money before they join the board. Stock compensation to board members generally comes with a number of restrictions. It tends to take the form of deferred or restricted stock that might only vest when the director leaves the board, and very often board members are prohibited from using the stock as collateral.

The counterargument is that, by owning company stock, board members can no longer be deemed independent and they might be tempted to act in their own interest rather than the company's. For instance, facing a possible takeover by a competitor, board members who hold company stock might be unduly inclined to sell the company, or sell it at a discounted price, and earn a personal windfall.

Yet in practice board members have more at stake than just financial risk by holding the company stock. Ultimately, their reputations are on the line if things do not go well during their tenure. If they are seen to have failed in their custodial role, the damage of that perception far outweighs any short-term profits.

On balance, I believe that owning stock in the company focuses a director's mind and does relatively little harm, particularly as most board members are unlikely to amass enough stock to allow them to wield disproportionate influence. There are also numerous checks and balances that ensure that board members do not put their own financial benefit ahead of the company. Fiduciary duties make it illegal for directors to act against the interest of the company and transparency measures make it highly visible if they try to break the rules.

The question of who should sit on the board is of perennial interest—and specifically whether employee representatives, founders, and activists should be granted board seats. The German two-tiered, dual board structure allows for up to 40 percent of board seats to be employee held. This means the perspectives of employees are voiced directly and considered in many of the important decisions made at the board level. This approach has not gained much traction in the United States or UK, but every now and then politicians do flirt with the idea. For example, in the UK, Theresa May's 2016 campaign pledge was unequivocal: "If I'm prime minister . . . we're going to have not just consumers represented on company boards, but workers as well." Nevertheless, by the time Prime Minister May left office in July 2019, she had not followed through on this pledge.

There is also considerable debate as to whether large shareholders in a company should be allowed to serve on the board, as they could exert undue influence on decisions, with primarily their own interests in mind. These investors come in two types: strategic and activist. Strategic investors usually gain seats on a board after the company has been acquired in a strategic deal, and therefore have likely operated a similar business. Activists tend to use financial tools such as repo markets to build up a stock position in the company. Strategic investors, generally, are focused on the long term, while activist investors can be in it for short-term stock appreciation. Many observers assume that strategic shareholders are always a constructive, positive influence, while activist shareholders are invariably negative and disruptive. However, the reality is far more nuanced.

Left unchecked, the disproportionate financial power of strategic investors can grant them too much control over critical decisions such as selecting the CEO, setting the company's strategy, and choosing whether to sell the company and at what price. On the board of SABMiller, for example, I served alongside two large strategic shareholders, who together owned roughly 30 percent of the company (and held five out of twelve board seats). Their influence on the company was always going to be substantial. And while strategy, CEO selection, and the eventual sale of the company elicited feverish boardroom debates, the board had to manage the optics of the outsize power that these strategic investors held compared to the rest of the shareholders, even if only on paper.

To head off this risk, strategic investor board members are deemed nonindependent and generally do not chair board committees or the board itself, nor do they occupy the lead independent director role. Furthermore, as nonindependent directors, they are often forced to recuse themselves from sensitive board discussions where they might exercise undue influence. Nevertheless, the long-term investment horizon of strategic investors aligns well with corporations and their other shareholders, such as pension funds.

Company founders are, in a sense, an extreme version of a strategic investor. Even if the founders' financial stake in the company is small, they can nevertheless wield enormous influence on a company and board since they are frequently understood as defining the company's culture. Having founders or family representatives serve on a board can be tricky, particularly if a board's responsibilities change dramatically—such as when a private company goes public.

Like strategic investors, activists take a notable stake in a company—as little as 5 percent will get them on the radar—but they are typically focused on short-term goals. According to analysis by Goldman Sachs, the length of time that activists trade from when they first get a stock to when they exit averages twenty-eight months. Activists are generally attracted to companies that have had weak financial performance, measured as total return on a stock—which they will compare to past performance and the target's peer group. They are also drawn to companies with a complex portfolio of assets or business lines.

Activists often seek board seats, promising a fresh (and unbiased) look at the company. On occasion, they get their wish, with boards capitulating and even increasing their size to accommodate the activist. For example, asset manager Trian Partners was able to gain board seats on Procter & Gamble and GE, and investment manager Third Point placed its representatives on Sotheby's, Sony, Campbell Soup Company, and Nestlé.

In principle, the new and unfiltered perspective offered by activists should add value to a business. After all, the activist's goal is usually a quick increase in the company share price. However, activists have earned a reputation for being disruptive and making costly demands that eat into management's time—and that, in many cases, run counter to the long-term interests of the company. For example, Procter & Gamble and the activist investor Nelson Peltz spent $100 million each advocating for their separate interests during a proxy battle in 2017. The board likely spent a significant proportion of this sum on advisors to help navigate the proxy fight. After a close result in favor of the company, Peltz was awarded a seat on the board.

Even when not battling with activists, companies increasingly hire bankers, financial consultants, and lawyers to advise them on how to handle an activist incursion, should one arise. Meanwhile, activists spend a considerable amount of money acquiring the necessary stake in a company and working to bring other shareholders around to their point of view: that the company is in need of urgent change, which they stand ready to deliver.

In addition to demanding board representation, more aggressive activists agitate for the removal of existing board members, the chairman, and even the CEO. For example, in 2020, the hedge fund Elliott Management Corporation attempted to remove Twitter's cofounder and CEO Jack Dorsey. The two sides ultimately settled, granting Elliott seats on Twitter's board but allowing Dorsey to remain CEO. The activist's playbook tends to also demand changes to the company strategy, which can entail corporate restructuring and asset sales or even selling the company entirely.

No company is too big, too complex, or too regulated to avoid being the target of an activist; virtually every industry has seen activists gain board seats. Some well-known corporations that have engaged with activist investors include food producer Nestlé, with Third Point; confectionary maker Mondelēz, with Trian; and retailer JCPenney, with the hedge fund Pershing Square. I directly experienced the interventions of an activist company, Sherborne Investors, while serving on the board of Barclays. Sherborne's approach faced much regulatory scrutiny and media attention, and in many respects was a source of board consternation.

However, a board's engagement with activists does not necessarily have to be adversarial. In 2016, while I was serving on the board of the Silicon Valley technology company Seagate, the board opted to willingly invite in ValueAct Capital, an activist investor. The two entities worked productively together, demonstrating that the relationship between the company board and the activist can be collaborative and constructive. This kind of outcome is more likely if the activist is open about when and how they built up a sufficient stake in the company: Did they purchase the stock outright, or indirectly through the repo market or using stock options? Additionally, it matters if the activist makes a concerted effort to engage with the board to express their concerns, rather than airing them publicly in the media.

There can be some resistance to activists joining a board. Sitting board members often worry that activists' thinking may be shaped by erroneous or outdated information, or that they will too readily discount the board's judgment. After all, in many cases the board has already explored the possibilities the activist is pushing for and decided against them—for good reason.

There is no doubt that activists are having an impact on boardrooms, even if their record of success is mixed. Activists can be catalysts for difficult but necessary change. This might include cost cutting that involves job losses or restructuring that involves the sale of a business unit. Even so, the hard-nosed, purely numerical approach that tends to guide activist investors often neglects the broader societal considerations that boards need to bear in mind.

A similar conundrum of divided loyalties is presented by the question of whether the same person should serve as board chairman and CEO. In lieu of separating the two positions, US corporations place considerable emphasis on the role of the lead director. The lead director's primary job is to act as a liaison between the chairman and the rest of the board. This individual, known in the UK as the senior independent director, is selected from the board members as their representative. Having worked on boards that use both models—separate and combined chairman and CEO roles—I have not seen any strong evidence that one format is superior to another, so long as the lead director is independent. The best lead directors avoid swaying decisions one way or another, often going so far as to vote only after other board members have expressed their views. It is also the lead director's job to present the board's feedback and review to the chairman, along with any concerns or criticisms they might have about the chairman's performance. It also falls to the lead director to relieve the chairman of their duties when the rare occasion arises.

Regardless of model, the chairs of the various committees are always appointed by the board chairman, who essentially goes through a matching exercise, selecting those board members with appropriate backgrounds and experiences to chair committees. For example, a board member with notable experience in auditing or accounting is usually chosen as the chair of the audit committee, and a member with a strong finance background or specific experience on remuneration issues is usually chosen as the chair of the compensation committee.

It should therefore be quite clear why boards tend to favor members who are CEOs or have otherwise served in the corporate C-suite. If one were to rank board members according to whom the CEO would be most likely to call for advice, those who have previously served as CEOs would, to my mind, be at the top of the list. The fact that different directors have different roles on the board means that not all board members are equal, which partly explains differences in board fees and compensation. Even so, in business, just as in sports or politics, a team is most effective if its members work together seamlessly. This is particularly important for corporate boards at times of high stress or change.

If one observation can be drawn from the many different varieties of board structures, it is that their differences often reflect the idiosyncrasies of the companies they oversee. Even so, across a wide variety of corporations, concerns related to board staffing remain a constant.

Staffing the Board

In his seminal book, *Good to Great*, Jim Collins describes the ideal way to build a management team using the metaphor of a bus. The leadership wants to first be sure they have all the right people aboard; only then can they move on to making sure those people are occupying the right seats. This framing applies just as well to the boardroom. After all, the board, too, is tasked with ensuring it reflects a mix of skills, talent, and experiences that enable it to address the challenges of the day. For this reason, filling their own ranks is a top priority of boards, and one that can involve a complex process of recruiting, vetting, and matching skills and personalities with the needs of the board and the company.

Most companies have just twelve board seats to fill, so it's imperative that they think long and hard about whom to pick. A CEO will want a certain portion of the board to have experience with the peculiarities and challenges of being at the helm of a company: people who have been CEOs themselves. Board members who have served as CEO—even in a different sector—will bring a wealth of transferable experience and knowledge with them. They will be ready on day one to give advice about motivating the employee base; executing the strategy; navigating regulators, investors, and other stakeholders; preparing for difficult economic circumstances; and, of course, managing their colleagues on the board.

Then there is the matter of stocking the board with technical expertise. In general, most companies reserve board seats for directors who have decent audit and financial skills. After all, one of the board's key functions is signing off on company financial reports. Yet other technical skills can be beneficial, too, particularly in industries with a more difficult or complex business model.

This is the case for many global financial institutions focused on warehousing, trading, and otherwise making money from complex derivatives. The boards of such companies need members with knowledge of how these products work and what risks they pose. It would be fair to say that having more directors with a deep knowledge of complex derivatives may have helped banks and insurance companies during the financial crisis. In contrast, a mining company's business model is much more straightforward—it mostly requires understanding that there is more value to be gained by taking a ton of copper out of the ground than by leaving it in.

Boards sometimes face pushback when they fill their seats with members whose experience is seen as similar to that of the executives managing the business day to day. These directors' contributions to board discussions may well duplicate the views of company executives rather than offering a fresh perspective or challenging the leadership team's logic.

Rather than seeking more of the same insights, boards should try to infuse their discussions and debates with knowledge that can drive the company in new directions. Consider, for example, the fact that some of the most well-known American companies derive over 40 percent of their profits from outside the United States. These include Ford (51 percent), IBM (64 percent), Intel (85 percent), Amazon (45 percent), McDonald's (66 percent), and Nike (50 percent). It would behoove these companies to have some board members with an international background and direct knowledge of the specific opportunities, risks, and complexities of operating in a global marketplace. This could come from managing a global employee base, with multiple jurisdictions governing the employment rights, or from experience with the political and economic risks inherent in global trade.

Achieving a balance of expertise in the boardroom is crucial. Often, in times of trouble, an imbalance in a board's composition can help explain why a company is facing challenges. For instance, in 2019, when Boeing was dealing with two fatal 737 MAX crashes, the company was criticized for having too many board members with financial backgrounds and too few who had engineering or technological expertise and may have been better equipped to grapple with safety issues. As part of the company's response to this criticism, in September 2019 Boeing created an aerospace safety committee on its board to oversee the development, manufacturing, and operation of its aircraft and services and to boost the transparency of engineering decisions.

In my own experience, I joined the board of Barrick, the gold producer, at a time when the company was dealing with a heavily indebted balance sheet and enormous cost overruns on its major capital projects. Some investment analysts complained that the board had too many directors with engineering backgrounds and too few with financial expertise that might have helped the company steer clear of its ongoing problems. In response, the Barrick board recruited directors with finance backgrounds who helped steady the company's financial situation.

But, again, the board's core should consist of people who have previously run large organizations and served as CEOs. This can be more difficult to achieve at certain times than at others. For example, there may not be a pool of candidates with relevant CEO experience at the precise time that a board is seeking a new member.

At least three trends have meaningfully shifted companies' approaches to staffing their boards in recent years. These are the need for geopolitical expertise, the need for technology skills, and the need for diversity—not just of race and gender, but of experience, bringing in the perspectives of regulators, government, customers, employees, and shareholders.

Geopolitical Expertise

Evidence of increasing de-globalization is unmistakable. Disruptive trends such as Brexit, rising populism, and protectionist economic policies are forcing corporations to find new ways to conduct global business. Increasingly, boards must consider their strategic choices and capital allocation in light of these fundamental shifts.

To do so successfully, changes to board membership may be necessary to ensure that there is sufficient geopolitical know-how in the boardroom. Global economic and political shifts demand that boards place an even greater premium on the type of experience and knowledge that has traditionally belonged to those working in public policy—including an understanding of areas such as human rights, social contracts, and the vested interests of domestic politicians. Shifts in the global policy regime could scupper board and management plans and even force multinational corporations to scale back and sell parts of their international operations.

Boards of global corporations are already contending with a host of geopolitical risks. These include challenges to the efficacy of multilateral institutions such as the International Monetary Fund (IMF) and World Trade Organization (WTO), which have governed the global system and brought stability over the past fifty years. Rising trade protectionism and mounting regulatory requirements are affecting all manner of industries and sectors, including banking, food, and technology. And of course, the 2020 COVID-19 pandemic highlighted how extreme global events could lead to international border closings and trade disruptions. These shifts are leading to a fall in global trade volumes, declining cross-border capital flows, and dwindling immigration. Boards would be wise to look for members who have a strong knowledge of worldwide economic trends and geopolitical dynamics and a network of political connections around the world.

Boards are also facing greater government encroachment. In 2014, for example, the UK government used political pressure to intervene in the attempt by Pfizer, the US pharmaceutical company, to buy British drugmaker AstraZeneca. The prime minister at the time, David Cameron, expressed concern about the deal's possible impact on UK jobs, and stated that the bid would likely be subject to a "public interest test," which would enable Parliament to intervene. Facing a steep uphill battle, Pfizer abandoned the proposed $106 billion deal.

Across the world, governments have long opposed takeovers that could make individual companies too dominant or even monopolistic. Today, states are increasingly citing national security reasons to probe, resist, and halt cross-border deals. The Committee on Foreign Investment in the United States (CFIUS) has blocked numerous M&A transactions in technology and infrastructure. The 2018 attempted takeover of MoneyGram by China's Ant Financial and of Qualcomm by Singapore's

Broadcom are just two of dozens of transactions that have been blocked by CFIUS over the past decade.

The CFIUS review process has also become more stringent. In 2018, the committee expanded its mandate to include reviewing bids for minority stakes in US companies, in addition to monitoring full acquisitions. It also resolved to target proposed deals from certain countries, notably China, and lengthened the list of national security concerns that can derail a deal. In a nutshell, not only are cross-border takeovers getting harder to execute, but it is becoming more difficult to do business in jurisdictions deemed to be a security concern, such as China and Russia.

These trends have far-reaching implications for a company's strategy. Given the circumstances, it is easy to see why a director with strong knowledge of intellectual property law and experience in dealing with cross-border M&As of assets in sensitive industries such as infrastructure, telecommunications, or technology would be particularly attractive to boards.

These tumultuous global shifts throw up additional urgent issues. Boards must interrogate the existing business to see what is at risk and determine how the company will fund itself when global financial institutions are squeezed on capital and liquidity. How will the head office get the right currency to the right businesses in the right countries on time?

As governments become more protectionist, boards will need to identify where their corporations could suffer substantial losses on capital investments that were previously made in good faith. Rising protectionism increases the threat of governments expropriating a company's assets and raises the risk that a company can lose its license to trade—that is, the right to operate in a particular country. Importantly, companies can effectively lose their licenses to trade even without a government's explicit withdrawal of permission. If a government simply imposes too many restrictive conditions, competition in a local market can become untenable. Google effectively shut down its Chinese search engine in 2010 after a cyberattack from within the country targeted it and dozens of other companies.

The increasingly siloed world also threatens how companies fund themselves. A "carry trade" is a strategy of borrowing at low interest rates in developed countries and investing in higher-yielding emerging markets. It is a strategy that many businesses engage in, but it may become increasingly untenable in the years ahead. The climate of global retrenchment has led to rising capital controls, which can hamper a company's ability to move money to its business units in other countries and repatriate any profits to pay its shareholders. Because the carry trade assumes that capital can move freely across borders, a world of separate, nationally focused financial institutions forces corporations to overhaul how they fund their operations and return capital to their shareholders.

If this trend continues in the extreme, corporations may have to abandon the global capital model in favor of a local approach. This would mean that rather than borrowing money in New York, investing in Brazil, and then returning the profits to the United States, corporations would raise and invest capital in Brazil, and profits would have to be distributed to local investors of the Brazilian subsidiary. Clearly, this would upend the current thinking within many boardrooms. But while this scenario may be hard for current leadership to fathom, boards should nevertheless explore how to maneuver in it so as not to destroy value or harm company operations.

Meanwhile, the tighter regulations on banking institutions that followed the 2008 global financial crisis should leave boards reflecting on how corporations will access capital to fund themselves. Greater capital and liquidity requirements could constrain a company's ability to access fresh capital, thereby making it more difficult to raise the money a global business needs to operate and invest. This could limit a company's growth, robbing it of the opportunity to expand into new markets or make an acquisition.

In April 2019, Jamie Dimon, the chairman and CEO of JPMorgan Chase, one of the largest global banks, cautioned, "When the next real downturn begins, banks will be constrained—both psychologically and by new regulations—from lending freely into the marketplace, as many of us did in 2008 and 2009." He went on to warn that "new regulations mean that banks will have to maintain more liquidity going into a downturn, be prepared for the impacts of even tougher stress tests and hold more capital because capital requirements are even more pro-cyclical than in the past. Effectively, some new rules will force capital to the sidelines just when it might be needed most by clients and the markets."

As it turned out, the global coronavirus pandemic hit less than a year later, in March 2020. Global economic growth forecasts were meaningfully reduced, and financial regulators responded by loosening the stress tests on banks, thereby enabling them to inject greater liquidity into the economy and avoiding the dire scenario that Dimon had foreshadowed.

Greater economic protectionism and mounting geopolitical risks affect where and how companies can successfully and competitively sell across borders. Boards need to make sure they have the talent and skills to understand how management should navigate and mitigate these risks. For instance, a board member with a strong financial background can help a company think through how to use financial-market tools to hedge against emerging risks and make the best possible investment decisions. Such an approach might include shifting company strategy from outright, large-scale investments across different countries to more joint ventures with local partners who would take on most of the risk.

As businesses reexamine their global footprint and consider the scale of their international operations, they must also consider the costs—not just the potential benefits—of cross-border investments. Overseeing a company's ongoing liabilities for international staff facing retrenchment, decommissioning international operations, monitoring environmental commitments, and meeting tax and regulatory obligations can expose a business to longer-term cash outlays and losses. A deft handling of geopolitical sensitivities—backed by requisite board experience, knowledge, and expertise—is essential.

When I served on the Barclays board, for example, we made the difficult decision to withdraw from Africa, a region the company had invested in for over one hundred years. My own experience—from having been raised in Africa and from my studies of economies in developing countries—helped the board look beyond the pure business aspects of the decision. In particular, my experience working for the World Bank allowed me to offer insights about how multilateral institutions and governments would react to this decision.

In the end, the board was able to understand the wider context of the decision, including the impact it would have on

African economies and communities and the potential geopolitical consequences, such as whether Barclays' withdrawal would create an opportunity for other financial institutions.

What initially appeared to be a relatively straightforward decision for Barclays turned out to be anything but—not least because the company had to negotiate sellouts from a dozen different countries. This meant negotiating terms with each individual government and mitigating the separation costs, which turned out to be considerable.

It was no accident that Barclays had recruited me; they had deliberately searched for someone with knowledge of emerging-market economics to join their board. More generally, all corporate boards benefit from meticulously cultivating the international expertise in their boardroom—that is, by attracting candidates from different parts of the world or with public policy experience.

Yet, in this rapidly shifting environment of global pandemics, environmental concerns, China's ascendancy, de-globalization, rising populism, and forecasts for slow global economic growth, geopolitical complexities are just the beginning.

Technology Expertise

Of the directors overseeing the world's biggest banks, only 6 percent have any technology experience. That figure, from an Accenture report, may seem surprising considering the increasing digitization of the banking industry. Yet banking is not the only sector to drastically undervalue this crucial type of expertise.

Technology is transforming the rules of business in just about every sector. As businesses decide on technology investments and contend with competition in the digital age, the board plays an important role in ensuring that the company's employees and operations are efficient and productive. Given the extent to which technological transformation can affect a board's ability to discharge its responsibilities—particularly in achieving the company's strategic imperatives—technological expertise should loom large when staffing a board. A background in technology might affect how a board director receives and interprets the information needed to make key business decisions on capital allocation, staffing, risk assessment, and, of course, technological changes.

How technological shifts will affect a company depends on at least two factors: whether technology is a strategic differentiator for the business, and the nature of the industry and market structure. After assessing the possible effects of a new technology on the company, the board can determine if it specifically requires technology expertise among its members—instead of, say, delegating technological issues to management, enlisting advisors to the board, or creating an independent advisory council that directly reports to the board.

The extent to which technology differentiates a business from its competitors can be viewed on a sliding scale. On one end, technology innovations and improvements simply ensure that a company remains competitive and stays in the game. At the other extreme, technology acts as a critical source of value creation and enhancement.

If technology merely serves to keep a company current— such as in a conventional utility company that provides water or electricity, or a provider of phone-line services—the board probably does not need to be actively involved in the day-to-day management of technology decisions and can comfortably delegate this responsibility to the executive management without requiring a tech seat on the board.

However, for businesses that derive a more significant part of their value from technology—and where technology can materially affect the company's strategic aims—a dedicated board seat with technology expertise could be useful. In this scenario, rather than use up a board seat, boards could, for example, use third-party independent experts who have a deep understanding of technology as a key driver of the company's fundamental value proposition. These outside experts would check and challenge management's recommendations.

Then there are companies whose core value proposition and viability depend on getting technology bets right. Obvious examples are technology companies such as Apple and Google. A conventional retail chain or supermarket that is competing aggressively with Amazon, such as Walmart or the UK's Argos, could also decide that technology is key to differentiating its services in the future. In these cases, technology decisions are a more significant part of the company's strategy, and thus fall more squarely within the board's oversight. This situation requires at least one director with the appropriate depth and breadth in the technology field.

The industry structure in which a business operates should also influence how a board assesses technology effects, and ultimately whether it could benefit from a dedicated technology seat.

For monopolies or companies with dominant market positions—such as a utility or power company—technology can enhance efficiency and increases worker productivity rather than differentiating it in the marketplace. In this case, the board can adopt a relatively arm's-length approach and delegate technology-related decisions to the company's executive leadership. This has been the attitude of most of the boards on which I have served. In most cases, the view was that the speed of technological change in both software and hardware means that any board member elected based on their technology expertise today could find their skill set rendered obsolete tomorrow.

The opposite is true for businesses operating in highly competitive industries—for example, wheat farming, where one company's product is essentially the same as the others' and companies have a nearly unlimited number of suppliers and consumers. Those boards need as much understanding of technology as possible, because for them, technology can be the differentiator in terms of reducing costs and increasing speed and efficiency. Of course, like most business decisions, the question of how to imbue the board with technology expertise depends on context.

Most companies, after all, do not operate on the extreme ends of this scale. The board of a monopoly can decide to delegate technology responsibilities if technology is seen as incidental to its core business. In contrast, a monopoly business that sees technology as a differentiator will want to have technology expertise on the board; many big tech companies are themselves examples of this kind of approach. In a similar vein, a company that operates in a competitive market but largely relies on technology just to stay in the game—for example, a mining or oil-and-gas business—can confidently delegate this responsibility. However, a business in a competitive market that draws appreciable value from technology—such as a financial services business—is best served by bringing independent technology expertise into the boardroom. Of course, the board needs to have clarity on what it expects from a board director brought on specifically for their knowledge of technology.

For the most part, today's boards tend to seek a director who will use their technology expertise to come up with fresh ideas to protect and operate the business and help sharpen the company's strategy. At a time when companies are allocating a greater proportion of their capital to technology—for purposes ranging from managing cyber risks, to increasing operational efficiency, to reaching their customer base—a board member with technology expertise can play a key oversight role in checking and challenging management decision-making.

Even so, boards must be aware that in today's world of ever-faster technological progress, there is no guarantee that the fresh perspective of a board member hired today will still be at the leading edge—or relevant at all—in a year. Their technology knowledge can quickly atrophy, going from the vanguard to obsolescence in little time.

Diversity and Inclusion

In May 2010, I joined a dozen board colleagues onstage at the annual general meeting of a board on which I served. During the question-and-answer portion of the proceedings, a shareholder in the audience posed a question to the chairman of our board. The shareholder asked, while gesturing at me, "What are the credentials of that statutory board member that she would be allowed to sit on this company's board?" I was, at the time, the only woman and the only visible minority serving on the board.

After some mild gasps from the crowd, the board chairman directed the insistent shareholder to the company's annual report, which, in addition to detailing the company's financial and operational performance for the year, laid out the relevant educational and work experience of all the board members. The shareholder sat down, seemingly appeased.

After I got over my instinctive embarrassment at being singled out in such an aggressive manner, I reflected on how unusual it was to see a woman or ethnic minority on a board. The experience was a further reminder about the urgent need for corporate boards to staff themselves with more women, more ethnic and racial minorities, and a generally more diverse group.

If we judge gender progress by representation in senior leadership positions, there is some reason to be sanguine. Women have made important professional strides over the past decade in politics and global policymaking. Prominent examples include European Central Bank head Christine Lagarde, former US Federal Reserve chair Janet Yellen, IMF head Kristalina Georgieva, long-term German chancellor Angela Merkel, New Zealand prime minister Jacinda Ardern, and numerous other female heads of state who have come and gone in Europe, Asia, Africa, and South America. In academia, the NGO world, and business sectors such as technology (old and new), automobiles, industrials, consumer goods, and even that bastion of masculinity, mining, the glass ceiling, while not shattered, is certainly cracked. Women have not just ascended into the C-suite, but in many cases have acquired the coveted CEO role.

This, in turn, means that the pool from which future boards can draw has expanded immensely. In fact, the number of women CEOs in the Fortune 500 has been rising steadily since 1998, when Jill Barad of Mattel and Marion Sandler, co-CEO of Golden West Financial Corporation, were the only female chiefs listed. The female Fortune 500 CEO population is now at an all-time high of twenty-four, and the corresponding figure in the S&P 500 is twenty-two—certainly a trend in the right direction. According to search firm Spencer Stuart, 26 percent of all S&P 500 board members in calendar year 2019 were women, and women made up 46 percent of newly appointed board members in the same year, up from 17 percent in 2009.

This represents progress, but there is still a great distance to go. Holding less than 5 percent of Fortune 500 CEO positions in 2019, women are still underrepresented in the C-suite and the boardroom. According to BlackRock's investment stewardship report, approximately 33 percent of the incoming director class in 2018 were women. Meanwhile, 52 percent of the ninety-four newly elected independent directors of real estate investment trusts in 2018 were women.

The debate on how to get more women on boards has moved speedily from the wish list to a high position on the board's agenda over the past five years. Numerous studies show that companies with female representation on their boards (and in their C-suites) tend to outperform companies that do not. In a 2015 report, *Diversity Matters*, McKinsey concluded that companies in the top quartile for gender diversity are 15 percent more likely to have financial returns above their respective national industry average. A 2014 publication by Credit Suisse found that companies with more than one woman on the board have returned a compound 3.7 percent per year over those that have none since 2005.

A gender-diverse board can help not just the quantity of earnings, but also the quality. In a 2016 study, *Putting Gender Diversity to Work: Better Fundamentals, Less Volatility*, investment-banking firm Morgan Stanley found that companies with high gender diversity display lower ROE volatility—

and thus higher long-term earnings quality—over a three-year time period, relative to companies with low gender diversity.

Meanwhile, a 2011 report on Fortune 500 companies by Catalyst, a nonprofit campaigning for better workplaces for women, shows that there are considerable advantages to appointing more than just one or two women to a board. The report, entitled *The Bottom Line: Corporate Performance and Women's Representation on Boards (2004–2008)*, found that companies with three or more female board directors over a sustained period significantly outperformed those with low female representation: by 84 percent on return on sales, 60 percent on ROIC, and by 46 percent on ROE.

The insistence on greater female board representation has, in part, been catalyzed by explicit proclamations from legislators. In August 2018, for example, the state of California announced a requirement that all companies headquartered there must have at least three women on their board. This policy follows a long line of similar quota-based approaches in Scandinavia and France. However, such an approach is not the only way to get more women into the boardroom. The 30% Club in the UK is an initiative to drive female board membership to at least 30 percent. Through mentorship, it seeks to broaden and deepen the pool from which boards can draw female talent.

Financial shareholders and large, influential asset managers are also pressuring corporations to place more women on their boards. In January 2018, the investment management corporation BlackRock wrote to the nearly three hundred Russell 1000 companies that had fewer than two women on their board, emphasizing the importance and benefits of board diversity. Financial shareholders wield enormous voting power and routinely use it to vote against board chairs and board members if they feel inadequate steps are being taken to redress issues of gender parity.

In addition to increasing the number of talented women members, boards are pursuing competent and experienced ethnic minority candidates. It is now widely considered best practice for corporate boards to reflect the diversity of the customers they serve and the communities in which they operate. For a company's board to truly reflect its consumers, it must be alive to not just gender diversity but diversity in race, sexual orientation, and thought as well.

The literature on the merits of board diversity in this more general sense is also well established. The McKinsey report *Diversity Matters* found that companies in the top quartile for racial and ethnic diversity were 35 percent more likely to have financial returns above their respective national industry medians. Companies in the bottom quartile for both gender and ethnicity/race were statistically less likely to achieve above-average financial returns.

Even so, ethnic minorities remain scarcely represented on the major corporate boards. In the UK, at the end of July 2017, only eighty-five of the 1,050 director positions in the FTSE 100 were held by ethnic minorities. Only 2 percent of director positions are held by UK citizens who are ethnic minorities, despite this group making up 14 percent of the total UK population. Fifty-one companies of the FTSE 100 did not have any ethnic minorities on their boards.

One attempt to remedy this gap came in the form of the October 2017 Parker Review, which concluded that UK companies should increase the ethnic diversity of their boards. In particular, the review proposed that every FTSE 100 board should have at least one director from an ethnic minority background by 2021 and every FTSE 250 board should do the same by 2024. Though this may not seem like an ambitious target, three years since the review's publication concerns are growing that many companies will struggle to meet the targets.

It would be a mistake to think that global corporations have reached a comfortable equilibrium on the question of diversifying their boards. However, it is fair to say the issue of board makeup is now receiving just as much attention from inside corporations as from without. That there should be more diverse representation among directors is largely unquestioned by boards themselves. It is the question of how to achieve this goal that is up for debate.

It is my sense that a great many people across different backgrounds hope to use their unique perspectives, talents, and experiences to contribute to the success of a company. However, it is also my sense that no one—including women and minorities—wants to occupy a board seat (or any seat for that matter) purely because of their race or gender.

Simply put, in order to operate, compete, and excel, corporations need the best talent. In theory, companies should not need to concern themselves with the question of whether an employee is Black or white, male or female. However, in the real world, the recruitment process has been beset by human failings, such as expedience, cultural networks, and historic connections, which have traditionally left many boards populated by members who look and think alike—a veritable death knell for a twenty-first-century company.

Enhancing board diversity is not without its challenges, and efforts can face pushback. Boards and companies must ensure that their attempts to combat homogeneity are not seen as reverse discrimination. And they must be careful not to implicitly prejudge excellent employees who did not choose to be male or white. Boards and executive management must be sensitive to this concern or they risk facing lawsuits similar to two that Yahoo faced in 2016. Two white, male employees sued the company, alleging discrimination and arguing that female management at the company "intentionally hired and promoted women because of their gender, while terminating, demoting or laying off male employees because of their gender." Both cases were dismissed by the courts, but nevertheless efforts to seek gender parity in the boardroom and broader workplace require sensitivity in all directions.

While rebalancing the boardroom to reflect modern society is an urgent matter of critical importance, it should not be pursued by driving out other members or sending the message that certain types of employees are no longer wanted. Doing so would create a run on talent and could sink the company. Talent should always welcome greater competition. The fact that companies can draw from an expanding pool is a good thing, but the board should not allow its diversity efforts to alienate any member of the workforce. Nor should the board let its message about increasing its diversity be interpreted as a signal to rule out others based on their gender, race, or any other aspect of their background.

Other Staffing Considerations

The benefits of refreshing a board's membership to better reflect global trends and modern societal demands are abundantly clear, but boards must also continually address their needs in areas beyond geopolitics, diversity, and technology.

For instance, boards frequently face pressure to integrate specific environmental and NGO experience into their membership. While this may, on a superficial level, seem innocuous, boards must always be sure to seek "T-shaped" directors: members who have broad enough knowledge and expertise to contribute on all the issues facing the board, but who also have deep capabilities and competence in particular areas—for example, auditing or technology.

The risk is that a single-issue board member could lack broader business perspective, and thus lack a nuanced understanding of the challenges of implementation that corporations face. This is particularly true for companies of greater size and scale. For example, a traditional chemicals company board might benefit from a member with experience running an environmentally friendly waste-disposal business, rather than an environmental activist.

As boards think about refreshing their ranks to better align with the times, the best boards will also look at staffing with an eye to different types of intelligence. An ideal board includes a mix of directors with conventionally defined raw intelligence and those with emotional intelligence, capable of reading the room and helping the board incorporate social and cultural considerations into its decision-making process. Interviewing potential board members to assess their problem-solving skills and intelligence is no doubt a difficult and fraught process. However, this sort of determination could be made by examining a candidate's experience. If the candidate has dealt with large, complex problems that required them to exercise shrewd judgment with little information, that is a good analogue for the sorts of problems that real-life board members deal with frequently.

Considering candidates through such a lens can be invaluable, particularly to new CEOs learning the ropes. A board should be capable of recognizing that the company's leadership rotates based on the challenges the board is facing. Its ability to solve a problem rests, in part, on the board identifying what kind of intelligence is required at that moment.

As business problems become ever more complex and multifaceted, boards must improve not only their ability to identify the biggest and most pressing issues but also their ways of thinking about the direction a corporation should take. The best boards equip themselves with different types of intelligence and strive to avoid groupthink.

Bringing Different Skills onto the Board

Bringing nontraditional talent into the boardroom requires a deliberate and concerted effort. Boards must permanently alter the networks they tap into when recruiting so that they can secure both the specialist expertise and the diversity that their companies require. Furthermore, board members may need to at least partially suspend their priorities—such as the preference for only C-suite experience—in order to secure high-caliber candidates with the expertise they need. For example, someone who is steeped in a technology company's inner workings—such as a senior marketing executive or the head of a division—can be a viable candidate for a technology seat even if they are not a technologist per se.

Expertise

There are at least three ways to add subject knowledge or expertise to a boardroom, each with its pros and cons. The most obvious path is for a board to create a position explicitly for directors with specific expertise. Experts can enhance oversight, arm the board with skills to challenge management assumptions, and keep the board updated on key trends. The challenge is to find board candidates with both expertise and broader business knowledge.

Some would argue, though, that dedicating a valuable board seat to a subject-matter expert is unnecessary. Boards could opt instead to delegate the requirement to management or to rely on specialist outside advisors and consultants. Both delegation and use of outside consultants work best if the specialist issue is peripheral, rather than core, to how the company derives profits.

Delegating expertise to management keeps responsibility and knowledge in-house with the managers who are more experienced with the underlying company structure. However, this approach increases the risk of an asymmetry of information between the board and management. It increases the board's dependence on management for expertise and impedes the board's ability to check and challenge.

If the board chooses to draw on independent advice instead, then it will rely on outside, third-party specialists to provide regular and objective insights on trends (say, in technology, geopolitics, or environmental shifts). The third-party advisor, which could be a committee of independent experts, reports directly and only to the board. The downside of this approach is that it can fuel mistrust and spark conflict between internal and external perspectives, further complicating board decision-making. External experts often give more generic advice because they don't understand the nuances of the business context gleaned from daily management. Overall, third parties can provide a valuable outside perspective but should be seen as complementary rather than substitutes for management's insider knowledge.

Addressing Diversity and Inclusion

The debate surrounding women on boards, in the C-suite, in business, and in the workplace more generally has traditionally centered on a handful of key questions. For example, the issue of how professionals should juggle demanding careers and family life. There is also the difficulty of breaking through traditionally male-centric institutional networks to even be considered for board seats. And there is a common refrain that, despite their best intentions, boards have difficulty finding suitably qualified diverse candidates.

These issues, and the barriers they have created for women, have been well documented in numerous studies. The good news is that in many companies there is no longer an explicit agenda to keep women out of important roles based on their gender. Governments and corporations have taken significant action that is starting to yield results, such as the mandatory quotas for board seats held by women.

Companies are also making their recruitment processes more transparent and sensitive to diversity and inclusion considerations. At the board level, this is achieved by insisting that the professional search firms that boards employ provide short lists that include a minimum number of female candidates. In some cases, corporations will stop doing business with board-recruitment firms that provide all-male and non-diverse short lists. The use of these third-party search firms is increasingly seen as best practice, since doing so makes the recruitment process more transparent and keeps selection committees from relying solely on private networks. Additionally, most boards are determined to develop a pipeline of candidates through mentoring and sponsorship schemes, not only for board refreshment but also for management succession. Enhanced transparency and disclosure help track progress on recruitment objectives.

Of course, women, too, have responded. Calls for women to "lean in" have led many to take a more active role in their own career management, and to rely less on their boss or organization. The clear-eyed understanding that a diversified workforce is simply good business has spurred women to more actively pursue opportunities and manage their careers.

As corporations have begun to focus on greater female board representation, they have also looked to add ethnic minorities and to ensure that diverse ideas and thinking are represented on the board. In this regard, many of the tools used to recruit diverse talent apply to all underrepresented groups.

The demonstrations in May and June 2020 triggered by the death of George Floyd awakened long-standing concerns and frustrations around racial injustice and inequity, including in the corporate world. The demonstrations yielded a strong response from the private sector, with corporations swiftly conveying that they would not stand for racial injustice, and that they would actively work—unilaterally and in concert with others—to give racial minorities more access and opportunities. In essence, businesses began acknowledging that there are systemic issues around race that they must help resolve.

Perhaps unsurprisingly, much of the initial response featured lofty proclamations that few people would find objectionable. For example, in the wake of the protests, Sundar Pichai—CEO of Google's parent company, Alphabet—recognized that "the black community is hurting" and pledged $12 million toward organizations that address racial inequality.

Some corporations launched public initiatives to help Black people progress within their company ranks, while others created multimillion-dollar funds that target minorities. On June 3, 2020, Goldman Sachs established a $10 million fund to help address racial and economic injustice. SoftBank, a Japanese company focused on technology, launched a $100 million fund to invest in start-ups led by Black Americans and people of color. CEO Tim Cook announced the investment of $100 million in Apple's racial equity and justice initiative. Beyond this, many executives spoke of the need to educate themselves about the realities of daily racial injustice.

However, the global nature and scale of the demonstrations mean that corporations must move from large proclamations and statements to actions—from tell to show. At the company level, this is about moving beyond macro or high-level pronouncements such as "attract, promote, retain." Boards can help companies address issues of racial inequity in at least two ways: by holding someone senior in management accountable for achieving diversity, and by charting progress to that end.

On accountability, boards should no longer merely encourage but rather force corporations to identify someone in senior management to diversify the workforce, suppliers, and business partners. In recent years, it has become fashionable for companies to appoint a chief diversity officer (CDO), a company executive that leads diversity and inclusion initiatives.

However, given the urgency of the problem, there is a strong case for the CEO and other senior managers in the executive team to take ownership of this issue now. There is, after all, a worrying sense that the CDO position is largely window dressing, lacking in stability and subject to high turnover.

According to a 2018 report by Russell Reynolds Associates, *The Emergence of the Chief Diversity Officer Role in Higher Education*, CDOs at universities have an average tenure of just 3.5 years. Still, according to some estimates, roughly 20 percent of Fortune 500 companies employ diversity officers, although there remains vigorous debate about the appropriate background, education, and credentials for this role.

Boards should also work with management to identify more explicit, transparent, and trackable metrics to measure progress—or lack of it—around the issue of racial diversity. They can also suggest remedies, such as a program offering specific internships targeting underrepresented racial groups. Boards should also insist that companies collect and act on data regarding their suppliers so that minority-owned businesses—such as those that provide recruitment, legal, portfolio management, accounting, transport, and food services—have an equal opportunity to partner with the company.

Ultimately, this kind of tracking and transparent data is critical for any corporation taking the need for diversity seriously. We have seen corporations adopt and adapt these methods to achieve considerable milestones on other social objectives, such as women in the workplace and environmental concerns.

Corporate boards have the power to effect change in a material way, and thus there are reasons to be optimistic that they can create a more equitable workplace and business environment in the future. For instance, boards retain ultimate control of management compensation, so achieving a truly racially diverse workforce could be a consideration when setting senior-level pay.

Wells Fargo CEO Charlie Scharf announced that members of the firm's elite operating committee will be graded annually on how much they increase workforce diversity. The reviews "will have a direct impact on year-end compensation decisions," he promised. However, only 3 percent of S&P 500 members include some form of diversity metric in their executive compensation plans, according to Bloomberg.

Given what is at stake, it should be the board's responsibility to focus the minds of senior management, much in the same way as when the board charges management with cutting costs, growing revenue, and driving profits. After all, when senior management have their feet held to the fire, more often than not, they deliver.

It is right that corporations should rethink their business models to address difficult social concerns and avoid damaging their reputations by ignoring them. It behooves boards to drive deep-seated changes in their corporations to promote racial justice and a more equitable way of doing business. Yet, in the rush to remedy past flaws and imbalances, boards must be on guard. Not least because virtually all hiring decisions made from desperation yield bad outcomes. Thus it seems clear to me that no board should hire a candidate just because they are a woman or a minority and just because hiring them makes their diversity numbers look good.

Some diversity campaigners argue that the objective of having more female or diverse board representation means that identity should take precedence over skills. In other words, they argue that because women and minorities have been excluded from the boardroom for many decades, today's boards should only select candidates from those groups in order to right the ship. This argument holds that even if such an approach leads to performance issues for the board and suboptimal outcomes for the company, the moral urgency of committing to diversity is worth the cost.

This is dangerous terrain. It can quickly and erroneously conflate incompetence with race or gender. It can also lead perfectly competent minority candidates to be tainted as only occupying their board seat because of their race or gender and not because of their ability. This can harm not only the candidates but also the board's ability to work together. The trust that keeps a board functioning as a team will erode if members start to doubt their colleagues' qualifications or question why a certain board member might be in the room in the first place.

There are other challenges as well. Boards primarily focused on selecting women and minorities could choose candidates who are already sitting on an excessive number of boards, which could result in insufficient time to fulfill their duties. Furthermore, there is a risk that a board member could feel that their opinion is being overlooked in discussions and that they are merely in the room because of their race or gender, rather than their skills and talent.

There is an often-expressed sentiment that corporations cannot easily find competent and skilled diverse talent to fill board seats. But this is simply not true—it is still possible to find strong candidates. Success in recruiting depends greatly on where recruiters put their energy. Even if you accept that the pool of women and minority candidates within today's C-suite is limited, there are numerous other trained and experienced business professionals such as accountants, lawyers, and business executives who still have valuable contributions to make. Rather than hiring a board candidate because of a quota system, boards would be better off committing their time and budget toward identifying the women and minorities with the best potential to rise to a seat on the board.

The cost of a search for the best and the brightest women and minority candidates may be high—particularly if the criteria for a board seat is narrow. However, with determination, boards can identify candidates with diverse backgrounds and experiences and reduce their board-search costs without creating suboptimal results. Quotas should only be used to help identify talented, competent, and experienced candidates who had previously gone unnoticed. Quotas that advocate for female or minority representation regardless of ability and potential contribution seem to me shortsighted and against the long-term interests of the business, society, and even the individual who ostensibly benefits from the arrangement.

Today's corporations, for the most part, have a clear-eyed appreciation of the importance of a diversified workforce. However, the multitude of efforts that have been made to achieve this goal are not enough. In May 2018, *Fortune* magazine outed twelve Fortune 500 companies that had all-male boards. Clearly, much remains to be done.

What Makes a Good Board?

This chapter has explored the selection of leadership as one of the key functions of a corporate board. The board's ability to select the right CEO and replenish itself with new board members who have the skills the company needs can mean the difference between success and failure—between a good board and a bad one. But how can we tell the difference?

A good board can be identified by the way it goes about its business. One overriding principle should be that independent board members are there to oversee management, not to manage the day-to-day operations of the company. In this respect, you know a good board when you see it.

Other necessities include transparency in the board structure, clear delineation of the roles and responsibilities among board members, and strong, independently minded, and engaged directors. The chairman plays a central role in guiding and chaperoning board members, helping them navigate the board agenda, and making sure the board fulfills its mandate. The chairman's leadership ensures that all matters are discussed fully—but prevents spending limitless time on individual agenda items—and that all members make useful and valuable contributions to board discourse. In short, a good chairman makes certain that the board gets the best out of all its members.

Nevertheless, bad things do happen to good boards. There are many times when boards are asked to suspend their ideological views for the sake of the company's future. In these moments, the judgment of the board—both individual members and the board as a collective—becomes critical. For example, when presented with complex decisions, the board generally exercises its judgment and discretion under a shroud of uncertainty, since board members simply do not have all the information they need. At these moments, it is the judgment of the board that reigns supreme and ultimately seals a company's fate.

Beyond natural attrition owing to age limits and term limits, refreshing the board is considered a best practice for leading corporations. Through annual performance reviews, boards go through membership changes and succession across committees. This process allows renewal of the board and is a natural way to avoid free riding and encourage active participation. Of course, this mechanism also allows for adjustments to be made when directors are not a good fit with the rest of the board. It is fair to say that many of the positive and negative attributes of a board are only visible internally—among the board itself, to the senior management team, and on occasion to third-party advisors. However, I would argue that any strengths or weaknesses of the board are reflected in the culture of the company more generally, in the way that the board sets a tone from the top. As the next chapter will explain, boards and all stakeholders—shareholders, employees, regulators, customers and clients, NGOs, and even lay citizens—are increasingly asking tough questions about corporate cultures.

CHAPTER 3

A Culture Revolution
Enters the Boardroom

THE NOBEL PRIZE–WINNING ECONOMIST MILTON FRIEDMAN ONCE OPINED, "There is one and only one social responsibility of business—to use its resources and engage in activities designed to increase its profits so long as it stays within the rules of the game, which is to say, engages in open and free competition without deception or fraud." He went on to conclude that a business's sole purpose is to generate profit for shareholders. For many decades after Friedman articulated this view in his 1962 book *Capitalism and Freedom* (popularized in a 1970 *New York Times Magazine* article), the doctrine stood as the overriding philosophy of the business world.

But times have changed. A clear rebuke to Friedman's view was issued in August 2019 by the Business Roundtable, a body of CEOs of major US companies. Their statement on the purpose of a corporation effectively ended adherence to the old philosophy of shareholder primacy. The 181 CEOs who signed the agreement committed themselves to working for the benefit of all stakeholders—customers, employees, suppliers, and communities—as well as generating long-term value for shareholders. The signatories included representatives from some of America's biggest corporations, such as JPMorgan Chase and Johnson & Johnson, as well as the largest asset managers, including Vanguard and BlackRock.

The consensus about the larger purpose of business is still evolving as boards wrestle with what the primary social responsibility of the twenty-first-century corporation should be. Corporate culture is a long-standing board responsibility, but the meaning of culture itself is changing. This term has shifted to include the fair and equitable treatment of employees, clients, and customers; an adherence to the spirit rather than just the letter of the law; and the notion of a broader duty as a good corporate citizen. Amid new societal pressures for environmental consciousness, gender and racial equality, and employee advocacy, some corporations are now looking beyond financial returns and shareholders and toward the greater good.

Whereas in the past a corporation's culture may have emphasized honesty and fair dealing with customers, now the concept of culture involves a much broader idea of social responsibility, making the board's duties even trickier.

Of course, these broadening demands for social responsibility are not exclusively the board's responsibility. Corporations are confronting them as a whole, from frontline managers on up. However, the trickiest and most complicated questions that arise—governing the company culture, overseeing cultural adherence throughout the organization, and balancing the corporate culture with commercial goals—are ones where boards have to weigh in.

This has invariably placed boardrooms under pressure to ensure that management articulates the role the corporation is meant to play and the ways it benefits society. Previously, the board operated under the narrow mandate of satisfying shareholders, who in large part tend to be professional institutional investors such as multibillion-dollar asset managers, pension funds, mutual funds, and insurance companies. These groups will certainly continue to play a dominant role by providing the capital for corporations to fund their operations and future growth. In exchange, corporations pay them a share of their profits—for example, through dividends. Yet these transactions do not happen in a vacuum.

Public opinion also plays a role. The blowback from the 2008 global financial crisis stoked popular anger about worsening inequality, perceived corruption in business, and the notion that capitalism was degrading the environment and hastening climate change. Together, these converging perceptions shone a light on the role of corporations in society, leading to greater expectations for what companies should do for broader society—expectations that boards must now navigate.

From the boardroom perspective, there is an overwhelming sense that companies are collectively taking up a broader societal mission. But in doing so, they face a deeply complex balancing act if they are to survive. As the concept of shareholder primacy fades, it is replaced by the competing and sometimes conflicting priorities of employees, consumers, governments, and shareholders. The danger is that if a company adjusts too little, it leaves itself at risk of losing its license to trade—either as a result of government intervention or consumer boycott. But adjust too much, and the company risks becoming uncompetitive.

Boards are watching and responding to the rapidly changing cultural landscape, increasingly recognizing the important role that culture plays in determining a corporation's future. In this sense, culture—defining it, monitoring it, and overseeing it—has evolved into a more central board responsibility. Boards are giving more credence to management thinker Peter Drucker's proclamation that "culture eats strategy for breakfast."

Netflix, for instance, made its corporate culture a matter of public record. In 2009, the company released a presentation entitled "Netflix Culture: Freedom & Responsibility," which outlined seven fundamental aspects of the company's culture, for example, paying top dollar for talent, placing great emphasis on personal initiative, and refusing to hire "brilliant jerks." Perhaps reflecting the appetite for a twenty-first-century approach to corporate culture, the presentation has been viewed more than nineteen million times in the past decade.

One reason that culture has been more frequently discussed in the boardroom is that it reflects a company's level of integrity and is a central part of how the company establishes and maintains its reputation. As recent upheavals at Wells Fargo, WeWork, the Weinstein Company, and others have shown, culture directly affects profitability and shareholder value, and ultimately determines whether a company lives or dies.

Headlines may give the impression that the cultural issues challenging corporations are purely the result of scandalous or illicit behavior on the part of individual managers or employees. However, other forms of culture—say, a lack of innovation or an overabundance of bureaucracy—can ossify and become equally damaging to the long-term prospects of the business. This type of cultural erosion tends to be much subtler and harder to detect than any onetime scandal. When even more salacious behaviors become culturally ingrained in a company or industry, the results can be catastrophic, as the 2017 #MeToo backlash showed.

You would be hard-pressed today to find a company that does not have some public, bold, codified statement of the company culture that expresses its values and guiding principles—the nonnegotiable tenets upon which the employees will conduct business. Such a values statement can also serve as a North Star, guiding employees who face ethical or moral quandaries when engaging with clients and colleagues. Among the board's central mandates is to uphold these stated values and principles. A company's board sets the tone from the top down by not only articulating the company's culture but also embodying it both individually and collectively. Done successfully, this helps retain employees and keep them engaged, makes customers happy, and protects the company's reputation.

The board's responsibilities when it comes to culture involve two broad categories: nonnegotiable aspects of culture—professionalism, ethics, and trust—and issues that are on the cultural frontier. The nonnegotiables are the principles that govern and define the model company. They are generally uncontroversial, and can include a vast range of virtues: ethics, respect, integrity, honesty, excellence, service, accountability, responsibility, professionalism, teamwork, and, above all, a commitment to doing the right thing. But if the board and the company it serves hope to keep pace with changing times, they must go further. They must reckon with the new corporate cultural frontier, going beyond the narrow definitions of professionalism to embrace human rights and the company's responsibility to benefit the communities where it operates.

Companies frequently affirm their commitment to these issues by pledging to conduct business in a socially and environmentally responsible manner. At times, a company will enshrine its values by signing on to global initiatives like the UN Global Compact on human rights or the Extractive Industries Transparency Initiative (EITI). Established in 2003, the EITI sets parameters for disclosure of the activities of more than eighty member companies in the mining, oil, and gas businesses.

Very often, the board's process of defining these two sets of values will unearth questions for which there are no easy answers. Nevertheless, seeking solutions is vitally important for companies in the fast-moving cultural landscape of the twenty-first century.

The Nonnegotiables

Putting a company's guiding values into writing is a time-tested method of defining corporate culture. Long before Netflix existed, in 1979, Goldman Sachs codified its fourteen business principles. These forty-year-old principles, which range from putting the client first to a commitment to teamwork, are still widely used in all sorts of corporations today. Most companies are also governed by a code of ethics. This often boils down to a list of guiding principles. For any company wanting to stay in business, such a definition of the basic elements of corporate culture is pretty uncontroversial. Nevertheless, boards face two significant challenges: First is the task of embedding the desired cultural values so that they permeate every layer of the organization. Second is the challenge of ensuring adherence to those values.

Embedding Corporate Values

In a recent Columbia Business School study, 92 percent of senior executives said that improving company culture would increase their organization's value. Only 16 percent said that their culture was currently where it should be. The disconnect, according to survey respondents, was due to organizations failing to put their stated values and policies into practice. Articulating what a company's culture should be is, in some respect, the easy part; embedding the culture is much harder.

Together with management, many boards spend an enormous amount of time crafting and honing their company's cultural message. However, the real task is making sure that, once specified, the culture will permeate the multiple layers of an organization. The scope of this task depends on the kind of organization. It is a different proposition to establish a culture in a new and ambitious start-up than to change the culture at a large and established global corporation.

The task of transforming a company's cultural agenda differs considerably between new and established companies, between midsize entities and large-scale ones, between founder-led companies and those with outsider CEOs, and between private and public organizations. The cultural transition is hardest for large, public companies that carry heavier regulatory responsibilities and have a higher profile in society. Smaller, private, and founder-led start-ups, on the other hand, have much less scrutiny and therefore more latitude to make mistakes.

At a start-up, the founder, for better or for worse, typically imposes their own values and beliefs onto the company culture. For example, WeWork—a company founded in 2010 that provides shared work spaces—has a stated policy that bans meat products on their premises in an effort to address environmental concerns. In an email to about six thousand employees in July 2018, the company announced that it would no longer reimburse employees for meals that include red meat, poultry, or pork and would stop serving meat at company events. Employees who needed medical or religious allowances were referred to the company's policy team.

The founder's influence can extend well beyond the start-up phase. A statement of values of a very different kind can be seen in Chick-fil-A, a well-established US fast-food chain, which has maintained a closed-on-Sunday policy for over fifty years, partly as a reflection of the founder's Christian faith.

The bulk of my board experience has involved working to alter and improve the corporate culture of established companies rather than start-ups. This is extremely challenging, not least because modern corporations are geographically diverse. For global companies, instigating culture change requires the board and management to navigate many different cultural norms and hurdles.

Changing a company's culture involves resetting values and behaviors and often discarding norms that have taken root over several decades. For this reason, some believe that it will always be a struggle to change an organization's culture without first changing its people. Of course, to jettison the old guard would likely be destructive, since it would mean removing numerous experienced and competent employees from the business in one fell swoop.

But change we must if companies are to thrive and survive. More and more board directors understand that culture undergirds all of management's goals. A positive culture can drive innovation or the successful execution of a strategy, just as a poisonous culture can impede a company's progress.

Microsoft's Satya Nadella credits the work of Stanford psychology professor Carol Dweck with transforming his company. Microsoft's senior leadership team determined that Dweck's growth mindset, founded on the principle of continuous learning, would become core to the company's culture, helping it to grow and innovate. For the company's over 130,000 employees, this meant tying their behavioral habits to a growth-oriented culture of perpetual learning, which proved critical for the technology company's fortunes. Within five years after the cultural shift, Microsoft saw its market value rise by a quarter of a billion dollars.

Because not all companies are the same, approaches to embedding culture will necessarily differ. For example, when a risk of fatalities exists—such as in a mining or construction company whose employees operate heavy machinery or drive long distances in areas with poor infrastructure—companies benefit from a dogged focus on a culture of safety. In my experience, these companies focus heavily on reinforcing messages that appeal to workers to "get home safely." In work environments that involve life-or-death situations, such as hospitals and military operations, culture is driven home by the use of checklists and strict procedures that require team members cross-check and verify one another's work.

Office-based roles—such as at financial firms or professional services companies, where people's lives are rarely at stake—tend to take a different approach. Here, compensation is more commonly used as a lever to drive preferred cultural outcomes.

On some boards on which I have served, companies have allocated as much as 20 percent of an employee's compensation to be determined by cultural factors.

In global organizations, the challenges of achieving cultural excellence are even more complex. A single organization can legitimately encompass many cultures, just as different units employing different business models can exist within the same company. Indeed, distinct, and often competing, subcultures exist in every organization.

Take, for example, a universal bank. Such an organization has a retail operation—offering mortgages, checking accounts, and personal credit cards to individuals—and an investment-banking unit serving corporations. There is an obvious difference between the more sedate, courteous, and collaborative approach of an employee engaging with retail customers and the aggressive, cutthroat mentality of a trader who works in the anonymous financial markets.

Because distinct subcultures can exist in a company, it is the board's duty to help harmonize and unify the overall corporate culture. The board must define the tenets that apply across the whole organization, such as a customer-first focus, integrity, respect, and excellence. In practice, boards can tolerate competing subcultures as long as they do not counteract or undermine the overall corporate values—though, ideally, they should actively uphold the agreed-upon norms.

Companies operating across multiple countries and continents have the daunting task of persuading employees with starkly different national, cultural, religious, and ethnic backgrounds to adhere to one set of harmonized values. Where the corporate norms fly in the face of local custom, employee disagreements and divisions can ensue. Workers may choose not to comply with the company culture or decide to subscribe to other values. One example is national differences in standard workday times.

Boards also have to be mindful of cultural fit when merging with or acquiring other businesses, which can introduce a harmful culture to the company. When a large company acquires a small one, it is not unreasonable for the larger company to impose its culture on the newly combined business. However, if the cultural gap between the two companies is too big to bridge, the acquisition could take value away from the company rather than add to it.

For example, more established technology giants have acquired many up-and-coming start-up companies in the hopes of remaining competitive by taking control of their newfangled products. Often, these smaller companies have a high-pay, low-bureaucracy start-up culture that enables an innovative approach and allows them to get new products into the market quickly. When such a company is ingested by a larger, older company, the risk is that the start-up's innovation will be blunted, key people will leave, and the culture of speed will be choked, eroding the value of the acquisition. The board of the acquiring company must ensure that management preserves the acquisition value by both guarding the innovative culture of the start-up and working to integrate its best aspects into the acquiring company's dominant culture.

The merger of two companies of comparable size also carries the risk of a culture clash. This is why scrutinizing the cultures of both organizations is integral to the due diligence process. Even when the strategic and financial picture of a merger suggests a good fit, the prospect of a cultural misalignment can be a deal breaker, or at least a cause of consternation. Here, the task of the merged board is to draw on the strongest cultural attributes of both companies, in the same way that it will look for cost benefits and operational synergies.

A 2018 *Harvard Business Review* article entitled "One Reason Mergers Fail: The Two Cultures Aren't Compatible" detailed the challenges of Amazon's acquisition of Whole Foods in 2017. The authors contrast the relatively loose culture of Whole Foods (which they characterized as more fluid, eschewing rules and valuing openness and creativity) with the tight culture of Amazon, which values consistency and routine, with greater emphasis on generating predictable outcomes. Tight company cultures tend to have little appetite for rebellious behavior and instead rely on strict rules and processes as the basis of their operations. In the several years following the Amazon–Whole Foods merger, reports of culture clashes have continued to emerge.

Cultural assimilation issues apply in areas beyond M&A —a change in the CEO can be culturally disruptive as well. As they recruit, boards must bear in mind that a CEO who fails to buy into an existing corporate culture, or whose cultural philosophy is different, or who simply does not fit, risks "organ rejection"—that is, the rest of the organization remains out of sync with the leader, undermining the company's culture and productivity. This is one reason boards tend to prefer CEO candidates who came up in the company and are therefore already familiar with the institutional culture. In such a case, the board needs to ask whether their pick for CEO can really impose a new culture if needed. If the CEO is hired from outside, the board needs to ask whether the candidate can truly embed in and reinforce the existing corporate culture.

The use of third-party providers, such as contractors and consultants, also creates difficulties in managing corporate culture. The presence of a significant number of outside workers running core operations—such as a customer call center supporting a bank or mobile phone company, a courier network attached to a large corporation (think drivers for Uber or delivery agents for FedEx), or engineers subcontracted to a mining company—should raise concerns for boards about how to ensure that the contractors live by the cultural values of the host company. In particular, whenever a large-scale outsourcing proposal is put to the board, directors must ask for an assessment of the likely impact on the company culture. The cultural implications of outsourcing have been brought into greater focus with the rise of zero-hour contracts, where an employer is not obliged to provide any minimum working hours, and the worker is not obliged to accept any work offered. These contracts, by their very nature, create a revolving and transient worker population that never fully latches onto the host company.

A sudden change in working conditions can also risk tainting or even poisoning a company's culture. In the face of the 2020 coronavirus pandemic, companies across the world rapidly switched to employees working from home. As the relationship between remote workers and leadership shifted, maintaining discipline and productivity in the usual ways was, for many, no longer an option. Suddenly, companies faced the fundamental question of how culture could be sustained in light of such a dramatic shift. Boards need to be vigilant about the implications of such remote arrangements for the company as they balance managing the company's costs, expenses, and health and safety on the one hand, and defending the company's inherent cultural values on the other.

Even the board itself—if it is diverse—can be home to different cultures. Not only have most board members forged long and successful careers in other organizations with strong cultures, but their own cultural background and nationality can influence their approach to cultural oversight. For example, board members may have differing views on CEO compensation: those with an American, market-capitalist background, where a higher remuneration is common, may clash with those who have a European view, which tends to be more socialist and egalitarian in nature. In such cases, even if there are no explicit rules on compensation, board directors can still be guided by their own unique backgrounds and cultural contexts.

Adherence

Whether companies like it or not, a proliferation of publicly available rankings in recent years signals to the world how well (and whether) the board, management, and the company are adhering to the values that today's society deems important. Examples include the *Forbes* list of "Most Sustainable Companies," the *Fast Company* list of "Most Innovative Companies," the Reputation Institute's rankings of "The World's Most Reputable CEOs," and Glassdoor's list of "Best Places to Work" (or their ranking of the "15 Companies with the Best Parental Leave Policies"). Even companies that are not ranked are affected by their conspicuous absence.

When it comes to cultural issues, social media can intervene in a swift, if not instantaneous, manner—acting as judge, jury, and executioner. Even if boards were to choose to ignore the cultural revolution that is afoot—though no board I have served on has—online surveys such as Glassdoor, Blind, and TheLayoff.com collate detailed information on companies from current and former employees, including information on the corporate culture. From these sources, boards can get a firsthand, unfiltered view of how their employees feel about management, company processes and bureaucracy, and the efficacy of the culture strategy. The reality is there for all to see.

Even more important, boards must measure and monitor their company's progress on their stated cultural values, and make sure employees adhere to those ideals. The hope, of course, is that the outside world's perception of the company will match the internal reality. As a practical matter, boards rely on surveys, scores, and assessments to gauge internal sentiment and employee performance. Employee engagement surveys are a commonly utilized barometer of how much the workforce understands and supports the company's mission and values. These surveys can also help the board and management glean whether employees believe the company culture is clearly defined and whether it is helping or hindering their ability to achieve business success.

Employee surveys often cover other areas too—such as motivation, work-life balance, and, increasingly, mental health. Though they do have limitations, these surveys can prove extremely valuable in revealing broader trends and sentiments in an organization. They can, for example, reveal huge problems that need to be addressed—Gallup's *State of the Global Workplace* report in 2018 revealed that 85 percent of employees worldwide were not engaged or were actively disengaged in their job. All combined, the data gleaned from surveys paint a picture for the board of whether employees are working in a positive environment that reflects the company's values.

Boards also see extensive data on employee performance, including individualized performance data for senior executives and aggregate employee data across business units. This information can shed light on an employee's conduct, their reputation in the organization, and how they behave around colleagues who are both senior and junior to them, which helps the board assess how well they embody the values of the firm. This assessment feeds into the overall picture of the employee's work performance and can ultimately inform their compensation, a tool boards and management are increasingly using to embed culture throughout the organization.

Another way to measure adherence is the cultural audit, which allows the board to see how its defined culture is permeating the company. There is broadening consensus about the value of audits, disclosures, and transparency of this sort. Much like audits conducted on a company's finances and controls, cultural audits are an independent inspection (conducted by internal and external auditors or consultants) of how well and how fast a certain culture is being adopted within an organization. These audits provide boards with a regular, often quarterly, sense of the extent to which employees are embracing or rejecting culture values.

Although cultural audits and compliance teams can be helpful, ultimately the board must rely on each and every employee to behave in a manner that embodies the company's values. In this regard, employees are the bedrock of company culture. Without every employee epitomizing and living the company values, the board's efforts on culture will fail.

Moving beyond metrics and measurements, there are a variety of tactics that companies can employ to enact change and enforce cultural norms across the workforce. These include incentivizing good behavior with inducements such as bonuses and so-called nudging, with punishments for employees if they abandon company values, and with more severe disciplinary actions (such as firing) for breaking laws or regulatory codes.

The simplest and arguably most common way to influence corporate behavior is through compensation. Companies have long used bonuses, promotions, salary raises, and other incentives to encourage certain behaviors. In much the same way that compensation is used to drive sales or revenue, it can also be an effective tool to promote adherence to cultural norms. Organizations can reward people with higher pay and bonuses for being cultural carriers. Boards can influence this because they have important oversight and decision-making rights on how much compensation is paid (as, generally, boards must approve the compensation pool) and how pay is distributed.

A subtler approach is to "nudge" the employee base. Here, with the board's oversight, management tries to influence people to behave differently through positive reinforcement and indirect suggestions. For example, company leaders could publicly commend an employee or team for exemplary behavior, signaling to the broader workforce the sorts of values they want employees to emulate.

Corporations regularly try to rally employees around a common narrative and appeal to reason. It is not uncommon for companies to adapt easily memorable slogans to drive home the cultural imperative to its employees. Some better-known examples include Google's "Don't be evil," Apple's "Think different," and BP's rebranding as Beyond Petroleum. By and large, even in cases where management has taken the lead on the culture message, boards will likely have a hand in overseeing the direction of a company's culture.

Companies can also discipline employees for deviations from stated cultural standards or for breaking legal and regulatory rules. Punishments can apply to rule violations beyond lawbreaking, such as violating a code of behavior that employees have signed. For example, a romantic or personal relationship between employees may contravene a company policy but not break the law. At the extreme, companies can also set expectations for how individuals should behave ethically and morally. Most companies have clear systems for punishing unethical actions, and these processes can be extended to breaches of corporate culture. Punishments can escalate from a simple rebuke to a formal warning and suspension, culminating in outright termination of employment.

For the board, the stakes are high: when corporate scandals tear a company apart, the offending behavior can almost always be traced back to a failure of culture. In particular, the failure to embed a positive culture can leave a vacuum in which a destructive one grows. Even when a company's cultural goals appear explicit, they may not be enough to protect a company from the erosion of values. Enron, for example, had its four values—integrity, communication, respect, and excellence—carved into the marble wall of its lobby in Houston. When the company fell to fraud and deception, these made for a bitterly ironic epitaph.

Large institutional shareholders are increasingly asking questions about culture, notably about how effectively companies adhere to their established values and to the new cultural frontier, and boards should take heed. For example, in

2019, State Street, one of the largest institutional investors in the world, gave notice to companies it was invested in that it would be seeking detailed insights into how their boards monitor corporate culture. Specifically, State Street Global Advisors published a letter to board members entitled "Aligning Corporate Culture with Long-Term Strategy," stating, "This year we will be focusing on corporate culture as one of the many, growing intangible value drivers that affect a company's ability to execute its long-term strategy."

The global accounting firm EY recently found that "intangible assets" such as culture make up, on average, 52 percent of an organization's market value (and in some sectors as much as 90 percent). Researchers have documented that, in the United States and UK, value is driven more by intangible, rather than tangible, assets—further underscoring the importance of corporate culture. In a nutshell, boards are taking the view that an increased focus on corporate culture not only supports a company's strategy but is essential to sustainable, long-term value creation.

Efforts to establish positive cultures in corporations should be seen not as a one-time exercise but rather as a continuous process. As much as corporations strive for operational excellence, they should also seek to achieve cultural excellence. Boards play a pivotal role in this by overseeing cultural programs and setting compensation, as well as by monitoring and evaluating progress and, when necessary, stepping in to support management in implementing cultural change.

The New Cultural Frontier

Today's corporations are being called on to say what they think about emerging societal issues, matters about which governments would traditionally be expected to lead and legislate. Pay parity, obesity, gender equality, racial equality, gay rights, gun control, climate change, mental health, worker rights, parental leave, and sexual harassment are among the issues on the long list shaping a new cultural frontier that go well beyond the nonnegotiables described above.

Milton Friedman's doctrine of shareholder primacy has lost its luster in recent years amid the growing expectation that corporations should contribute more to society and social progress via the environmental, social, and governance (ESG) agenda. Warren Buffett, chairman and CEO of Berkshire Hathaway, has questioned the legitimacy of corporations taking a moral view on questions facing society. He argues that social change should be led by governments, not corporations.

The pressing question is whether Buffett's stance is now behind the times. Even if boards agree that the responsibility for social change lies with government, the reality is that in the years ahead, corporate winners and losers will increasingly be decided by their willingness to adapt to the new cultural frontier. In effect, for corporations, subscribing to the ESG agenda grants them the license to operate.

The results of a 2019 Fortune 500 CEO poll underscored just how much these executives have moved beyond Friedman's narrow framework. Only about 5 percent of today's CEOs believed that their "company should mainly focus on making profits, and not be distracted by social goals." Roughly half the CEOs believed their "company has a responsibility to address social problems through charitable activities, but not as part of our core business strategy," while 44 percent— up four points from 2018—felt that their company "should actively seek to solve major social problems as part of our core business strategy."

Today, people seek leadership from CEOs on society's most pressing questions. The 2019 Edelman Trust Barometer reveals that, by a double-digit margin, the majority of people believe that CEOs can create positive change. On specific issues, about 65 percent of those polled felt that CEOs can make a difference on pay equity, prejudice and discrimination, and training for the jobs of tomorrow, 56 percent believed so on the environment, 55 percent on personal data, 47 percent on sexual harassment, and 37 percent on fake news. In short, respondents believe in the ability of corporations to effect change, despite the appearance that trust in corporations is low.

What is a corporation's social responsibility? It is increasingly apparent that companies are taking on a more central role in addressing social concerns and thereby coming closer to meeting the demands of society. Around the world, many citizens have become skeptical of capitalism, the pursuit of economic growth, and the dominance of the private sector. This widespread mistrust of market capitalism means that conventional wisdom—such as Friedman's opinion on the narrow responsibility of a corporation, economist Ronald Coase's argument that the corporation is the best structure to lower costs, and general beliefs that only the corporate model can create real economic value at scale—is due for a reboot. Part of this rethinking is that corporations are now expected—by employees, investors, governments, and society at large—to become outright agents of change. This puts these cultural issues firmly on the board's agenda, with expectations that boards and management take action.

Boards recognize that there has been a loss of trust in corporations and that they must rebuild faith across society. Boards must therefore dedicate a greater share of their time and resources to addressing these issues. The corporate response to the 2020 coronavirus outbreak showed some companies' willingness to play a central role in finding solutions to a global problem and demonstrated how corporations can set aside commercial priorities in pursuit of greater social goals. As governments, for the most part, were slow to act to prevent the spread of the disease, companies took it upon themselves to mandate social distancing. Many professional services firms required staff to work from home before any such restrictions were imposed by the government.

Outside an immediate crisis such as the pandemic, societal matters are becoming woven into common commercial practice through employment contracts and recruitment policies. Additionally, corporations know that their actions could affect their insurance policies and credit ratings, as well as their standing with shareholders, as often represented by proxy institutions such as Glass Lewis and ISS. Influential state-owned pension funds such as the California Public Employees' Retirement System (CalPERS) and the Dutch and Scandinavian pension funds, as well as sovereign wealth funds (for example, Norway), which manage trillions of dollars in assets, have also shown that they are willing to transform corporate behavior where they deem change necessary.

On one level, these new responsibilities may seem like common-sense priorities, but they can be difficult for boards and corporations to navigate. They introduce new complexities, trade-offs, and decisions—particularly as companies aim to compete in the global marketplace, because some countries have lower or different standards on these social issues. Even if boards and management are resistant to making changes, NGOs and the broad array of stakeholders—ratings agencies, governments and regulators, insurers, and even financial investors—are now united in demanding that boards and management take a broader view of social issues while running global corporations.

Of course, there are many areas in which governments have already passed laws and set regulations. Yet other areas remain—for example, obesity and mental health—where government intervention has been patchy and often limited, leaving corporations under pressure to fill in the void.

Governments, struggling with a multitude of challenges, often appear broken and incapable of providing quality services in a range of public functions such as education and health care. Corporations, facing charges of being overly driven by profit, see an opportunity to step in, make a positive contribution to society, and perhaps also be recognized for doing so. Yet corporations, too, have come under fire when they are seen as not doing everything within their power to help address many of these societal ills, even if these issues fall outside the company's primary purview.

Several US cities, including Boulder, Oakland, Philadelphia, San Francisco, and Seattle, have implemented a sugar or soda tax as a way to tackle obesity. Because obesity is not being addressed systematically at either the state or federal level, these cities have taken matters into their own hands and imposed an additional tax on businesses. This increases expenses for companies in one jurisdiction but not another, and companies have taken action in response. For example, Coca-Cola has broadened its suite of products to include less sugary drinks.

While there is a commercial imperative to adapt to updated consumer tastes—and, in some cases, to pressure from local governments and employees—corporations have taken the lead where broader public policy has taken a back seat.

Public policy has generally been slow to address climate change concerns about meat production, but companies have taken the initiative to create vegan, nonmeat, and plant-based options. Even where governments may be lagging on broad-based environmental policies, companies are imposing green initiatives to address climate concerns in their business models. Getting rid of single-use plastics, such as straws in fast-food chains, is one very targeted intervention in this drive.

If the goals of today's company are to retain and engage employees, keep customers happy, and burnish the organization's reputation, then the era of prioritizing profits above all else is over. Amid the clamor for progress on social and cultural issues, the question for boards is straightforward: Will the efforts to meet these goals ultimately hurt the business, or are these issues a jumping-off point for innovation and an opportunity to establish new businesses and products that reflect twenty-first-century norms?

Boards must always consider the larger societal ramifications when making decisions. When considering whether to establish a mine, drill a well, or open a branch, they must answer three questions: Is it legal? Does it make financial sense? And is it moral or ethical?

Take the example of a mining company deciding whether to dump toxic waste in a river in a poor, developing country where it operates. Discarding waste in this manner may be legal in a country with limited environmental protections. Dumping toxic waste in this way may help the company's bottom line by reducing the costs of shipping the waste to a designated disposal site. But from a board's governance perspective, even if such an action is legal, it is unequivocally unethical because the toxic waste would certainly harm local people and their environment. Moreover, boards must factor in the very costly fact that reports of waste dumping would likely cause the company significant reputational damage.

Boards must ensure that their calculations reflect the true cost of their business operations and practices, including hidden or second-order costs that may wreak havoc on society. For example, a pulp and paper company that cuts down too many trees in a developing-world rain forest will attract criticism for deforestation. However, the harm caused by this decision does not stop there: cutting down trees may also create optimal conditions for the spread of mosquito-borne diseases and expose local populations to a heightened risk of illnesses like malaria.

A Confluence of Complex Issues

A decision about whether or not to dump toxic waste should ultimately be an easy one. But not every decision is so clear-cut. Today's boards face a multitude of complex puzzles they must address.

Pay Equity

Reasonable people can rally behind the simple idea that workers should earn a fair wage. But in fact, compensation is among the most complicated issues that reach the board level.

CEO pay ratios are just one example. Boards are increasingly having to consider whether the disparity between the CEO's pay and the salary of the company's lowest-paid employees (or the company's median, or the national average income) is defensible. Inflation-adjusted CEO pay has grown 940 percent since 1978, while typical worker compensation has risen only 12 percent. According to the Economic Policy Institute, the ratio of CEO pay to average worker pay rose from 33 to 1 in 1980, to a peak of 376 in 2000, before lowering slightly to 276 in 2015.

In 2019, Abigail Disney (an heiress and relation to the founders of the Disney company) targeted skewed compensation, calling the chief executive of Disney's pay a "naked indecency." She went on to recommend that the company begin remedying the problem by slicing executive bonuses in half and distributing the money to the lowest-paid 10 percent of its workers. In the past, CEO pay was decided based on performance and internal pay scales. More recently, boards have tended to determine CEO compensation based on what other companies of the same industry or size are doing. Critics have argued that this shift has contributed to the considerable rise in CEO compensation and its sharp divergence from average worker pay.

Boards face fierce pressure to ensure that pay and performance are properly aligned, and that they steer clear of rewarding poorly performing CEOs with outsize compensation packages, so that pay structures reflect the quarter-by-quarter and year-by-year performance of an enterprise. This can be done through long-term incentive plans and deferred compensation, which ensure that CEO pay is aligned with the long-term interests of the company and discourage CEOs from taking a short-term approach to their role. In this system, CEO compensation is set based on well-defined goals and scorecards reflecting targets based on short-, medium-, and long-term goals.

There are a range of things that a board's compensation committee will want to get right as it discusses effective remuneration. As well as paying attention to regulation, the view of consumers, and the wider public opinion on pay, boards must take into account the perspective of the company shareholders, who will want to see that the board is tightly managing the company's expense base. The compensation pool should not rise at the same rate as profits or revenues, and fixed pay increases should be controlled so that base pay increases do not regularly outstrip inflation.

The board will want to make sure that bad times are shared—if it is going to cut the shareholder dividend and limit investment, then it seems fair that personnel incentive pools will also be reduced. On the flip side, boards will want to avoid giving the impression that compensation automatically rises for all employees—including the CEO—if the company's revenues and profits go up. Executives should not benefit more than shareholders when a company is flourishing.

Given that boards are in the business of managing a company for future success, they should be mindful that high-performing junior and middle managers should be paid, rewarded, and favored over the old guard—today's middle managers will be running tomorrow's businesses. Boards should match employees' performance records with their pay, make sure the best pay is going to the people they expect to shape the company's future, and not exorbitantly compensate people whom management is planning to fire or push out.

At the most senior levels, C-suite employees' compensation should be linked to the performance of the whole company, since they are in charge of running it. Boards should also retain some powers to reclaim a portion of executive compensation at a future date through "malus and clawback" clauses, which allow the company to claim back compensation if a senior officer's misdeeds are revealed in the future.

Of course, boards update and refine their approach to remuneration as they consider what peers and competitors are doing to attract, promote, and retain employees. Boards have been under pressure in recent years to more transparently explain their compensation formulas. Stringent new rules are increasingly allowing company shareholders to check the board's oversight of the company's compensation. "Say on pay" gives a company's investors the right to vote on the remuneration of executives and is designed to tackle the problem of a corporation's managers overpaying themselves.

In analyzing ten years of say-on-pay votes, up to the end of 2018, Harvard Law School found that over 40 percent of Russell 3000 companies had received an "against" vote recommendation from ISS, the proxy vote service.

Some boards have responded by laying out fair-pay agendas, publishing compensation ratios, and releasing other information about their compensation practices, such as how many employees were paid over $1 million in a year. Shareholder votes do matter, and boards ideally should secure a minimum of 90 percent approval from shareholders for executive pay proposals. But even in the face of pushback, boards still need to use their best judgment to determine what they think compensation should be, resisting pressure from the media, regulators, or society that pushes them toward a policy that seems inappropriate.

Pay structures are not as simple as merely determining base pay and cash bonuses. The compensation committee has to approve the package, and the full board has to sign off on aspects of remuneration such as stock options, restricted stock, pensions, and insurance. Stock options can be a particularly valuable form of compensation when the stock price increases. However, a sharp rise in the share price disproportionately benefiting the CEO can lead to critiques from outside the company. While many large investors and institutional shareholders understand the complexity of CEO pay, some argue that the process for determining it is too complex and insufficiently transparent to be understood by individual investors, regulators, and the wider public. Above all, the board should make sure that CEO stock options do not incentivize short-term thinking linked to quarterly performance.

In the absence of government intervention, companies are increasingly pressured to think and act as if they were the policymakers. Sometimes this extends to a company investigating what a fair minimum wage in a certain place should be, or publicly opining on everything from ensuring a living wage to explicitly linking executive and employee pay. One step an assertive board can take is to promote greater transparency on compensation. Ideally, clear pay structures will offer employees opportunities to progress through the organization and earn more, while better understanding the board and management's remuneration decisions.

Gender Equity

Gender parity efforts also exemplify the practical challenges that boards face in seeking to do what is right from a societal perspective. In principle, the idea that women and men should be compensated the same amount for the same work of the same quality seems both easy to address and pretty uncontroversial. But, although the majority of boards have acted swiftly and energetically to attempt to remedy the problem, gender inequity still exists. For example, in its 2017 gender pay report, the BBC said that out of the ninety-six highest-paid BBC employees, sixty-two were men and thirty-four were women. The study revealed numerous examples of men earning significantly more than women for doing the same job, such as copresenting a show.

In the pursuit of gender parity, deep questions often emerge, and their solutions may fall outside the corporate board's purview. For instance, it is well known that girls and women have not traditionally been encouraged to pursue science, technology, engineering, and mathematics (STEM), which often lead to well-paid careers. Resolving that problem would surely help achieve gender equity, yet boards can hardly be expected to have such a dramatic influence over society.

Maternity leave stands out as a key gender equity issue. Companies have reported hearing differing—and sometimes conflicting—answers from focus groups of women about what they feel would be most effective in achieving gender parity. Some women want longer maternity leave and would like corporations to insist on paternity leave for new fathers. Such a policy, they argue, would remove the stigma of professional women choosing to take time off around the birth of their children. Meanwhile, other women, albeit a minority, have questioned the very notion of maternity leave, arguing that it unfairly designates childcare as purely a women's issue. Others would like corporations to keep their seats warm in their absence, so that their specific job with their particular clients remains intact. Another model proposed is the idea of shared parental leave, where new mothers and fathers have an equal right to spend time with their families. A related question that emerges as the population ages is whether employers should accommodate needs of employees as caretakers—for example, to look after aging parents. Given the plethora of arguments and views being put forward, boards face an immensely complex task in putting a workable policy in place.

A number of more recent approaches—such as flextime and allowing people to work at home—also have mixed support among women employees. Some fear that not having a physical presence in the office could be deleterious to their career in the long term, even if a policy that allowed them to work from home would be beneficial to their family. These views constitute a clear reminder that the quest for gender parity, while laudable, demands more than just a single, simple solution.

More starkly, the lack of gender parity, as well as the underrepresentation of minorities, reflects a deep-seated crisis of opportunity and access. And even gender pay equity does not address more systemic issues such as overpromoting men and leaving women in lower roles with few avenues for advancement. While many companies have board-endorsed mentor programs and outright stipulations that appointment and promotion lists must include women candidates, even the best of these interventions skirts over more fundamental issues, such as the lack of women in STEM. Crucially, while boards can arguably make a dent in these areas, they cannot redress the failures of the whole system on their own.

Along the same lines, corporations are increasingly taking on the mantle of building and re-skilling the workforce of tomorrow by supporting youth development through financial assistance and internship programs—initiatives that should, at the margin, help redress the dearth of adequately skilled women (and men) in the pipeline. However, these initiatives cannot achieve the necessary changes without broad and active public policy efforts.

There are plenty of subtler challenges to achieving gender parity. For example, the same qualities are often unfairly interpreted differently based on gender. Women's workplace temperament is seen as different from that of men. Not better or worse, just different. And whereas men are praised for confidence and assertiveness, women are labeled bossy and aggressive. Even more trying for boards seeking gender equity across their organizations is that women tend not to put their hands up to flag interest in a promotion, better pay, or other opportunities. Thankfully, this sentiment is changing.

Calls for women to "lean in" and ask for what they want—and to strive to stay in the workforce come what may—do resonate with many. The best corporations are constantly exploring innovative ways to circumvent the old boy network by remaking interview and recruitment processes to be more gender-neutral. For example, Harvard's Iris Bohnet has written about the potential of blind interviews, which screen candidates without information on their race, gender, or religion. In the era of technology, artificial intelligence (AI) recruiting tools, while not without their limitations, are already showing promise of enabling more objective screening processes that give women a fair shake.

But here again, society has an important role to play in fundamentally recasting how we raise girls and young women. Risk-taking will forever be a feature of corporate success. It would certainly improve the lives of women workers if more girls from a very young age were encouraged to take risks. But altering traditional societal expectations surrounding gender roles and behaviors is hard work. Nevertheless, it is worth pursuing as a collective effort of governments, businesses, and society as a whole.

Boards and the corporations they lead must continue to evolve. Corporations can (and are) making noteworthy and considerable progress to ensure that management is not blindly following an unexamined company culture that leads to over-promoting underperforming men and overlooking talented women. Boards are becoming increasingly interested in the more tacit ways that a business's culture is established and sustained. Many boards have committed to ensuring that the work environment is not biased against certain segments of the employee population and that it reflects appropriate and inclusive perspectives from the entire employee base.

For all their efforts to seek gender equity—not just in the boardroom, but throughout their organizations—boards have relatively few levers to make change directly. For example, any company can pick off the most talented women with a STEM background from other companies, but this does not address the systemic societal need for a pipeline of skilled women. Thus, as boards look beyond Band-Aid solutions to achieving gender parity, they must partner with governments, policymakers, and civil society organizations that are also aiming for lasting structural change.

Social and Environmental Effects

Board members are not deaf to the loud calls for corporations to take the lead in addressing social and environmental concerns. Every single board that I have served on in the past decade has engaged in considered and constructive debates on these issues. On most occasions, these discussions have led to sweeping changes in product design, sales practices, recruiting and promotion methods, and the tone and culture of the organization itself. But here, too, the speed and manner of change must be weighed against a corporation's immediate mandate to deliver its prescribed goods and services in a safe, cost-effective, and efficient way.

Moves to address societal concerns must be made constructively and methodically. If they are undertaken hastily and without proper consideration, they can bring considerable costs that may actually hurt, not help, society at large. While it has become fashionable to campaign for the breakup or even shutdown of companies and whole industries, there is often little thought given to the consequences. For example, large, traditional energy companies are facing spirited and virulent campaigns undertaken by environmental lobbyists calling for the companies' shareholders to divest and for banks to stop lending to them, on the grounds that they contribute to climate change. These actions would lead to the destruction of enterprise value, lost jobs, lost revenue to governments, and many other second-order effects that could permanently harm whole communities. Moreover, such efforts actually undermine progress toward cleaning up the environment as well as toward finding better, cleaner, and more efficient sources of energy by defunding the scientists and engineers who are at the forefront of discovering those sources.

Nevertheless, more and more boards are being confronted with their company's impact on society, notably in the areas of environmental and social concerns. In order for the company to survive, boards must reallocate human and financial capital to avoid being out of step with societal shifts and capitalize on these trends by going into new business lines. Take the example of a fast-food chain. Its core business relies on producing and selling millions of hamburgers. This satiates a need and meets the demand of a well-established market. In 1994, when McDonald's stopped publicly updating the number, the company had sold ninety-nine billion hamburgers in roughly forty years.

Think about it: such an expansive global operation delivering a consistent, cost-effective, and tasty offering requires that the board work with management to monitor and oversee employee matters, supply chains, health inspections, costs, the company's reputation, and long-term strategic planning. Under these pressures, staying in business is already a demanding balancing act.

Yet issues of societal and environmental import are also creeping onto the crowded board agenda. These may take the form of concerns about global obesity: At a time when around one billion people are deemed obese, how does a fast-food company justify selling its products? Or they may revolve around hunger: When forty-two million people (roughly one in seven) struggle with food insecurity in a developed economy like the United States, what is a company in the business of feeding people doing to fight hunger? There are also questions about the environment: Livestock are estimated to contribute around 14.5 percent of the world's greenhouse gases every year. What, then, are food companies doing to offset those emissions?

All these factors have a direct impact on the company's core business: the production and supply of hamburgers. Rapidly shifting customer preferences, changing policy decrees, and the advent of technology will each surely play a role in complicating the food business's future. Estimates in the United States and UK suggest that a third of consumers are cutting down on meat. In response, the appearance of the meatless Impossible Burger on fast-food menus is thought to have attracted new customers and improved profit lines. Policymakers might institute new laws that materially change the business model—such as higher taxation or even outright bans on meat—and of course technology could usher in future substitutes that affect the company's strategy.

Surprising as it may seem, the world's largest institutional investors are now placing greater demands on boards and corporations to address a multitude of social issues. Since 2012, Larry Fink, the founder and CEO of BlackRock, has published a letter to CEOs in which he outlines key areas of focus for his company, which is one of the world's largest asset managers. His yearly letters have included calls for a new model of shareholder engagement (2018) and a call for companies to fulfill their purpose and responsibility to stakeholders (2019). Also in 2018, a group of the world's biggest investors—including BlackRock, other asset managers like Vanguard and Schroders, and several large pension funds—called on companies to commit to a common set of metrics for societal and workforce issues. The signatories to this agreement, which became known as the Embankment Project for Inclusive Capitalism, together control more than $30 trillion. Collectively, they agreed to push companies to disclose hard-to-quantify measures such as staffing, governance, and innovation, as well as societal and environmental impacts. In 2017, the investment firm JANA Partners and pension and health-care fund CalPERS, both major shareholders of Apple, urged the smartphone maker to create ways for parents to restrict children's access to their mobile phones.

They also pushed for the company to study the effects of heavy smartphone usage on mental health.

Another instance of this sort of pressure went public in December 2018, when the oil company Royal Dutch Shell agreed to link executive pay to carbon-emissions targets. This followed pressure from shareholders, led by the Church of England and Robeco (a Dutch asset-management fund) and supported by Climate Action 100+, a five-year initiative to engage with companies around the world to achieve the goals of the Paris climate agreement. Significantly, just five months earlier, Shell's CEO had appeared to oppose such a proposal and had reportedly said that setting hard emissions targets would risk exposing the company to litigation.

It may not be such a surprise that big investors can get results, but there are deeper stirrings of dissatisfaction too. Larry Fink's 2015 letter to CEOs may well have proved to be a tipping point in prompting investors to force corporate action on a slate of issues from environmental sustainability to female representation on boards. However, one underlying impetus for investor action is no doubt a recognition that members of the millennial generation—now the largest population cohort in the United States—have different priorities for what they deem societally acceptable.

Given the magnitude of these changes, boards will most certainly need to act. But how a board goes about changing its business requires consideration and reflection. There is, after all, a workforce to manage, a company to operate, and customers who are still willing to pay you because they want your hamburgers. While management is the first part of the company to deal with many social issues, in our highly challenging times, these matters are also of immediate concern to the board, since they go to the heart of governing and overseeing the company strategy, succession, and culture.

A thoughtful board will weigh its current strategy and consider whether it needs to change. Perhaps such a change includes selling different products. As mentioned above, conventional energy companies are facing increasing challenges due to environmental concerns. Warnings from international agencies and governments are forcing boards and corporate leaders to embed explicit environmental agendas into their strategies. In October 2018, a report from the United Nations Intergovernmental Panel on Climate Change demanded the urgent phasing out of fossil fuels, stating that coal-fired electricity must end by 2050 and that the world has just twelve years to limit a climate catastrophe. This was part of the UN's wider call to reduce greenhouse gases by 45 percent and limit the rise in global temperatures to 1.5 degrees Celsius. In November 2018, a US-government-sanctioned report cautioned of the significant damage that climate change will unleash on the country, both environmentally and economically. Policymakers in China, the UK, and France have already made proclamations that they plan to ban fossil-fuel cars by 2040.

All this necessarily forces energy companies to recalibrate their strategy, even at a time when the global demand for oil-based energy continues to rise. Boards and management of energy companies have been forced to invest in alternative energies—geothermal, wind, solar, battery, biofuel, nuclear—that have emerged as contenders to meet the needs of the future.

Even in the absence of detailed environmental law, energy companies are responding to customers' changing sentiment and their desire to reduce their carbon footprint. This trend has far-reaching implications for the boards of airlines and car companies, as customers pledge to scale back on air travel and appear keen to use more shared ground transportation. Of course, the boards of global banks are also affected, since they are under increasing pressure to reassess their lending to the energy sector. Already, some financial companies have committed to curb or eliminate lending to the coal industry.

Yet, cutting against the environmental needs, these same companies face an entirely different challenge: today over 1.2 billion people around the world lack access to reliable, clean, and affordable energy. This puts the livelihoods and futures—the education, health care, and commerce—of billions of people at stake, mainly in the world's most densely populated and poorest regions. Grinding poverty, greater disorderly immigration, and slowed human progress are all direct consequences of a world where conventional forms of energy and the companies that deliver them are banned. Given that forecasts suggest a nearly 50 percent increase in energy use by 2050, the boards of energy companies do not have the luxury of doing nothing.

The broader takeaway is this: virtually every board, in every company, in every industry is contending with sometimes conflicting demands for environmental and social change with urgency. One would be hard-pressed to find a board of any reasonable size, stature, or recognition that was not reviewing and considering the ramifications of their corporate actions on society—socially, environmentally, and beyond.

Capital allocation and company portfolios reflect the changes that these boards are making. Hamburger companies are expanding their menus beyond meat, and energy companies are investing billions in R&D and alternative energies. These boards and corporations get it—their long-term success, and even existence, depends on having an open mind. The goal, of course, is to deliver the food that customers clearly want and the energy that people clearly need in a way that protects the environment and does not contravene today's norms. This in part explains why corporations are making public commitments to defending high standards on human rights, fighting corruption, supporting labor rights, and advocating environmental protections such as the UN Global Compact.

A Shifting Work Environment

The corporate workplace has not been immune from cultural changes. Employees' ways of engaging and operating at work are vastly different from those of yesteryear. In the past, there was a clear delineation between how people behaved at work versus in their private life. In many corporations, this is no longer the case.

The fact is, people spend a large proportion of their life at work. By some estimates, the average person spends ninety thousand hours (or over 3,500 full workdays) at work over their lifetime. The blurring of the lines between home and work—encapsulated in the call to "bring your whole self to work"—is aimed at making employees more authentic in the work environment. Yet these changes throw up a multitude of issues for which traditional board thinking might be ill-equipped.

Bringing one's whole self to work is likely to lead to more frequent power struggles between employers and employees. Employees' reactions to their peers breaking certain behavior codes—such as those prohibiting sexual harassment—are increasingly playing out in public, rather than behind closed doors. On May 23, 2019, protests against the alleged sexual harassment of McDonald's employees took place in thirteen cities, and workers filed a total of twenty-five sexual-harassment complaints against the company that week. Public disagreements between management and employees over business principles are also being aired for all to see. Even when management makes moves that are perfectly legal, some workers may vocally protest against business practices they consider undesirable. While boards often leave it to management to deal with such frustrations, the new work environment can sometimes produce challenges that the board cannot escape.

For one thing, there is the rising risk that, in the name of preserving and defending individuality, some employees may refuse to work on certain projects or for certain clients. In 2019, for example, employees at Google refused to work on any government contract pertaining to the US Department of Defense. In the end, Google's management relented and did not sign the contract.

Campaigns for employee self-advocacy can clash with management's responsibilities, stressing the organization's power dynamics and placing its operations at risk. When this happens, the board must become involved. These issues are difficult to navigate. Any efforts by employees to strip senior leadership of its responsibility to strategize for the company have to be addressed. Of course, not all self-advocacy efforts are confrontational—in fact, drawing on the economic theory of Pareto efficiency, a board might decide that the pursuit of personal agendas by individual employees is harmless if the whole company can be better off without any one employee being worse off. Additionally, in order to help circumvent worker apathy, boards and management must strive to make the case for why people should want to work at their company and should make sure they are continuously matching employees with the work they enjoy.

Michael Moritz, the former managing partner of Sequoia, a leading venture capital firm in Silicon Valley, has penned a number of spirited articles highlighting the risk that the US technology sector will become less competitive than China's. In an article titled "Silicon Valley Would Be Wise to Follow China's Lead," Moritz argued that differences in attitudes about work-life balance between US and Chinese companies place the former at a distinct disadvantage.

The Chinese work culture in tech start-ups, which can involve putting in fourteen-hour days six or seven days a week, stands in stark contrast to California's tech scene, where companies juggle parental leave demands and workers prioritize the need for greater work-life balance. The grueling schedule adopted by Chinese companies is known by the shorthand "996"—that is, 9:00 a.m. to 9:00 p.m., six days a week. In another article, Moritz explained that Chinese technology companies are on track to become increasingly dominant globally: In a ranking of the top fifty start-ups by value, twenty-six were companies from China and only sixteen were from the United States. Of the top twenty, eleven were from China. This is despite, or perhaps because of, China's demanding work environment. Moritz's observations point to a concern already being expressed in some boardrooms: that increasing societal demands domestically could undermine the competitiveness of US companies globally. The accuracy of this view can be debated, but any board member would be shirking their duties if they neglected the risks posed by increasingly aggressive global competition.

Emerging Issues for the Board

It is practically impossible to produce an exhaustive list of all the cultural and social issues that boards are being asked to address. Issues such as gun control, mental health, and provenance (that is, the origins of the inputs used in products companies make) seem likely to appear with greater frequency on the boardroom agenda going forward.

In the case of gun control, for example, the boards of companies that sell guns are caught in the middle of a tug-of-war between the constitutional right of US customers to bear arms and the rising calls for greater restrictions on the sale of guns. Boards and company leaders are being forced to choose sides in the debate.

In September 2019, Walmart announced it would limit the sale of guns and ammunition. DICK'S Sporting Goods, a well-known gun supplier, stopped selling guns in over one hundred of its stores and destroyed $5 million worth of weapons in a declaration of its anti-gun stance. The leaders of both these publicly traded companies were reacting to a spate of deadly shootings across the United States, including one that killed twenty-two people in a Walmart store in El Paso, Texas, in August 2019.

Mental health will also likely be on future board agendas. In May 2019, the French telecommunications company Orange, along with its former CEO Didier Lombard and other members of its senior leadership team, faced a trial in which they were charged with "moral harassment" related to changes in the company in 2008 and 2009 as it was privatized and reorganized. These changes involved job cuts and repeated staffing adjustments, all of which allegedly led to the suicides of as many as thirty-five employees. The World Health Organization has forecast that depression and anxiety will cost the global economy $1 trillion a year in lost productivity and has urged employers to take a central role in addressing mental health issues. Similarly, a November 2018 report published in the *Lancet* forecast that mental health disorders would cost the global economy $16 trillion by 2030.

Corporations are likely to bear much of the economic cost of society's mental health troubles—whether indirectly via higher tax burdens to help governments fund treatment, or directly as boards and corporations contemplate taking greater responsibility for the management of their workforce's mental health. With this in mind, and recognizing that these issues are no longer solely the purview of the state, boards are being prompted to consider the costs of mental health difficulties and devise plans to address them.

With regards to provenance, consumers are demanding greater transparency when judging which products they will buy. They want more information about how and where a company's goods and services are produced. They want to know what wages are paid to employees, what conditions are like for workers, and what impact companies are having on the environment. These demands are coming particularly from younger consumers, and boards and corporations must be attentive to their preferences. As Generation Z (those born between 1996 and 2014) was expected to become the largest consumer market by 2020, their buying choices will be of great importance. Estimates from GreenMatch—an advocacy group that promotes the use of green energy products—suggest that 72 percent of Generation Z would spend more money on a service that is sustainably produced.

Boards should note that the sentiments of younger, up-and-coming generations—whether regarding gun control or environmental concerns—have been catalyzed in an era of hyperconnectivity and social media, which will have a considerable impact on business agendas in years to come. Boards need to reflect on how technology and social media are making it easier for consumers to form strong opinions quickly. Through technology, they can better understand where goods and services come from and more easily find out how businesses are conducting their operations. Armed with this information, customers are demanding answers and threatening to walk away if they don't get them.

Boards Under Siege, but Moving Forward

At times, looking at the many social and cultural demands on corporations, it is hard not to feel that boards are under unrelenting siege. But just because these are difficult issues does not mean that boards can avoid them. Society is holding companies to account precisely because these issues are important and not going away. In fact, the emphasis is likely only to increase.

My sense from the boardroom is that criticism can, in some cases, be too harsh and even unfounded. Critics have a way of constantly moving their goalposts and lodging complaints without a good understanding of companies' limitations. In reality, one would be hard-pressed to find any board that neglects to consider the ramifications of its actions on society. However, boards are being asked to do a lot—including some things they cannot really do by themselves, often in areas where public policy should be taking the lead.

Many companies are already making progress, providing excruciatingly detailed information on how they produce and deliver their goods. Shareholders and consumers alike are demanding answers: How much carbon dioxide was emitted? How much water was used? What is the average wage of the people who worked to get this to my doorstep? Boards and their corporations, meanwhile, are responding in unprecedented ways. During the 2020 global coronavirus pandemic, corporations sacrificed a great deal of economic vitality in the name of broader societal health. For example, hotels in the United States, the UK, and Germany turned their rooms into makeshift hospitals to help medical authorities cope with the surge of patients.

Still, boards should also take into account that emphasizing sustainability need not reduce returns and that sustainable corporations will likely gain market share and appeal to more customers. Indeed, some advocates argue that the idea of a choice between returns and sustainability is a false one, since Western companies have a duty to set standards globally. They point to the 1977 Foreign Corrupt Practices Act (FCPA), which stipulates that US companies cannot pay bribes. Even though US firms were held to this higher standard, global demand for US products has increased over time and the FCPA ultimately did not harm their competitiveness, their corporate profitability, or their success.

However, the intensity of global competition has grown in the past forty years. There will be a limit to how far corporations want to go in pursuit of sustainability goals, and how long society wants sustainability to remain a priority if it comes with economic consequences. Where this limit lies will become clearer as the threats from global competitors take effect. This is particularly the case when Western companies are forced to compete against rivals in countries where norms and regulations allow them to focus exclusively on financial returns. In this scenario, boards will likely have to ask if they should push back against campaigns around social issues.

In some respects, businesses have been here before. This is not the first time they have faced pressure to help employees and society, even if doing so diverges from their primary purpose. For example, in the years after World War II, it became standard practice for companies to offer workplace pensions. Pension entitlement had the benefit of offering employees financial security and incentivizing them to commit to their employer in the long term. However, in the early 2000s, a number of industrial giants—most notably automotive companies Ford, General Motors, and Chrysler—learned the limits of such largesse. As these automakers struggled to stay afloat under the weight of their unsustainable pension liabilities, less constrained global competitors took market share. Today, many newer companies do not offer pensions, while older ones are reducing and capping their contributions for new employees to prevent ballooning pension liabilities, particularly in this era of historically low interest rates. Of course, global competition was not so acute sixty years ago when pensions were introduced. Today, it is a formidable threat.

There is space for corporations to improve their records on the suite of social issues. This is why many companies take seriously the perspectives of stakeholders and partner with organizations and campaigns in cases where constructive progress can be made. But although many campaigners push for change in a constructive way, others have taken a far more aggressive approach. The nature of their demands suggests that they are trying to undermine the corporation's business model and even drive it out of existence. Real risks can emerge when these critics actually get what they wish for.

Take the hypothetical case of a US mining company operating in a poor emerging country. NGOs lobbying against the company's mining practices ultimately force it to shut down its operations and leave the country. But when it becomes clear that a Chinese mining company will be coming in and resuming operations, the NGOs ask the US company to stay, concerned that the Chinese replacement will be even less receptive to their concerns.

As campaigners and lobbyists pressure the boards of global companies to change their ways, it is crucial not to lose track of the fact that corporations do bring substantial benefits to society. These include not just economic growth but second-order benefits—such as wider investment in people, innovation, and infrastructure—that the average citizen does not always ascribe to corporations. Balancing between garnering higher returns and adhering to ever-greater levels of social responsibility involves difficult decisions. If lobbying leads companies to scale back too far, the benefits they previously brought may disappear.

Even if the emphasis on social issues does not immediately threaten the viability of companies, it will likely increase the cost of business operations, raise the barriers to entry, and hurt competition. All of this will increase the costs to consumers and affect smaller companies more acutely, which in turn will reinforce the case for consolidation across industries. Already there is considerable data showing that many industries are consolidating to a point where sectors are acting more as national monopolies or global oligopolies. As the literature in economic theory makes abundantly clear, such systems are far from the ideal of perfect competition. The result is that the cost of goods and services will be determined by fewer and fewer corporations, to the disadvantage of the customer. Beyond that, many consumers would understandably disapprove of our society depending so much on a handful of massive corporations.

There's undoubtedly a need for broader engagement from government and society in addressing many of the cultural issues set out in this chapter. Nevertheless, given the cultural shifts occurring across the business landscape, corporations must adapt, and boards will have to become more assertive in how they respond to new cultural norms. Whether this involves companies changing their underlying business models, engaging more with employees and institutional investors, or taking a more expansive role in social issues, it is necessary. If they do not, companies will lose customers, employees, and investors, and ultimately face demise.

The first three chapters of this book have examined how boards carry out their responsibilities of overseeing strategy, managing board and CEO succession, and navigating the rapidly shifting cultural landscape. Now, we must turn to the future risks a board should devote itself to tracking as it continues its work as the custodian of the organization.

CHAPTER 4

Five Critical Issues No Board Should Ignore

WHEN BOARDS THINK ABOUT THE TRENDS THAT COULD DISRUPT GLOBAL commerce, they tend to focus on an immediate set of risks that are likely to affect their organization's operational and financial performance, say, over the next year. These can include macroeconomic issues, geopolitical concerns, or the threat of changing customer preferences. Yet it is just as important for boards to scan the horizon for slower-moving issues that have the potential to reshape the business landscape in the long term. Focusing too intently on the immediate future can mean boards miss emerging obstacles that can harm a company.

Unlike the usual set of issues that boards are accustomed to dealing with, the risks explored in this chapter transcend the short term. These are the factors that determine the fortunes of companies over years—not just a few months or quarters. Boards need to anticipate these critical issues and develop sound plans for navigating them.

Boards of the past had to deal with the major macroeconomic and geopolitical challenges of their eras: the Spanish flu, the Great Depression, the First and Second World Wars, the oil-price shocks of the 1970s, and the collapse of the USSR, to name a few.

Today, the corporations that will truly differentiate themselves are those with boards and management teams that are focused on five factors: the risk of a more siloed and protectionist world, massive changes in the investment landscape, new technological developments, the global war for talent, and, ultimately, short-termism itself. In many ways, these risks are not discrete but rather overlapping and interrelated. Short-termism, in addition to affecting board thinking directly, is also a precondition of the other four risks. All in all, these seismic shifts are defining the business environment of the future, and how boards respond will determine the winners and the losers.

1. The Risk of a More Siloed and Protectionist World

Liberal democracy has existed as a dominant political ideology for just 1 percent of human history, and even now only about 30 percent of the world's population enjoys living in a liberal democratic society. Nevertheless, liberal democracy, combined with market capitalism, has delivered greater economic success for its citizens in the postwar era than authoritarian and state-led regimes.

However, in the past couple of decades, the desirability of market capitalism has diminished. Mature democracies in the West have suffered both economic and political upheaval, as manifested in the 2008 global financial crisis and the populist backlash that led to Brexit and the 2016 election of US president

Donald Trump. Concurrently, states that de-prioritize democracy, such as China, have recorded unprecedented economic success. In many respects, the world economy is de-globalizing already. This is evident in the breakdown of many international agreements and the trend toward more bilateral ones—for example, the United States' decision to reject the Trans-Pacific Partnership and the revisions to the North American Free Trade Agreement that resulted in the 2020 US-Mexico-Canada Agreement.

Threats to multilateralism are visible across Europe, where an unprecedented sequence of disputes has led to fractures within the European Union. The fallout from Greece's debt crisis in 2010, Britain's decision to leave the union in 2016 after forty-five years, Italy's budget dispute in 2018, and skirmishes in 2020 between the richer and poorer European countries on how to finance coronavirus-related spending have all chipped away at the EU's previously unified, multilateral approach. Additionally, Poland and Hungary have presented a challenge to the EU's core principle of free movement, and concerns are rising about the health of German industry—which has underpinned the EU's economic might for decades. Altogether, these developments signal the reemergence of assertive national power in Europe.

Meanwhile, China is working to establish a multilateral world order of its own to rival the dominance of Bretton Woods institutions such as the IMF and World Bank. This effort has included the creation of development institutions such as the New Development Bank and the Asian Infrastructure Investment Bank. China is also seeking to gain a greater global foothold in trade, capital flows, and investments through the multi-continent Belt and Road Initiative, which includes infrastructure investment across sixty-eight countries in Asia, Africa, Europe, and the Middle East to develop improved trade routes by land and sea. As a result, a growing proportion of the global economy will be guided by China.

The 2020 global COVID-19 pandemic initially showcased the power authoritarian governments have over governments that rest on democratic freedom. An authoritarian government could quickly apply the levers it had—such as the ability to restrict freedom of movement and quarantine its population by decree—to control the spread of the disease, while governments in the United States and Europe hesitated before imposing similar restrictions in the hope of preserving individual freedoms, a bedrock principle of democratic capitalism.

But the bigger point is that amid the greatest global health crisis in a generation, it has been nation-states that have taken the lead. Multilateral institutions such as the World Health Organization, World Bank, and IMF have acted, but they played less of a core role than they might have in the past. It is a perilous moment. Present trends suggest that long-standing principles of free trade and free movement of capital, labor, and ideas are unwinding—as is the ideal of small, fiscally disciplined government.

Boards must determine whether their companies will be able to survive in a new world order where the liberal, market-capitalist construct is replaced. Companies will be forced to fundamentally rethink and adapt their business models, a seismic shift that may be difficult for them to come to terms with. The very idea that the political and economic systems that they have known and operated in for decades are vulnerable is hard to accept.

Company leaders often place a premium on the notion of permanence. They behave as though the global liberal economic system is here to stay, discounting the idea that another system could supplant it as the dominant global framework. As a result, boards and management risk being unprepared for a fundamental change to the economic and political system in which they operate.

Change should not be so hard to envision for companies that have been adapting their business models to ever-accelerating technological shifts. Today's boards and executives have operated in a world where innovation and technological progress have always been constants—even if the scale and scope of this change has accelerated in recent years. Nevertheless, democracy and capitalism have remained largely stable for so long that systemic change can be harder for companies to imagine than technological innovation. If today's global economic and political system is upended, boards will have to rethink their business models or risk failure.

The prevailing globalized economy has allowed corporations to tap relatively cheap capital, deploy it around the world, and garner higher returns (the carry trade), while hiring and recruiting the best talent internationally. Multilateralism has significantly lowered the costs of global supply chains, enabling companies to manufacture goods in low-cost environments and sell them at higher prices in developed markets—as Apple has done with its iPhones. This has driven trade and investment, and thus economic growth, at a global scale to levels not previously seen. But in a rapidly de-globalizing world, these benefits could quickly disappear. Corporations would lose these benefits of multilateralism and be forced to raise capital and invest locally.

If globalization is dead, or dying, boards must plan for the most harmful consequences, including the disruption of the global supply chain, which would invariably send the costs of production soaring. Over the last five years, for example, rising wages have increased production costs in countries like Argentina and India; both are experiencing double-digit wage inflation. This forces business leaders to consider the viability of their operations in these countries, and whether they will be forced to move out.

The new decade is already characterized by rising economic complexity and geopolitical divisions: escalated US-China tensions, populism and nationalism in Europe, and the continued threat of a global recession. Amid this turmoil, forward-thinking business leaders are developing strategies to mitigate the long-term risks of de-globalization.

Naturally, they are concerned about trade protectionism and the revenue a company could lose in potential tariff wars. However, there is another, subtler danger associated with de-globalization: many global corporations are simply not structured in a way that will allow them to compete in a de-globalized world. It is increasingly understood that this new, siloed business environment will directly affect three pillars of global corporations: technology, global recruiting, and the finance function. Later in this chapter, we will examine in greater detail the particular risks stemming from fast-evolving technology and the war for global talent. For now, however, we will look at how technology and recruitment are themselves at risk from de-globalization.

In recent years, corporate leadership has rightly prioritized addressing cyber risks, the threat of technological obsolescence, and the consequences of a jobless underclass as a result of increased automation. However, there are now mounting concerns that something more fundamental is at risk. Many observers have begun to wonder whether global supply chains—a critical factor in the success of many multinational corporations—will continue to function as they once had.

Over the past fifty years, multinational corporations have built and relied on global supply chains to source goods from low-cost regions and sell them in other countries for higher prices. This drove the success of many companies—catalyzing their profits by lowering costs, helping to drive global GDP, and underpinning the economic success of many emerging economies such as China's.

In the last decade, however, this powerful profit trend has reversed. Global trade growth has flatlined in the past decade at around 3 percent, and there are real concerns, given the threats of de-globalization and protectionism, that it will continue to do so. In January 2019, the McKinsey Global Institute revealed that the share of goods produced around the world and traded across borders has fallen sharply, from 28.1 percent in 2007 to 22.5 percent in 2017. In the report, McKinsey suggests that the unwinding of global supply chains may partly reflect the political backlash against trade and globalization (such as the imposition of tariffs and trade barriers). However, it may also reveal rising consumer demand in China and other developing countries, where citizens are buying more of their own locally produced goods, as well as improved domestic supply chains in those countries.

Another explanation is, of course, that increases in wages have eroded these poorer countries' once-glaring cost advantage. If foreign trade is being driven less and less by the search for low wages, it would explain why, according to McKinsey, less than 20 percent of trade today is based on labor-cost arbitrage. The prospect of seeing the profit gains of low-cost production all but wiped out is just another strand boardrooms must confront. Ultimately, companies are left with a choice between absorbing these higher costs or passing them on to the consumer.

Yet another threat to global supply chains is the emerging "splinternet"—an increasingly fragmented internet with competing China-led and US-led platforms. This technological fragmentation has the potential to dramatically disrupt global supply chains by eliminating centralized procurement and thereby raising costs and reducing the efficiency gained from shared global services. Furthermore, a balkanized internet promises to increase the complexity of companies' operations and erode their ability to respond quickly to market forces. In such a world, companies will need to choose between the US and China camps or bear the costs of operating in two adversarial technological worlds, each with its own regulatory and operating standards.

Already, the first signs of such divergence are being felt across corporations concerning the issue of data privacy. Most Western companies make every effort to protect individual privacy—a stance that arguably places them at a distinct disadvantage to their Chinese competitors, who operate within a less stringent data-privacy regime. The relatively light data-privacy rules in China enable access to large data sets with more individual information. This can speed up innovation, enabling cutting-edge drug discovery, which in turn helps push costs down for the end consumers and makes a company more valuable.

Greater immigration controls are another aspect of the move toward de-globalization. The recent shift in the political mood in the United States and Europe against immigration has intensified the global war for talent and threatens to undermine corporations' ability to hire across borders.

In the United States, the government has undertaken protectionist measures to restrict the movement of labor. For example, in the wake of President Donald Trump's April 2017 executive order to "Buy American and Hire American," US Citizenship and Immigration Services has held up record numbers of H-1B visa petitions, such that the denial rate for first-time H-1B applications has increased from 10 percent in 2016 to 24 percent in 2018 and 32 percent in the first quarter of 2019. Recruitment, particularly at senior levels, depends on access to global pools of talent; executive teams that are composed of different nationalities and backgrounds are widely seen as a source of competitive advantage. Mounting restrictions on immigration also limit the opportunity for tomorrow's business leaders to learn how to navigate across cultures and mean fewer opportunities to share best practices and transformational ideas.

A more fragmented world also significantly complicates the task of managing global corporate finances and adds considerable costs. Global companies derive enormous benefits from a centralized finance system. Today, many companies raise capital relatively cheaply in financial hubs such as New York or London and invest it across their global operations. In most cases, this centralized model means corporations are able to borrow at a lower cost than they would if their regional and national subsidiaries had to raise money from local currency markets, which tend to carry greater risk and volatility. A more siloed world means corporations will struggle to extract their investment capital and return profits to shareholders. Boards, therefore, would be wise to consider whether the corporations they oversee should change their structure and consider becoming less centralized and more federated.

Global companies' responses to de-globalization will likely need to include an overhaul of their business, funding, and operating models, moving away from a centralized treasury that directs cash around the world and toward a model in which the company merely owns subsidiaries that individually raise capital and invest locally. While this framework may be more expensive than a globalized system, it could at least allow the company to survive. However, even then, corporations could face the prospect of capital controls that limit or even prevent their local operations from sending profits back to the group center and on to investors as dividends and returns.

The shift from a more centralized to a more federated model brings additional complexity, as business leaders will be forced to contend with an increasingly complicated web of independent processes and regulations in different jurisdictions. To reasonably manage or mitigate threats will require extraordinary levels of highly specialized knowledge at the local level, making it nearly impossible for headquarters to understand the necessary risk budget, let alone adequately hedge those risks.

As power continues to move away from multilateral organizations—such as the EU and WTO—and devolves to national governments, global corporations will likely find it harder to maintain effective government relations across different countries. Of course, multinational corporations already have to abide by the various regulations of the markets in which they operate, and therefore need deep local knowledge to be effective. But as protectionism leads governments to subscribe less often to global rules, national regulatory bodies will become paramount and corporations will need ever more specific knowledge to operate and succeed. This growing complexity on matters of taxation, tariffs, quotas, and environmental regulations will force corporations to contend with the question of whether their organizational structure should become more diffuse.

The rationale for global corporations' existence is that their leaders are able to observe the world and marshal capital, labor, and production in ways that lower costs, increase efficiencies, and enhance value. As it becomes increasingly difficult to transfer these production factors across borders, it is reasonable to ask whether a global corporation is even the structure best suited for succeeding in a de-globalizing world. This question becomes even more urgent in light of the fact that global corporations across such sectors as consumer goods and finance are seeing their fiercest competition come from large local or regional competitors, rather than other traditional global companies.

This is another reason for corporations to operate in a more federated structure, as a collection of independent, loosely affiliated, locally run companies. These subsidiaries would enjoy the benefits of sharing knowledge among a larger network of companies, but most capital allocation and human-capital decisions would be delegated to the local level. Perhaps these subsidiaries could even list and trade independently on local as well as global exchanges.

Ultimately, the way forward will depend on whether a company's leadership considers de-globalization to be an enduring phenomenon or a passing trend. If business leaders believe a siloed business world is here to stay, then they must give real consideration to upending the prevailing corporate structure. If, however, corporate leaders believe that the push toward a more fragmented world is temporary and will soon pass, then their responsibility is to navigate the de-globalization risks while retaining their global business model. Either way, leaders should be alert to the idea that if they are wrong, the corporations they serve may not survive.

In the face of these questions, boards have to make difficult choices. A board can't get every decision right, but when its members are facing a pivotal choice, they should ask themselves a few questions: Are they making decisions with a long-term view? Are they making decisions based on what's best for the firm? Are they avoiding the impulse to follow the herd—recognizing that the company's fortunes may be linked to the wider industry in a way that's not immediately obvious, as was the case with banks during the 2008 financial crisis? Are they managing the underlying risks as well as the highly visible ones? Are they updating their risk models?

Today, boards face uncertainty about how the international trading environment will fare in the years ahead. Several scenarios are possible. For example, the world may make a fundamental long-term shift toward more state-led capitalism, where rigid national borders and protectionist policies place severe limitations on global trade, forcing companies to reassess their strategy. Another possibility is that protectionism will plateau and we will avoid any further limitations on international trade, which would require a less drastic strategic response. Still another scenario is that protectionism will quickly lose credibility and businesses will be free to resume an open trade agenda within a relatively short period of time. Each of these outcomes has its own challenges, but only a board that contains a breadth of knowledge and experience will be able to plan for all of them effectively.

2. Sea Change in the Investment Landscape

In addition to de-globalization, boardrooms are noticing and discussing the concentration of capital and its corresponding effect on investor power. Boards face formidable challenges in responding to investors' desire to see corporations focus more on a broader utility function and social good. As we saw in Chapter 3, some of those priorities can be addressed through internal company policy, but there are many that can only be dealt with by transforming the business landscape. When it comes to investments, boards must reckon with more vocal institutional investors, the risk of outside activists, investors excluding their companies from key funds, the rise of machines, the effects of algorithmic trading, and capital drying up for public companies.

More and more corporations and their boards are being forced to pay attention to the largest institutional investors, who wield considerable influence and refuse to be ignored on the issues that they deem important. According to estimates, for example, the three largest institutional investors—BlackRock, Vanguard, and State Street—control 15 percent of the investable market and 5 percent of trading on the world's financial markets. In 2017, BlackRock and Vanguard attracted $1 trillion in new flows of capital, further concentrating their power. It should come as no surprise that a handful of investors consistently appear at the top of almost all large company share registers. According to Jan Fichtner at the University of Amsterdam, BlackRock, Vanguard, and State Street are the largest investors in about 90 percent of companies in the S&P 500.

Smaller investors often decry this concentration of power, claiming that the playing field is not level and that institutional investors command too much control of the boardroom. Some even say large index investors should not vote in shareholder meetings precisely because of their disproportionate power. But the opposite argument has won out in recent years—namely, the idea that large investors should be able to vote because they provide permanent, stable capital. If these investors have the clout to effect positive change on social and environmental issues, proponents argue, why shouldn't they?

Large institutional investors can make other demands, too, such as direct access to senior management and board members. In contrast, someone trading stocks at home would find it very difficult to secure a meeting with the CEO of a Fortune 500 company. In theory, all shareholders are alike and ought to be treated as such. In practice, however, boards are being forced to prioritize, and they will take notice of the whims and cares of the largest and loudest investors. Importantly, this privileged access helps large investors make better-informed investment decisions, in addition to allowing them to influence the company's strategy.

Outside the large institutional investors led by the big three of BlackRock, Vanguard, and State Street, the multitrillion-dollar universe of investors includes sovereign wealth funds, pension funds, insurers, private equity funds, hedge funds, endowments, and foundations. Investors of all types are becoming more active and aggressive, agitating for corporations to change what they do and why and how they do it. Further complicating matters is that, although human employees are still largely responsible for executing trades on behalf of these entities, increasingly automated forms of trading—such as algorithmic and high-frequency trading (HFT)—are becoming commonplace, transforming how boards interact with investors. The bottom line is that boards will need to reckon with a new universe of investors in a more active and assertive manner.

Boards will be primarily concerned, naturally, with the most vocal investors, including those that dominate the share registers and therefore pose a threat to the status quo. Of these, passive funds, active funds, and activist investors are emerging as the most prominent figures wielding influence over boards and management.

Passive funds tend to track a stock market index such as the S&P 500 or FTSE 100. These indexes ascribe weights to different companies based on their market capitalization; as such, passive funds echo the risk and reward profiles of the index they track by holding a certain number of different companies' shares. Passive funds are viewed as permanent capital, in that they buy and hold long-term stock investments in corporations.

The amount of money invested in passive funds has been rising in recent years. According to Moody's, the value of passive funds is on course to surpass active investments in US equities, and it will make up 25 percent of European equity investments by 2025. One explanation for the popularity of passive funds is that they generally charge investors lower fees and often match or exceed the performance of active funds. However, this trend could reverse in favor of active investors if the US ten-year treasury yield spikes and interest rates rise above, say, 4 or 5 percent. If this happens, investment flows will likely be redirected into active funds.

In active funds, portfolio managers use their experience and judgment to regularly buy and sell the company shares in their multibillion-dollar portfolios. Although these funds have become less attractive as cheaper passive investments have been introduced, boards know that these stock-picking investors have the ultimate sanction available: they can sell a company's stock if it is underperforming or if it does not fit their view of the world.

The third type of investor, the activist, campaigns to change the direction of the companies they invest in. As discussed in Chapter 2, these investors typically build up large equity stakes of at least 5 percent in a corporation and then seek to influence company strategy, often looking to gain a seat on a board.

Boards should be assertive in dealing with all these types of investors. The increasingly vocal passive class and the directly confrontational activist class will inevitably bring their own agendas with them, and board members will have to strike a balance between these investors' interests and the broader shareholder base. But the shift toward passive funds and away from active investing is having a profound impact on the relationship between investors and boards, leading to a reordering of stock ownership and share registers so that boards are expected to engage with their shareholders in ways not previously seen.

The growing scale of passive investors, combined with their status as holders of permanent capital, means they wield ever-greater power over boards and corporations. According to a January 2020 *Bloomberg Businessweek* article entitled "The Hidden Dangers of the Great Index Fund Takeover," passive funds form the biggest shareholder group on the S&P 500, with 22 percent of these companies' equity typically held by three investors (BlackRock, Vanguard, and State Street), up from 14 percent in 2008. The sheer dominance of these investors is raising questions of possible anti-competitive behavior and concerns that concentrated ownership can lead to higher prices and reduced innovation.

Large passive investors are increasingly exploiting their power to make demands about a company's governance, role in society, and strategic direction. In general, these investors tend to focus on making sure that a company is well managed and seek to build a long-term relationship. Because passive funds consider themselves permanent capital, they will only sell a stock when a company falls out of an index or no longer meets some other predetermined set of criteria. The result is that, rather than simply selling shares in a company a manager disapproves of, these funds will instead seek to influence the company. For example, by the start of 2020, BlackRock had built a specialist investment stewardship group of more than forty executives dedicated to engaging with companies on governance issues and delivering sustainable growth. In extreme cases, passive investors might agitate to change the makeup of the board or even remove the current management.

Traditional active investors, for the most part, take a different tack. Because they are looking to pick winners and losers, and given the relatively short time horizon of their portfolios, active fund managers are more likely to sell out of a company stock if they feel the company and board are performing poorly, rather than embark on a campaign to alter the company's leadership or strategy. Even so, a growing number of active funds advocate that better governance leads to better performance.

Both passive and active investors can, and do, vote against company wishes on specific proposals. On executive pay, for example, large investors may use say-on-pay initiatives to exert influence on a matter that has traditionally been the sole purview of the board. In part, these institutional investors are responding to pressure from their employees, society, and their clients—such as public-sector and corporate pension funds.

Activist shareholders bring a more radical approach to how they engage with a board and a corporation. They will often quietly build an equity stake in a company, either by directly holding the company stock or through stock options, and they will generally seek to accumulate at least 5 percent of the company's stock before trying to exert influence. At this point, they will publicly declare their holding and explicitly make known their demands and expectations. Very often, activists find a company's strategy objectionable or they will complain that management is moving too slowly to execute a plan. It is also common that activists will seek to change the board or management.

Recent history indicates that activists expect a relatively high return on their investments in a short period—their average time between entering and exiting an investment is twenty-eight months—and boards anticipate that an activist investor will be motivated accordingly. Effective activists run campaigns to win over a target company's largest shareholders to build support for their plans for change. Sometimes activists raise capital to fund their stake from the same institutions that hold direct shares (for example, through passive investments) in the target company—something that will cause consternation and mistrust on the part of the board. This is why activists' engagement can lead to very ugly, public proxy fights.

Moreover, because activists are seeking to make key changes to strategy and implementation, addressing their concerns inevitably consumes vast quantities of the board and management's time and energy. This gives the board the sense that investors are encroaching on the decisions and judgments it has been mandated to make without a full grasp of the subtleties involved. At times, activists are advocating for a strategy change that the board has already examined in depth and rejected for sound reasons. Importantly, if the company has convinced investors that it has explored and rejected certain strategic ideas, it will be far easier to dismiss a challenge from an activist.

In the most extreme cases, an activist might campaign to break up a company, which can lead to conflict with the board. In July 2018, food group Nestlé was called to task by an activist investor, Third Point Management's Dan Loeb, who accused the company of being "insular, complacent, and overly bureaucratic" and of "missing too many trends." He proposed the company sell assets in noncore areas such as frozen foods and confectionary. Nestlé pushed back, emphasizing its decade-long record of strong shareholder returns.

Even more famous is the tussle between Pershing Square activist Bill Ackman and Herbalife, the multilevel marketing company. Ackman took a short position on the stock and launched an aggressive public campaign, claiming that the company was a predatory pyramid scheme and arguing that its value would fall to zero. The revelation of Ackman's short position in 2012 prompted Herbalife CEO Michael Johnson to call up business news channel CNBC to defend the company and attack Ackman, kicking off a five-year battle. In February 2018, Ackman disclosed that he had unwound the position in Herbalife, with both sides effectively claiming victory: Herbalife was forced to settle with US Federal Trade Commission regulators for deceptive sales practices and pay a $200 million fine, but it continued to trade and was able to avoid fulfilling Ackman's prediction that it would become worthless.

As we have just seen, the relationship between a board and an activist can be fraught. One source of tension can be the manner in which activists build up their stake in the first place, especially if they use options or borrow stock in the repo market rather than own the shares outright. This approach can lead to skepticism among board members and management and concerns that an activist's motives are not aligned with the longer-term aims of the company.

The rise of shareholder activism over the last decade has coincided with an era of low returns on investments in the years following the financial crisis. The activist strategy is thus largely seen as an artifact of this low-interest-rate environment, as investment managers look to find returns. Pressure on investors to deliver their own higher returns has incentivized some to take a bolder, more aggressive activist approach.

It is not surprising that investors are wielding their power, given the uncertainty that characterizes the overall economic outlook. A 2016 report by McKinsey forecast that a confluence of macroeconomic factors—including high debt and slow economic growth—will lead to an era of low investment returns. By 2036, real equity returns in the United States and Europe—which averaged 7.9 percent between 1985 and 2014—are projected to be between 4 and 6.5 percent. No company is immune, and as low growth and low returns are forecast to continue, it seems likely that activists are here to stay.

Today's boards are exploring whether greater engagement with investors is the answer to keeping shareholders happy. This could be part of the solution, but navigating the (often hidden) links between shareholders can place boards at a distinct disadvantage. When boards receive mixed messages about different investor intentions, it makes engagement significantly more complicated.

One scenario that is particularly harmful to constructive dialogue is when passive investors team up with an activist against a company. These passive funds are often publicity-shy and have sought to effect change behind closed doors by engaging in constructive discussions with boards. But passive funds have shown they are willing to make "requests for activists"— effectively, soliciting more vocal and aggressive investors to agitate on their behalf.

One example of this is pharmaceutical company Bristol-Myers Squibb's acquisition in 2019 of Celgene. One of Bristol-Myers's long-term passive investors, Vanguard, was understood to have a healthy relationship with the company's board and management, and observers assumed it supported the deal. At the same time, Wellington Management, which managed a health-care fund for Vanguard and had a stake of nearly 8 percent in Bristol-Myers, publicly opposed the transaction through a statement filed with the SEC. Wellington's statement surprised the financial markets; it was seen as a notable change of practice because Wellington criticized Bristol-Myers publicly instead of engaging with the board directly. Vanguard's public silence on its own position created ambiguity. Nevertheless, the $74 billion transaction closed in November 2019.

Boards and company management are further challenged because they are increasingly called upon to respond to two different constituencies within large institutional investors. These factions often have competing agendas, even when they represent the same institution. On the one hand, there are the conventional portfolio managers, who focus on traditional metrics of performance such as the company strategy, business model, and financial and operational performance. On the other hand, there are the environmental, social, and governance managers, who are guided by priorities of their own. Although it can be difficult, boards should strike a balance between the competing agendas of ESG advocates and traditional portfolio managers.

Some institutional investors are taking a unified stance and joining with their peers of comparable scale and stature to form coalitions to push for changes in corporate governance. One such coalition, Investor Stewardship Group (ISG), includes more than sixty organizations, with combined assets in excess of $30 trillion. The group's aim is to codify a framework of basic investment stewardship and corporate governance standards. ISG has put forward six principles that it believes are fundamental to good corporate governance at US-listed companies, including that institutional investors should attempt to resolve differences with companies in a constructive and pragmatic manner.

However, across the ESG landscape, there are estimated to be at least 250 organizations looking to engage with boards and companies. These organizations have varied agendas and no uniformity on their metrics or standards, which makes it difficult for boards to figure out which issues to prioritize.

Additionally, proxy advisors such as ISS and Glass Lewis, who vote on behalf of some shareholders and advocate their views to other investors, have become increasingly influential and have come to be seen by some as disruptive. In November 2019, the SEC submitted proposals to make it harder for shareholders to demand changes at companies. For example, the new rules would make it harder for proxy advisors to resubmit proposals designed to effect change at companies: as of late 2019, a proposal to restructure the board needed only to gain 3 percent investor support for it to be resubmitted the following year. The new rule would require 6 percent support to be resubmitted the following year, then 10 percent in the second year, and finally 30 percent in the third year. This change would make it harder for a loud minority to dominate the agenda of the board and senior leadership team—and therefore recognizes the importance of allowing competing voices to contribute to the direction of company strategy.

Another recent change is that specialist institutional investors such as hedge funds were previously able to make outsize returns by gathering higher-quality information on individual companies—essentially capitalizing on an asymmetry of information and gaining insights not widely available in the market. But as technology has become more sophisticated and information has become more easily available, the advantage previously enjoyed by those funds has eroded. For example, data on shipping volumes in a certain port could yield information about makers of certain goods and about oil and gas companies. In the past, this data would be collected locally by investors with the resources to hire individuals or local agencies to report on the shipping volume. Today, GPS technology means that this information is readily available to anyone.

Without the ability to profit from an asymmetry of information, investors have found a new approach called factor investing. This is a strategy that picks stocks by screening for certain factors. There are four specific, observable factors that fifty years' worth of studies have shown to be indicative of better returns: momentum, value, size, and quality. Momentum refers to stocks that have performed strongly in the past, and which offer attractive returns going forward. The value factor targets bargain stocks—those trading at low prices relative to their fundamental value. Size takes into consideration how company size, defined by market capitalization, drives stock returns; an investor's strategy can target large, midsize, or small companies. In terms of quality, factor investing ranks companies highly if they demonstrate low debt, stable earnings, consistent asset growth, and strong corporate governance.

Factor investing has become more common over the past decade. In 2018, it accounted for 16 percent of asset allocation by institutional investors, according to a global study by Invesco. Its growing role means that the factors most attractive to investors will be of increasing importance to corporate boards in coming years. The ascent of factor investing will require boards to think carefully about how their company fits into investors' portfolios.

Boards will have to consider the lens through which investors are assessing and classifying them as they make tactical and strategic decisions, and also when thinking about which investors to actively court.

In terms of momentum, boards should monitor their stock's trajectory over time and versus the company's competitors. For value, boards should emphasize their company's strengths when the stock is undervalued. For quality, boards should help manage a disciplined debt load, company ratings, and balance sheet, particularly when they consider acquiring new companies. For size, boards can sometimes be lulled into the view that bigger is better. However, the evidence from factor investing indicates that investors may reap higher returns from including smaller companies in their portfolios, rather than choosing big companies alone.

In one sense, these factors act as a check on board decisions, reducing the risk of pursuing high-paced growth fueled by debt for its own sake. However, the deeper concern for boards is whether investors are thinking about these factors in the short term only. If they are, boards could end up stalling on borrowing or not making investments designed to yield returns in the long term, instead prioritizing maintaining their quality metrics or earnings momentum in the short term. Ultimately, this is about trade-offs that the board must make and again emphasizes the importance of the board's judgment.

From the board's perspective, technology presents both opportunities and risks, which we'll consider later in this chapter. But certain technological innovations, such as AI, are also influencing and adding risk to the new investment landscape. More and more, the trades being made in the financial markets are being executed between machines, with few human decisions involved.

Using preprogrammed, algorithmic trading instructions, automated trading enables the purchase or sale of stock orders that are too large to fill all at once—transactions that are sometimes in the billions of dollars. This sort of trading has become extremely common. In 2006, a third of all EU and US stock trades were driven by automatic programs. At the London Stock Exchange, over 40 percent of all orders were entered by algorithmic traders that year. According to a 2019 report by Coherent Market Insights, computer-led or algorithmic trading now accounts for 60 to 73 percent of all US equity trading.

Algorithmic trading is widely used by large institutional investors—such as pension funds, mutual funds, investment banks, hedge funds, and insurance companies—that need to execute sizable orders in the financial markets. Through algorithmic trading, these institutions can minimize the cost, market impact, and risk inherent in the execution of particularly large trades. Computers have the advantage over humans of being able to rapidly trade based on large amounts of information. They can react faster to the temporary mispricing of stock and are able to compare stock prices from different markets simultaneously.

High-frequency trading strategies, which have garnered a lot of publicity in recent years, use this speed advantage to achieve a profit. In 2009, studies suggested HFT trades accounted for 60 percent of all US equity trading volume. That number fell to approximately 50 percent in 2014, in large part due to high infrastructure costs.

From a board's viewpoint, algorithmic trading matters because it can move the company's stock very quickly, without the board necessarily knowing who the counterparty is. The more information a board has about the shareholder buying or selling the company's stock, the more the board is able to address the concerns of the investors, assuming they are human. Where the board has little or no sense of who is buying or selling—particularly large stakes—it is left with no real opportunity to influence the decisions being made by the agents placing orders.

When a board makes a decision that triggers a sell order by an algorithm, for example, it has no ability to communicate or explain the nuance behind that decision. Whereas a human-to-human discussion could yield a wholly different decision, and might prevent the sale of the stock, an algorithmic decision is unavoidable—as are its consequences on stock value.

Imagine a company that has established a reputation as a top dividend payer—say, with a track record of not having reduced its dividend in more than twenty years. But now, conditions are such that it behooves the company to pursue long-term investment and growth plans by cutting dividends rather than taking on more debt. The algorithm yields a binary buy-sell decision and is unable to consider the logic behind the board's action. Thus, algorithmic trading feeds into the long-standing concern that the boards of these "dividend aristocrats" are, in effect, hamstrung. They are forced to make expedient and suboptimal decisions—such as paying a dividend instead of making a long-term strategic investment—for fear of provoking a harmful response from automated investors.

As algorithmic trading continues to grow and to become more sophisticated, the role of the board becomes more difficult. Globally, regulation is helping preserve some transparency in this trading space, but the opacity of algorithmic trading will no doubt remain a challenge to most boardrooms. These computer-led trades are truly outside the control—and line of sight—of the board, as high-frequency trades can occur with counterparties that board members have no way of engaging.

Another change to the investment landscape is the increasing popularity of exchange-traded funds (ETFs). These collections of securities are like mutual funds, except they are listed on the stock exchanges and trade throughout the day. In 2011, ETFs surpassed $1 trillion in assets, challenging the dominance of traditional mutual funds. By November 2019, the value of ETFs reportedly passed $6 trillion. ETFs have shifted the investment landscape by making it possible for investors to gain exposure to certain sectors without having to invest in individual companies.

Amid the broader boom in ETFs, investors flooded into commodity funds—notably in gold and oil—to gain exposure instead of buying shares in gold miners or oil producers. Around this time, I was serving on the board of a large gold company. My colleagues and I were understandably curious about the possible impact of capital diverted out of company shares and into commodities. The board understood that ETFs create greater competition for investor capital and require management to make an ever more compelling case for investors to buy the company's stock.

Fundamentally, boards—and not only boards of natural resource companies—are right to consider whether their corporations must fight for capital as investors seek out alternative asset classes. Already, large investors have been putting increasing levels of capital into private equity. In May 2019, estimates from data provider Preqin suggested that global private equity funds have around $2.5 trillion of capital ready to deploy to buy out companies, real estate, infrastructure, and debt. The value of leveraged buyouts reached $256 billion in the first half of 2019, the highest since 2006. If investors are migrating toward private companies, it suggests that competition for capital for public companies is getting tougher.

Boards should also take heed of the fact that, as the amount of capital in private equity and other asset classes is increasing, the overall number of public companies has declined. The number of publicly quoted US companies fell by 50 percent between 1998 and 2016. According to the Wilshire 5000 Total Market Index, the number of publicly listed US stocks peaked at a record of 7,562 in 1998. At the end of 2016, there were just over 3,600. This shrinking of the stock market should prompt boards of listed companies to think carefully about strategy, but it could also create opportunities. Companies staying public could perhaps gain scarcity value, and therefore access capital at more competitive terms and even cherry-pick investors. However, it is fair to say that the greatest advantages would accrue to the highest-quality companies and those that are best able to deliver their message. Ultimately, every company is accountable to its investors—and they will make the decision to buy or sell a company stock on their own terms.

In light of this, boards should expect to devote more time and attention to keeping the majority of their shareholders happy and dissuading them from moving their investment capital to private companies. Beyond simply keeping investors updated on strategic direction, boards have to be alert to issues and concerns important to shareholders, such as corporate culture, environmental protection, or matters of pay.

Boards must also consider how to prioritize their investors' differing goals. Should they listen to the passive and traditional active investors that hold vast amounts of company shares and often have a longer-term view? Or should boards prioritize the louder, more outspoken activists who are often looking for a more immediate share turnaround? Companies try to operate with the interests of all shareholders in mind but can be forced to placate the more vocal ones. This is a difficult balancing act.

3. New Technological Developments

Today's boards are living in a world of extremely rapid and deep technological change. The pace of this change is forcing boards to reconfigure their organizations in at least three ways: first, enhancing competitiveness through digitization and adopting new technologies; second, ensuring that the company remains operationally resilient in the face of new technological threats; and third, future-proofing the company so that it can remain agile and adapt to ongoing changes in the global technological landscape.

On the first point, boards are already having conversations about how best to exploit new technology to be more competitive, such as through growing revenue by selling to more customers, cutting costs, and remaining operationally efficient by increasing worker productivity. When boards discuss these issues, they must go beyond merely thinking about how to keep the company alive and instead focus on how the company can use technology to overtake its competition. Of course, past generations of boards have wrestled with similar questions about technological change. But today, the rewards for companies at the frontier of adopting technology are bigger than ever before.

Boards will have to wrestle with how much to spend on technology and where to deploy it—whether data privacy, cyber risk, or operational efficiencies. The most assertive boards are looking at their companies, regardless of sector, as technology-driven entities and as such will not shy away from the enormous changes that the future demands. In February 2020, Microsoft CEO Satya Nadella projected that technology spending as a percentage of GDP would double over the next decade and that the primary trend driving this would be the increasing rate of digitization—which would, in turn, drive productivity growth in all industries.

The topic of AI has also taken a central role in the discussion, as boards and companies look for ways to incorporate new technology into their operations and seek to understand how it will change the ways they compete with their peers and engage with their customers. AI—which has come to encompass automation, analytics, and machine learning—will likely transform all critical business areas, including information, business processes and workflow, the workforce, and risk management.

Automation, especially, can be difficult for boards to manage. For example, despite the financial upside of cutting personnel costs through automation, boards must consider the broader social ramifications of reducing a company's employment levels. Many boards and companies struggle to automate their operations because the new business model can threaten existing businesses that are generating enormous profits. Older companies' reluctance to innovate and embrace cost-cutting technologies is what gives newcomers an opportunity to disrupt whole industries.

Another innovation, blockchain, also promises to upend traditional business processes. Blockchain is the decentralized, secure record-keeping technology behind cryptocurrencies like Bitcoin. It can be used to speed up global transactions, such as a US-based company buying a barrel of oil from the Middle East. Where a transaction like this has traditionally taken many weeks or even months, with lots of paperwork and numerous middlemen—including accountants, lawyers, and banks—blockchain makes it so that it can be done in a matter of minutes.

The application of blockchain that has been the subject of the most heated debate in recent years is, of course, cryptocurrencies. These currencies promise to fill the gaps in the traditional financial arena. For example, many securities transactions still take a long time—up to two or three business days—to fully settle. Similarly, real estate transactions can take months to complete, due to a protracted verification process. And small businesses often face expensive transaction fees from their banks. Cryptocurrencies like Bitcoin can address these issues. They can also facilitate transactions in a war-torn country or where the government has ceased to function. In this situation, cryptocurrencies offer the same benefit of traditional money in that they are a unit of account, a medium of exchange, and a store of value.

Supporters of cryptocurrencies argue that the governments behind today's dominant currencies of global commerce—the US dollar, the euro, and the yen—are managing them in a reckless way, with high levels of debt that will cause inflation and ultimately undermine the currencies' value. Even so, it is hard to see how cryptocurrencies could replace or challenge the dollar, euro, or yen in a way that today's boardrooms should be worried about. Although cryptocurrencies appeal in certain circumstances, there are reasonable doubts about their universal application.

In addition to examining technological opportunities for revenue growth, cost cutting, and efficiencies, boards must ensure operational resilience and safety in the face of technological change. Boards should support management in guarding against cybercrimes and technological warfare, which can lead to debilitating data-privacy breaches that compromise customer loyalty and regulatory trust. In extreme cases, malware ransom attacks can hold a company hostage and permanently halt operations.

The 2013 data breach of US retailer Target ultimately led to the hijacking of 110 million customers' banking and personal data. Another example is Equifax, one of the largest credit agencies, which in 2017 suffered a data breach where 143 million customers' personal information was stolen. Boards need to be vigilant against cyber threats—not only because companies are subject to multimillion-dollar fines for these breaches, but also because rebuilding operations and repairing the reputational damage involve enormous costs.

Cyberattacks come in different shapes and forms and can be carried out by a range of parties with different motivations: from state actors to disgruntled employees to rogue hackers. In its 2016 cybersecurity intelligence index, the US technology company IBM revealed that 60 percent of all attacks were carried out by insiders, with three-quarters of the attacks involving malicious intent and one-quarter being inadvertent.

This era of technological change and hyper-connectivity is coming at the same time as a period of greater transparency.

Customers are increasingly demanding more information from corporations about their operations: how much employees are paid, what conditions workers face, and how much of an impact they have on the environment. Through technology, employees also have the power to offer public feedback on social media and review sites, whether companies want it or not. Prospective employees can then use this data to decide whether to join the company without managers ever knowing.

In some cases, companies and employees are also embracing technology that allows for more flexible work environments. GitLab, a technology company that hosts and manages coding projects for businesses, describes itself as all remote, with employees of all levels spread across sixty countries and no centralized headquarters. GitLab's founder and CEO, Sid Sijbrandij, is so confident that remote working is the way of the future that the company has published a publicly accessible guide to managing and operating a remote workforce.

The 2020 COVID-19 pandemic made it clear that working from home may be the most effective option for millions of workers across virtually all sectors. Government requests for people to shelter in place accelerated boardroom discussions around remote workforces, which centered on several important questions: how managers can best manage workers from afar, how to maintain workforce productivity, how best to mitigate cyber risk and ensure data privacy, and how to oversee health concerns including the mental well-being of all employees. Companies have turned to technologies that allow them to support more employees, oversee company controls and processes, and facilitate remote collaboration. Even so, implementing these changes, particularly at an accelerated pace, has been a challenge for companies and boards.

Although current technological challenges are more than enough to fill a board's agenda, company leaders must also look to the changes ahead and focus on future-proofing their organization. They should be particularly attentive to what this means for the organizational structure and the nature of management. In this regard, GitLab's organizational approach could serve as a model for other companies transitioning from rigid hierarchies to flatter and more informal organizational structures.

As discussed earlier in the chapter, some technology leaders have highlighted the risks of the splinternet—the emergence of separate US-led and China-led internets, each with different regulations and limited access between them. Technology insiders suggest that this internet balkanization could take root within this decade.

Such a split would be disruptive for multinational companies that rely on an effective and functioning global system, as it would harm supply chains and shared services such as procurement. Moreover, the splinternet could make it harder to manage a company's workforce across entrenched borders, to share best practices, and to embed the corporate culture.

Global technological tensions and competition necessarily throw up questions of surveillance, counterterrorism, and regulatory creep. Boards and management often find these to be among the hardest questions to answer, as they can pit moral and ethical views against the imperative to grow the business and achieve commercial success.

Take the matter of data use. At a conference in Orlando, Florida, in 2019, Tim Cook, the CEO of Apple, declared data privacy to be the most important issue of the century. Western society assumes that an individual's personal information is theirs and theirs alone and should be protected. This notion was enshrined in the European Union's 2016 General Data Protection Regulation (GDPR), which forced companies to reevaluate their data management. The law gives individual citizens control over their personal data, restricts its transfer, and provides data protection and privacy. GDPR has, however, been met with mixed reviews, accused by many of being burdensome and complicated to implement and of throttling investment and growth, particularly of small and medium-size businesses.

While Western countries take a more restrictive view of personal data use, this is not the case everywhere, presenting moral quandaries for multinational corporations. A hypothetical global company might be able to make a drug breakthrough with the help of extensive personal data gained from its operation in China, where data-privacy rules are relatively less stringent. However, because of the norm around personal-data protection in the West, despite having done nothing illegal the company risks being criticized by employees and customers in countries where data-privacy laws are tougher. This leaves the board with the question of whether to retain the moral high ground at the possible expense of a large commercial success.

Similarly, the success of the leading technology companies today—primarily social media platforms and search engines—has brought into question whether it is legitimate for businesses to collate, use, and manipulate individual users' data to the extent that they do. Outrage on this issue has been vocalized in books like *The Age of Surveillance Capitalism*, which went as far as to call for breaking up large tech companies and instituting much tighter regulation. From a board perspective, I believe that the question of data privacy is much more complex than these discussions make it out to be. In fact, I see two specific issues that complicate the immediate instinct to pass judgment on matters of data privacy.

First is the matter of network effects. The efficacy of search engines or GPS-based maps relies on pooling vast amounts of data to verify and enhance the results. Even if we can accept that these network effects are crucial to the instantaneous retrieval of high-quality information, it is not so simple to conclude that technology companies are justified in collating and utilizing an individual's data. Furthermore, it is an open question whether technology companies are within their rights to block users who do not grant access to their private information. For many companies, user data is fundamental to their core business, and the demand that they keep individual data protected and private might threaten the viability of these businesses upon which we have come to rely. This complicates how boards think about strategy and where the legal and ethical lines should be drawn for a company to use data commercially.

A second issue pertains to China. Any mention of China is a jumping-off point for a debate around ideology, but matters of data privacy doubtlessly influence the competitive landscape between US and Chinese companies. The question of data privacy brings into stark relief the difference between the Western notion that the individual is paramount and the Chinese view that the good of broader society trumps any individual's interests. The fact that Chinese companies have access to big data sets and more latitude on their use gives those companies a distinct advantage over competitors that have to abide by more stringent data-privacy laws.

This raises a crucial matter in the boardroom: Will US technology companies be able to compete and even lead in areas of technology such as AI, facial recognition, machine learning, and big data if their access to data is curtailed because of data-privacy laws? Furthermore, does China's implicit advantage mean that Western companies are placed at a disadvantage in the long term, or possibly precluded from competing at all? Boards of technology companies have to think about the implications of China's access and approach to data and what this means for businesses that rely on data sets drawn from fields like medicine, logistics, and avionics.

Boards and companies across industries will need to make tough calls and often irreversible decisions on data privacy that will determine the fate of a company for decades to come. As boards consider how to navigate data privacy, they should of course think about the explicit regulatory landscape (such as Europe's GDPR). However, they must also weigh the opinions of their consumers, some of whom will be protective of their personal data and some of whom will be willing to share it—not just for money but for the advance of science, as with drug trials.

A middle ground is achievable on data privacy. Corporations can find their way by agreeing to a data-sharing protocol with their customers or perhaps anonymizing the data. But even this will have its supporters and detractors. The ethical complexity of these matters will be a formidable issue for boards, and they must ensure that they are prepared.

To be truly competitive, boards cannot just remain defensive on technology. As companies seek to win market share, increase profits, and remain relevant, boards must embrace a more offensive stance to align with technological change. This change will require a transformation of organizational structures and company DNA. But perhaps most importantly, technological shifts will distinguish winners from losers and determine which companies will still be around twenty or thirty years from now. Ultimately, boards must oversee these technological transitions by ensuring that their companies absorb new technologies and implement the best and most modern practices to maximize efficiency and mitigate risks.

4. The Global War for Talent

According to the Organisation for Economic Co-operation and Development, for the first time in American history, this generation of Americans will be less educated than the preceding one. This trend happens to be occurring just as automation is accelerating and as global corporations' need for highly skilled workers is becoming more acute. The demand for STEM skills such as coding is rapidly shifting how companies operate and what sort of workforce they require to succeed.

These trends have led to a tougher and possibly more expensive hiring environment for corporations. As a consequence of a shrinking and tighter workforce, they could be forced to pay higher wages and thereby face the possibility of considerable cost inflation. A 2018 study by management consulting firm Korn Ferry argued that a sustained rise in salaries, driven by a shortage of highly skilled workers, could add $2.5 trillion to annual global payrolls by 2030, harming companies' profitability and threatening business models.

Company leaders regularly lament that it is increasingly difficult to identify and hire enough people with the requisite skills—especially in highly valued areas such as science, mathematics, and technology. This is becoming a cause for greater concern in boardrooms as companies seek competitive advantages in areas such as data analysis, coding, and programming.

In a 2013 report, the McKinsey Global Institute estimated that by 2020 there would be a global shortfall of eighty-five million high- and middle-skilled workers. McKinsey also reported that almost 40 percent of employers say a lack of skills is a reason for entry-level vacancies. At the time of this writing, these figures had not yet been updated.

Cognizant, a US-based company, has extensively researched the sorts of jobs, skills, and employees that will become increasingly important in the coming years. Crucially, Cognizant's research has shown that technology and AI will not so much replace humans as create new roles for human workers alongside machines. In the report *21 More Jobs of the Future: A Guide to Getting—and Staying—Employed Through 2029*, Cognizant suggested a range of new roles—from cyberattack agent to virtual identity defender and machine risk officer—that could become common in the workplace of the future. This is unfolding alongside a number of other employment trends that corporate boards should be attuned to, including the development of the information gig economy, the trend of working beyond traditional retirement age, and changes in workplace behavior and dress.

Securing top talent is becoming tougher in part because of greater competition for fewer high-quality candidates and rising barriers to immigration. But, perhaps more crucially, it is also becoming harder at precisely the moment when the knowledge economy is taking off. Investment in intangible assets—for example, R&D, strong brands, and intellectual property—has doubled as a share of trade in recent years, from 5.5 percent to 13.1 percent. A 2019 McKinsey report underscored this point, explaining that "value creation is shifting to upstream activities, such as R&D and design, and to downstream activities, such as distribution, marketing, and after-sales services." This trend indicates that the market leaders of the future will be those able to secure the best talent, rather than the cheapest.

Against this backdrop, global corporations are responding by increasing their investments in training both current and prospective employees. The intention is to create the skills they need, particularly in highly technical technology-based areas, and to compensate for the weaknesses from traditional education. Some companies are also lowering the minimum qualifications for jobs. For example, Apple, Google, and IBM have joined the ranks of other global corporations that no longer require professional employees (such as software engineers) to have college degrees.

In the longer term, as boards and executive teams contend with the dearth of global talent and barriers to immigration, they may have to explore changing their corporate structure to rely on local recruiting. Just as boards may be obliged to respond to de-globalization pressures by establishing a more devolved corporate structure, they could also use stronger local offices to recruit new employees so that hiring occurs on a more country-by-country basis.

5. Short-Termism

The final critical issue facing boards is short-termism. Myopia exacerbates some of the preceding critical issues, but it can also harm a board's decision-making on its own.

Politicians from Republican president Donald Trump to Democratic senator Elizabeth Warren have expressed concern that US public companies are overly focused on the short term and have suggested that the solution might involve reducing investor power.

In 2018, Senator Warren introduced the Accountable Capitalism Act, which would require all US-domiciled businesses with revenues exceeding $1 billion to grant at least 40 percent of board seats to employees. It would also require that board members take into account all stakeholders, not just shareholders, when making decisions. The goal of these proposals is to grant more power to employees and other stakeholders with a longer-term perspective, and to reduce the power of financial shareholders, who might prioritize shorter-term capital gains. President Trump, for his part, has advocated ending quarterly reporting in favor of half-year reporting to lengthen the investing horizon.

In business, too, the debate over short-termism has reached a fever pitch. Senior leaders including Jamie Dimon, Warren Buffett, and Larry Fink have all warned of the perils of short-term thinking. They and other CEOs have proposed ending the obligation to provide quarterly earnings guidance, which can lead management teams to manipulate earnings to avoid disappointing markets. Buffett has said, "When companies get where they're sort of living by so-called making the numbers, they do a lot of things that really are counter to the long-term interests of the business."

In a 2017 study published in the *Milken Institute Review*, the "Case Against Corporate Short Termism," the authors found that in the period between 2005 and 2015, the US economy might have grown by an additional $1 trillion and generated five million more jobs had companies adopted a longer-term perspective. A host of indicators reflect how deeply short-termism has become ingrained in the business psyche and the degree to which it influences board choices. The average tenure of CEOs has fallen dramatically in recent years—indicating that boards are dealing with succession more frequently—and company life spans have diminished as boards oversee more frequent opportunities for buying and selling their companies.

The tenure of Fortune 500 CEOs is becoming ever shorter—from an average of ten years in 1990 to 6.6 years in 2011 to around 4.4 years today—thereby creating significant volatility in management and corporate strategy. Meanwhile, the average time that a company exists has also contracted considerably, according to researcher Dick Foster at Yale University. The average life span of an S&P 500 company in 1935 was ninety years; in 2011, it was eighteen years, no doubt in part reflecting the churn of companies in the technology sector that go from start-up to acquired at what often seems like warp speed.

As a consequence, two things have happened. One, from 1998 to 2016, there was a 50 percent decline in the number of companies trading on public stock markets, which reflected that boards were deciding to consolidate their companies or take them into private ownership. This latter decision can be seen as pushback against the short-term focus of the market and reveals the desire of many boards to no longer be beholden to quarter-by-quarter earnings pressures.

Two, more and more, corporations have chosen to pay excess cash flows to shareholders in the form of dividends and share buybacks rather than reinvesting in the business. A share buyback generally occurs when boards decide that the share price is lower than it should be. Buying back a meaningful number of shares creates greater scarcity and will typically boost the price. Between 2007 and 2016, S&P 500 companies distributed $7 trillion in dividends and buybacks, the equivalent of 96 percent of retained earnings, according to a study by Harvard Business School.

There is a widely held view that the ultimate problem with short-termism is that it leads to reduced longer-term investment, which then harms a company's prospects for growth. However, short-term thinking has another, equally pernicious effect: it can mean the board fails to recognize a company's exposure to more deeply entrenched risks. This, like reduced investment, poses a threat to the existence of the company over the long term. Boards therefore must be cognizant that myopia itself is a risk they must manage. The salient questions are: What sort of risks does the board focus on? And which risks does the board miss if its thinking is too short-term?

Typically, boards focus their attention on risks that are urgent and visible. These include challenges related to geopolitics, reputation, expropriation of assets, and sustained market volatility. But the risks that are most likely to sink companies are longer-term problems that are not within the board's immediate purview, including technology obsolescence, weakening competitiveness, declining levels of competence, adherence to the wrong strategy, and the impact of regulation.

A classic example of this is widening company pension deficits. Companies are still struggling to manage pension obligations nearly twenty years after S&P first showed in a 2002 survey that more than three-quarters of large US corporate pension funds face deficits. Given that corporations have pension obligations and contractual commitments, there is relatively little they can do to unwind the agreements. Instead, today fewer companies offer retirement plans and those that do continue to manage their existing pension agreements as best they can, which proves particularly challenging in a world of historically low interest rates and compressed asset returns.

What this means is that boards can be ill-equipped to stress-test and risk-manage the most dangerous threats. In a world of short-termism, this focus on immediate risks leads to the board focusing on ensuring that its operations are resilient in the short term as opposed to addressing threats to the underlying business model that will manifest themselves in the long run. Long-term problems are hard to predict and their impact is hard to quantify, but there is a case to be made that risk-management tools ought to better incorporate these considerations. That is, the models that boards use should better capture the risks associated with low-probability, high-impact events, which are increasingly affecting companies.

The rise of populism and the ongoing threat of de-globalization demand that boards embed these risks into their discussions in a more systematic way. In the finance sector, for example, regulators in the United States and Europe have enforced annual stress tests to make sure that the banking system can withstand extreme market conditions, such as the disruption of trade due to protectionist measures. These stress tests allow boards to mitigate the danger of these risks. Insurance companies are also having to overhaul their models in order to charge the correct premiums for new levels of risk.

In short, companies have to think about both surviving and winning in all environments. Boards are charged with ensuring that management finds the right balance between short-term financial performance and long-term value creation. Boards should consider if stress tests—whether administered at the company level or assessed industry-wide—can enhance their risk management by incorporating more long-term thinking. Rising societal demands from employees, governments, and consumers are also likely to continue placing a natural check on short-term profit seeking.

The risk of short-termism not only threatens boardrooms— it plagues institutional investors as well. These are the investors who manage and oversee multitrillion-dollar hedge funds, pensions, mutual funds, and insurance assets. Short-termism, for some institutional investors, means holding stocks for less time. In 1970, the average length of time a New York Stock Exchange stock was held in a portfolio was seven years; by 2011, it was just seven months. High-frequency trading, which enables traders to take advantage of even the smallest stock moves using computer algorithms, means that portfolio managers today can hold stocks for as little as eleven seconds. Such trading volatility can make it challenging for companies to make reliable assumptions about how and when to finance their business activities from the capital markets.

Investor myopia can back board members into a corner where they must decide whether to capitulate to short-term shareholder demands or get out of the stock market altogether and become private. Short-termism on the part of institutional investors can place undue pressure on boards and corporate management teams to deliver profits sooner rather than later, forcing companies to meet the expectations of shareholders every quarter. Companies that stay in the stock market, especially mature companies, consequently face expectations to pay out dividends and buy back shares.

This pressure has likely contributed to companies paying out more in dividends than they retained in earnings in five of the six quarters leading up to June 2016. At its peak, the dividend-to-retained-earnings ratio reached 130 percent in 2016, up from around 60 percent in 2009, according to global communications firm WPP.

Some might argue that the trend of greater dividend payments has little to do with investor behavior and is more of a signal of increasing short-termism on the part of companies themselves. But no matter the cause, the result is that companies are choosing to pay profits back to shareholders—and keep them happy today—at the expense of investment for future growth.

Facing this pressure, many companies are choosing to move to private ownership and delist from the stock markets. This is a trend that is supported by a growing investor preference for private investments in equity and lending over public stocks and bonds.

Furthermore, the dominance of short-term thinking can hurt corporate investment and the broader economic growth prospects of a country. According to research from Stanford University, the pressure corporations are experiencing "to meet quarterly earnings targets may be reducing research and development spending and cutting U.S. growth by 0.1 percentage points a year." In contrast, private companies that are not subject to aggressive quarterly reporting cycles invest at nearly 2.5 times the rate of public companies in the same industry.

Boards of many listed companies have already done a considerable amount to address the issue of myopia by changing compensation structures to incorporate deferred remuneration and emphasize longer-term benchmarking. Nevertheless, boards need to remain open-minded about other aspects of day-to-day operations that could also benefit from this sort of approach.

Jack Welch, the late former chairman and CEO of GE, once noted that "if the rate of change on the outside exceeds the rate of change on the inside, the end is near." Accordingly, at the highest level corporate boards ought to concern themselves with an existential question: Is their company likely to disrupt, be disrupted, or stay the same? Put another, harsher way: Where will the company be in 2050? Innovating, acquired, or bankrupt?

Both the costs and the risks of global operations are shifting. Several challenges stand out: the impact of digitization, the war for talent, the changing expectations of society, the shifting behavior of investors, and the effects of de-globalization. Given the extent of global change, successful companies will have to revamp their business strategy more than once in the next thirty years.

Some might view these as esoteric issues, but the threats are very real. Given their pressing nature, the five critical issues just discussed should be on every board's docket. While it is management's responsibility to oversee an organization's day-to-day operations, the board should also heed the deep transformations that are underway, which will drastically alter how business is conducted. Is the company future-proof? Has the board adequately thought through long-term risks? Culture and corporate governance changes should make boards better equipped to tackle these issues. But, even if we accept the inevitability of these changes, the transition will undoubtedly hurt.

CHAPTER 5

Innovate or Die

The Existential Crisis of the Twenty-First-Century Board

THE ABILITY OF COMPANIES TO QUICKLY INNOVATE AND ADAPT TO A CHANG-ing world is now a matter of economic life or death. Yet nimbleness is not enough on its own—societal expectations about how, where, and with whom corporations do business are shifting as well, leading to demands for additional changes that must be deep, radical, and lasting. It is simply impossible for the modern corporation to undertake transformations of this speed and scale without also taking on the challenge of reforming the board of directors itself.

Corporate boards, like corporations, will face an existential crisis if they do not change with the times. Just as corporations must justify their continued relevance through real-world success, boards must justify their stewardship of corporations. When faced with twenty-first-century challenges, boards must make twenty-first-century reforms. The ways that boards respond to today's challenges will determine which companies survive.

Boards are tasked with overseeing three domains of corporate decision-making: strategy, leadership, and culture. Any reforms must enhance the ability of boards to deal with these three areas and to ensure that their companies remain competitive over the long term. Of course, the quality of a board's decision-making ultimately hinges on who is in the boardroom and the processes by which decisions are made. Thus, any improvement of the function of boards must also take on the question of how to improve recruitment efforts, upgrade board processes, and achieve the ideal board structure.

There is palpable impatience for corporations and their boards to reform, and to shed what many see as an old hierarchical framework that is slow to adapt and unwilling to collaborate with emerging political and economic systems and cultural and societal norms. Even when boards have the best motives and intentions, change can be difficult. Nevertheless, the sections that follow offer concrete proposals for how to upgrade corporate boards, thereby ensuring that they remain relevant and continue to support the competitiveness of the corporations they serve. If pursued with urgency and vigor, these proposals could help boards reimagine themselves to become more assertive and effective, and thereby improve the trajectory of their corporations.

Renewing the Approach to Strategy

In their position overseeing corporate strategy, boards can act boldly to oppose short-termism by continually setting their sights on long-term strategy. As we saw in Chapter 1, boards generally address underlying long-term trends and less-visible structural risks at an annual strategy meeting. But in the present environment, an annual review is not enough. The mandate of the board should be reformed to explicitly address long-term risks with greater frequency. In practice, this means updating the board agenda to review these risks during regular discussions and quarterly meetings. Many corporations have stand-alone risk committees that address these issues. But it is important that deep structural shifts receive visibility and discussion time at the full board level as well. Such an explicit mandate will materially alter the board's thinking about longer-term trends and ultimately improve its decision-making around investment, strategy, and operations.

Another potential board reform centers on data. Chapter 2 discussed the problem of asymmetry of information, and how even in the best of times boards are required to make decisions with limited information from a single source—that is, management. Critics of corporate boards argue that one of their greatest problems is their relationship to management—that is, management has full control over what information the board sees and what it hears about how the company is performing and the challenges it faces. The board's dependence on management creates an asymmetry that renders boards far less effective than they could be. The fact that management curates information for the board, and that the board lacks the ability to collect its own data, creates a blind spot that means any guidance the board gives will be colored by management's perspective. To counter this data deficiency, boards could more consistently seek additional third-party information, particularly regarding structural and long-term trends. Doing so will enhance board members' perspectives and serve to further assert board independence.

A third, arguably more far-reaching reform would require boards to take a more prominent role in setting the corporate strategy. In the conventional paradigm, management presents a strategy proposal, which the board then independently reviews, challenges, and eventually approves. While there may be pushback from the board on certain elements of management's strategic approach, the board is unlikely to upend the whole strategy itself. In this regard, the board acts merely to ensure that management delivers on certain preapproved tasks, rather than offering a full counterproposal.

Reimagining this process could mean that board members work on the company strategy parallel to management, during separate and concurrent working sessions. The two groups would then meet to compare the proposals and work through the benefits and disadvantages of each.

Ideally, through such a process the board and management would land in the same place on company strategy. But even if they did not, this approach would offer a more robust discussion about strategy. It would also require individual board members to be much more engaged and assertive without crossing into the operational obligations, but it would have the advantage of eliminating any accusation that the board is merely rubber-stamping management's agenda and could offer a more informed way for the board to support the CEO.

Upgrading Succession Planning

The board's second responsibility, for overseeing succession and board structure, is also ripe for reform. When hiring a new CEO, the board must always be particularly aware of a candidate's moral compass. As we saw in Chapter 2, many boards already consider the ethics of a prospective CEO during the recruiting process. But, in light of the changing landscape, a deeper form of assessment is in order. A more assertive board could alter its recruitment process so as to place a prospective CEO's ethics and values at the very heart of its evaluation, equal in importance to financial performance. Specifically, boards should incorporate metrics to gauge a potential CEO's values. Questions could probe topics such as a candidate's modesty and ego, their biggest mistake and lessons learned, how they spend their time and pursue continuous improvement, and how they innovate and improve in cultural terms.

One question I find interesting is asking a candidate about the worst thing they have done to another human being, which can shed some light on their perspective on right and wrong. Additionally, to avoid a future scandal, boards could adopt the vetting approach used by political parties in the UK, which ask if there is anything a potential candidate would like to tell them now that could come to light in the future and cause embarrassment.

At a time when discussions about cultural sensitivities are becoming more frequent within companies and boards, these questions will help the board identify the candidates best able to lead corporations in a rapidly changing cultural climate. Overall, the goal of the board is to vet and groom company leadership in such a way that builds a deep bench of talented candidates who know the inner workings and culture of the company and who can be promoted to higher levels with the least amount of friction.

Beyond CEO selection, a truly forward-looking board would reform recruitment for the board itself. Ultimately, boards need to refresh their ranks and recruit the best people. This means instituting active review processes rather than leaning on age rules. The most effective boards will be those that populate their ranks with specialists and people who are knowledgeable about the specific shifts and trends most likely to affect corporations in the years ahead. This could include members with geopolitical and technological expertise, as well as those with more diverse perspectives and backgrounds.

Board members need sufficient skills and direct experience so they can support and evaluate the performance of the CEO and wider management team with a high level of authority and credibility. Many boardrooms already have members with relevant skills in areas such as finance, accounting, law, and government relations. But to adapt to changing times, they need to go a step further and more accurately match the skills of board members to the specific areas in which the company is operating. For example, the board of a company that designs software should have a member who has experience not just in technology but specifically in technology design.

As we saw in Chapter 4, rising protectionism and de-globalization bring the risk that corporations will have to adapt their organizational structures to reflect a more siloed world, potentially creating separate boards to oversee individual regions—such as Asia or Europe—that would be connected to the global parent company through a federated structure. If this comes to pass, companies must consider whether the board structure, too, should change so that separate, local boards oversee each region. A decentralized structure may limit the board's ability to govern a global business, but, in such a de-globalized world, the potential gains of a unified board would also be inherently limited.

In a world where cross-border movement is impeded, regional boards could allocate resources and mitigate risks more effectively because they would have greater proximity to the local marketplace and operations. Many companies already have some semblance of this regional structure, but the localization is not mirrored in their governance system or boardroom.

Confronting Cultural Change

A third set of reforms would ensure that the board is better equipped to address the shifting cultural landscape. Boards are increasingly expected to make judgment calls on matters of morality, fairness, and ethics involving worker advocacy, pay equity, gender and race parity, data privacy, and the inevitable advances in AI and bioengineering. We saw the delicate tightrope boards presently navigate in Chapter 3, but there is more that could be done to take these challenges on.

Reformist boards could set up an ethics committee, or else clearly show what mechanisms they are using to tackle the current multitude of ethical dilemmas. In so doing, boards will enhance their oversight role at a time when ethical questions are coming faster to the fore. In particular, rapid advances in technology raise serious questions about how companies should use, store, and transfer data. Similarly, advances in medical sciences create questions around the use of human embryos and genetic engineering, at a time when society has yet to decide what is and is not acceptable. The addition of ethics committees need not be restricted to technology, pharmaceutical, and biotech companies. All companies, regardless of industry, face ethical questions, and these committees would take on these difficult conundrums before it is too late to change course.

There is an adage among some businesspeople: "You see one board, you see one board." It means, essentially, that corporations—and by extension, their boards—are inherently unique. Given the varying nature of the industries in which companies operate, ethics committees could have vastly different tasks. The ethics committee of a pharmaceutical company might be focused on data-privacy issues, whereas the ethics committee of a mining conglomerate might be occupied with whether to invest in countries led by governments that are seen as authoritarian or that have morally reprehensible human-rights records. A consumer goods company, such as a clothing chain, will be concerned with maintaining an ethical supply chain, in particular ensuring that no child labor or worker abuse takes place.

As we look to the future, 55 percent of US human resource managers believe artificial intelligence will be a regular part of their work by 2022, according to a survey by the talent-software firm CareerBuilder. As many companies start to deploy AI systems to recruit talent and run their operations, ethics committees could be called upon to ensure that human biases, particularly those on race and gender, do not seep into the organization. Reports have already emerged of such human biases making their way into AI systems. For example, in 2018, Amazon stopped using recruitment software to sift through résumés, fearing that it favored men over women.

Additionally, boards should support management in guaranteeing operational resilience against cyberattacks, staying current on technology, and ensuring supply chains are not disrupted, even when trade wars threaten them. Board ethics committees must ensure that the organization progresses and evolves in a manner acceptable to today's society. Technological change means that many industries—including food production, agriculture, and medicinal cannabis—will face debates that go beyond strictly technical and legal boundaries and into the realm of questions that push moral and ethical limits. Furthermore, ethics committees should consider whether companies' social and environmental goals might become mandatory.

Ultimately, assertive boards must recalibrate their mandate to ensure that they are acting as a change agent on ethical matters. After all, a transfer of decision-making from government to industry is underway on many ethical issues. This means that boards and corporations will have to lead in challenging areas such as environmental management, data privacy, and social justice, whether they like it or not and whether they are ready or not.

There is also an opportunity at the board level for better and more direct engagement with investors. As described in Chapter 4, boards face a fast-changing investor landscape and increasing demands from shareholders for clarity about the board's approach to governance, particularly on how it oversees culture. By directly engaging with investors, boards have a chance to get a sense of their concerns and priorities, and investors can gain a better understanding of how and why boards make their decisions.

To address these situations, boards could appoint a senior or long-tenured director to lead investor engagement, such as one-on-one meetings or board-only road shows. Of course, board members would not easily be able to meet with each and every investor, so such an approach could be seen to favor large institutions over individual retail investors. But even with this limitation, boards would get to know the company shareholder base better and would have a valuable chance to reaffirm that the company's and investors' interests overlap.

Primed for Change

Board members run the risk of being overly wed to the status quo, refusing to surrender their position at the pinnacle of the company's hierarchical structure that places decision rights at the top of the organization and not fully recognizing the threats posed by new changes on the horizon. But ignorance is no protection from the new world coming. All these proposals are worthy of consideration and reflection, but how and whether they are applied to a specific boardroom depends on the individual corporation. For example, companies that collate and handle private data—such as software companies, banks, and utilities—should more urgently pursue the possibility of establishing an ethics committee than, say, an infrastructure company that is more business-to-business focused. In a similar vein, corporations that derive a large share of their revenue from international markets should prioritize recruiting board members with global experience, which may not be that important to a largely domestic company. But no board can believe that it will survive the coming years without adopting some reforms.

In keeping with the view that boards—and by extension the companies they oversee—must innovate or die, the way boards make decisions and ultimately deliver on their mandate has to fundamentally change. A starting point for this might be evaluating the possibilities detailed above.

In order to innovate, boards must be more open to new and different ways of calibrating and assessing their organization's performance. For example, boards have generally calculated employee compensation by relying on metrics that capture the revenues, costs, and profits of existing businesses. An alternative remuneration approach that gives greater weight to innovation would instead reward employees based on how they drive the company toward new technologies, ideas, and business opportunities. Even if this means deprioritizing or cannibalizing existing businesses that are generating profits, taking bets on innovation and new technological trends is vital to ensuring that businesses remain focused on the future.

At least one major company has already taken up this tactic. Changing its approach to management compensation was a key element of Disney's strategic move toward streaming over the last several years—a shift that has been credited with adding multiple billions of dollars to the company's market capitalization. At the heart of this change was an overhaul in pay incentives for senior management, replacing the traditional approach with rewards based on employees' ability to build businesses for the future.

It is a herculean task to persuade staff and investors, who are generally focused on the short term, to back business models that are not yet clearly known and do not yet generate profits. It becomes less onerous, however, if management is highly incentivized and united in its determination to prioritize long-term company growth over short-term profits.

Without reform today, there's an ever-greater risk that boards will face questions about whether they should exist at all. How can boards assert their value over alternative governance structures and ultimately justify their existence?

Some argue that, even without a board, the market—in the form of customers and investors—would hold corporations accountable for operational and financial performance and guide company strategy. Furthermore, this theory holds, a combination of regulators, lawyers, and accountants sets guardrails and keeps the company operating strictly within the law. Some combination of excellent recruitment firms and consultants would be more than able to pick a CEO and evaluate their performance without the formalities of a board.

This view of corporate boards as obsolete and other negative perceptions should not be dismissed out of hand. They reflect the fact that laypeople and ordinary shareholders have seen immense wrongdoing—including value destruction and scandals—without any obvious repercussions for senior management or the board itself. If anything, some of the most common complaints are that management is regularly paid handsomely for poor performance and rarely fired for objectively egregious behavior. But more seasoned professionals and management executives are critical of boards too. Their views are often rooted in direct experience of working with weak boards or weak board members, who are seen by management to offer limited and unhelpful input in board discussions.

But these sentiments discount the value that a truly effective board can bring. Board critics should remember that good governance requires sound judgment and not rote compliance. Therefore, boards will become ever more important in a world of interlocking and clashing cultural values. There is no doubt that the best management teams comprise smart people who work tirelessly on numerous company issues. But boards have the advantage of a wider perspective, along with the nuanced understanding and judgment that come from it. When boards work well, they are a thing of beauty. When they don't, the results can be ugly.

Former president Barack Obama has observed that "by the time something reaches my desk, that means it's really hard. Because if it were easy, somebody else would have made the decision and somebody else would have solved it." His words capture the value of having an ultimate arbiter, such as a board, who takes responsibility for making the hardest decisions.

What all of this points to is that boards and their directors must continue to justify their existence and their authority. In order to maintain high standards, boards must be assertive in how they reform themselves in response to the transformation of the environment around them.

For now, the law of the land is very clear: the true north for a company remains shareholder value. But things are changing, and in the years ahead there must be more focus on social and environmental concerns. The best boards are not waiting for new laws; they are already reviewing their practices and experimenting with fresh ideas. Today's boards must be even more focused on how to prepare for the future.

Over the course of a board member's career, a board will likely be charged with making just one or two key decisions that have the potential to fundamentally change the trajectory of the company and seal its fate. Board members of today should remember that past boards built the foundation from which today's companies can grow and compete. They must recognize, too, that they will eventually pass the baton to the board of the future.

Today's board members are custodians whose job it is to strengthen the company's foundation, upon which board members of the future will continue to grow and run the business. Ultimately, this means corporate board members must embrace humility rather than hubris, remaining vigilant and malleable, as they lead in an increasingly chaotic world.

Acknowledgments

I am immensely grateful for the opportunity to have a seat at the board table of numerous large, global, and complex organizations.

I have been fortunate to work with board colleagues who time and time again have exhibited amazing judgment when the companies we serve have faced complex, tangled, and hugely consequential challenges. I have learned an enormous amount about how to think and be less judgmental, but at the same time how to sharpen my efforts to be thoughtful and form good judgment.

Ten years on, Andrew Wylie and the team at the Wylie Agency—James Pullen and Hannah Townsend—continue to be supportive, dependable, and so much appreciated. They are truth-sayers, which is priceless.

Lara Heimert is, as ever, superb—a true stalwart. It is an immense pleasure to work with her. I always learn so much.

Publishing a book truly takes a village.

Brian Distelberg, Conor Guy, Kaitlin Carruthers-Busser, Liz Dana, Edward Tivnan, and Tim Whiting all helped with the wizardry of taking this concept from idea, to proposal, through various draft stages, to publication, to bookshelf. I remain indebted to them all for support, candor, and encouragement.

Sanjana Balakrishnan was an immense help on research—thank you so very much.

Brandon Proia has been a constant and steady hand throughout this project—it is a true pleasure to work with him, and his contributions to enhancing the quality of this book are innumerable.

Jeremy Adams has again been an amazing, thoughtful partner, a confidant, and a welcome skeptic; he prodded and pushed me to think long and hard about the intersection of economics, finance, public policy, and the central role of global corporations. Without ascribing errors—which are mine alone—Jeremy deserves enormous credit for this book.

Team Versaca, you will never truly know how grateful I am for all of you: Charlton Antenbring, Deanne Buschbacher, Jeff Dunham, Jaymie Farr, David Jansen, Grace Martinez, Billy McGee, Keely Mulkerrins, Natalie Muscato, Trinity Nelson, Cristina Nunes, Louis Nunes, and David Taylor.

Kristi Brusa supports me every single day and has done so for over eight years—through the good, the bad, and the ugly. How she does this with a smile and so efficiently remains a mystery. Thank you, thank you!

Thank you to my family, old and new—my parents and siblings—who, through thick and thin, remain unwavering and steadfast in their love. To Jared and Barnaby goes all my love and eternal gratitude.

Bibliography

Aaronson, Susan A. "Corporations as Good Global Citizens." *YaleGlobal Online*, April 8, 2003. https://yaleglobal.yale.edu/content/corporations-good-global-citizens.

Acas and Government Equalities Office. *Managing Gender Pay Reporting*. London: Acas, 2019. https://archive.acas.org.uk/media/4764/Managing-gender-pay-reporting/pdf/Managing_gender_pay_reporting_07.02.19.pdf.

Accenture. "Bank Boardrooms Lack Technology Experience, Accenture Global Report Finds." News release, October 28, 2015. https://newsroom.accenture.com/news/bank-boardrooms-lack-technology-experience-accenture-global-research-finds.htm.

The Activist Investing Half-Year Review 2019. New York: Activist Insight, 2019.

AFL-CIO. "Executive Paywatch." https://aflcio.org/paywatch.

Allen, James, Frederick F. Reichheld, and Barney Hamilton. "The Three 'Ds' of Customer Experience." *Working Knowledge*, November 7, 2005. https://hbswk.hbs.edu/archive/the-three-ds-of-customer-experience.

Alphabet. "Google Code of Conduct." Alphabet Investor Relations. Last modified July 31, 2018. https://abc.xyz/investor/other/google-code-of-conduct/.

Amanatullah, E. T., and M. W. Morris. "Negotiating Gender Roles: Gender Differences in Assertive Negotiating Are Mediated by Women's Fear of Backlash and Attenuated When Negotiating on Behalf of Others." *Journal of Personality and Social Psychology* 98, no. 2 (2018): 256–257. http://dx.doi.org/10.1037/a0017094.

Amazon Web Services. "Teach Tomorrow's Cloud Workforce Today." AWS Educate. https://aws.amazon.com/education/awseducate/.

Americans for Carbon Dividends. "The Solution." www.afcd.org/the-solution/.

Anadu, Kenechukwu E., Mathias Kruttli, Patrick McCabe, Emilio Osambela, and Chae Hee Shin. "The Shift from Active to Passive Investing: Potential Risks to Financial Stability?" Supervisory Research and Analysis Working Paper, Federal Reserve Bank of Boston, 2018. www.bostonfed.org/publications/risk-and-policy-analysis/2018/the-shift-from-active-to-passive-investing.aspx.

Analysis: Diversity and Inclusion in the Media Industry. New York: ISS, 2019. www.issgovernance.com/library/analysis-diversity-and-inclusion-in-the-media-industry/.

Andilotti, Eillie. "The End of Capitalism Is Already Starting—If You Know Where to Look." *Fast Company*, September 18, 2017. www.fastcompany.com/40467032/the-end-of-capitalism-is-already-starting-if-you-know-where-to-look.

Andrews, Edmund L., and Jackie Calmes. "Fed Cuts Key Rate to a Record Low." *New York Times*, December 16, 2008. www.nytimes.com/2008/12/17/business/economy/17fed.html.

Ang, Yuen. "Autocracy with Chinese Characteristics." *Foreign Affairs*, May–June 2018. www.foreignaffairs.com/articles/asia/2018-04-16/autocracy-chinese-characteristics.

Anthony, Scott D., S. Patrick Viguerie, Evan I. Schwartz, and John Van Landeghem. *2018 Corporate Longevity Forecast: Creative Destruction Is Accelerating.* Lexington, MA: Innosight, 2018. www.innosight.com/wp-content/uploads/2017/11/Innosight-Corporate-Longevity-2018.pdf.

Anthony, Scott D., S. Patrick Viguerie, and Andrew Waldeck. *Corporate Longevity: Turbulence Ahead for Large Organizations.* Lexington, MA: Innosight, 2016. www.innosight.com/wp-content/uploads/2016/08/Corporate-Longevity-2016-Final.pdf.

Armitage, Jim. "Pfizer Drops AstraZeneca Takeover Bid: American Drugs Giant Admits Defeat and Scraps Offer for British Pharmaceutical Company." *Independent*, May 26, 2014. www.independent.co.uk/news/business/news/pfizer-admits-defeat-and-drops-astrazeneca-bid-9435767.html.

Arthur, Charles. "Nokia and Microsoft Join Forces in Bid to Win Smartphone War." *The Guardian*, February 11, 2011. www.theguardian.com/business/2011/feb/11/nokia-microsoft-deal-risks.

Artz, Benjamin, Amanda H. Goodall, and Andrew J. Oswald. "Do Women Ask?" Warwick Economics Research Paper Series 1176, University of Warwick, Coventry, UK, September 2016. http://wrap.warwick.ac.uk/81362/1/WRAP_twerp_1127_oswald.pdf.

———. "Research: Women Ask for Raises as Often as Men, but Are Less Likely to Get Them." *Harvard Business Review*, June 25, 2018. https://hbr.org/2018/06/research-women-ask-for-raises-as-often-as-men-but-are-less-likely-to-get-them.

Ash, Timothy Garton. "The EU's Core Values Are Under Attack as Never Before. It Must Defend Them." *The Guardian*, May 7, 2018. www.theguardian .com/commentisfree/2018/may/07/eu-core-values-viktor-orban-hungary -fidesz-party-expel-parliament-grouping.

Asl, Farshid M., and Erkko Etula. "Advancing Strategic Asset Allocation in Multi-Factor World." *Journal of Portfolio Management* 39, no. 1 (2012).

Babcock, Linda, and Sara Laschever. *Women Don't Ask: Negotiation and the Gender Divide*. Princeton, NJ: Princeton University Press, 2003.

Bank of England. "Climate Change: Why It Matters to the Bank of England." www.bankofengland.co.uk/KnowledgeBank/climate-change-why-it -matters-to-the-bank-of-england.

Barbosa, Talita A. "NYSE Decimalization: The Impact on Holding Periods." Master's thesis, Nova School of Business and Economics, 2017. https:// run.unl.pt/bitstream/10362/26129/1/Barbosa_2017.pdf.

Bariso, Justin. "Microsoft CEO Satya Nadella Credits a Book by a Stanford Psychologist for Taking the Company from Stodgy to Cool." *Business Insider*, January 18, 2019. www.businessinsider.com/satya-nadella -microsoft-mindset-book-2019-1.

Barrett, Annalisa, and Jon Lukomnik. "Age Diversity Within Boards of Directors of the S&P 500 Companies." *Harvard Law School Forum on Corporate Governance*, April 6, 2017. https://corpgov.law.harvard.edu/2017/04/06 /age-diversity-within-boards-of-directors-of-the-sp-500-companies/.

Barrionuevo, Alexei. "Enron Chiefs Guilty of Fraud and Conspiracy." *New York Times*, May 25, 2006. www.nytimes.com/2006/05/25/business/25cnd -enron.html.

Barton, Dominic. Presentation at Pi Capital, October 2013.

Barton, Dominic, Diana Farrell, and Mona Mourshed. "Education to Employment: Designing a System That Works." McKinsey & Company, January 1, 2013. www.mckinsey.com/industries/social-sector/our-insights /education-to-employment-designing-a-system-that-works.

Bass, Alexandra Suich. "Surrogacy Is Surging in the Tech Community." *The Economist*, April 30, 2019. www.economist.com/1843/2019/04/30/surrogacy -is-surging-in-the-tech-community.

Batish, Amit. "Berkshire Hathaway Adds Two New Directors as Buffett Eyes Successors." Equilar, January15, 2018. www.equilar.com/blogs/349-berkshire -hathaway-add-two-new-directors-as-buffett-eyes-successors.html.

BBC. "France Telecom Suicides: Former Bosses Go on Trial." May 6, 2019. www.bbc.co.uk/news/business-48175938.

BBC. "Google 'Retaliating Against Harassment Protest Organisers.'" April 23, 2019. www.bbc.co.uk/news/technology-48024849.

BBC. "Italy Budget: Rome Rejects European Commission Demands." November 14, 2018. www.bbc.co.uk/news/world-europe-46203605.

BBC. "A Quick Guide to the US-China Trade War." January 16, 2020. www.bbc
.co.uk/news/business-45899310.

BBC. "Timeline: How the BBC Gender Pay Story Has Unfolded." June 29,
2018. www.bbc.co.uk/news/entertainment-arts-42833551.

BBC. "Uber Investigated over Gender Discrimination." July 16, 2018. www.bbc
.co.uk/news/business-44852852.

Bebchuk, Lucian, John Coates IV, and Guhan Subramanian. "The Powerful
Antitakeover Force of Staggered Boards: Theory, Evidence, and Policy."
Discussion Paper No. 353, Harvard Law School, Cambridge, MA, March
2003. www.law.harvard.edu/programs/olin_center/papers/pdf/353.pdf.

Begbies Traynor. "Understanding a Company Director's Fiduciary Duties and
Consequences of Failing These Duties." Last modified February 25, 2020.
www.begbies-traynorgroup.com/articles/director-advice/understanding-a
-company-directors-fiduciary-duties-and-consequences-of-failing-these
-duties.

Bellstrom, Kristen. "WeWork Has an All-Male Board—and It's Not Alone:
The Broadsheet." *Fortune*, August 15, 2019. https://fortune.com/2019/08
/15/wework-%20ipo-board-of-directors-male/.

———. "Why One Diverse Candidate Isn't Enough: Broadsheet for June
24." *Fortune*, June 24, 2019. https://fortune.com/2019/06/24/why-one
-diverse-candidate-isnt-enough-broadsheet-for-june-24/.

Bellstrom, Kirsten, and Emma Hinchliffe. "Kim Kardashian Lawyer, Sudan
Protest, Ovia Health: Broadsheet April 11." *Fortune*, April 11, 2019.
https://fortune.com/2019/04/11/kim-kardashian-lawyer-sudan-protest-ovia
-health-broadsheet-april-11/.

Berman, Dennis K. "The Stock Market Has Turned into a 24-Hour Speakers' Corner." *Financial Times*, July 1, 2019. www.ft.com/content/dd822
d02-9bd5-11e9-9c06-a4640c9feebb.

Bezos, Jeff. Amazon letter to shareholders, 1998. http://media.corporate-ir.net
/media_files/irol/97/97664/reports/Shareholderletter97.pdf.

Black, Sandra E., Diane Whitmore Schanzenbach, and Audrey Breitwieser. *The
Recent Decline in Women's Labor Force Participation*. Washington, DC:
Brookings Institution, 2017. www.brookings.edu/wp-content/uploads/2017
/10/es_10192017_decline_womens_labor_force_participation_black
schanzenbach.pdf.

BlackBerry Limited. "Annual Report Pursuant to Section 13(a) or 15(d) of the
Securities Exchange Act of 1934," prepared for US Securities and Exchange
Commission, February 28, 2018. www.annualreports.com/HostedData
/AnnualReportArchive/B/TSX_BB_2018.pdf.

BlackRock. "Our Responsibility." www.blackrock.com/corporate/about-us
/investment-stewardship#our-responsibility.

BlackRock Investment Stewardship: Global Corporate Governance & Engagement Principles. New York: BlackRock, 2019. www.blackrock.com /corporate/literature/fact-sheet/blk-responsible-investment-engprinciples -global.pdf.

BlackRock Investment Stewardship: Protecting Our Clients' Assets in the Long Term. New York: BlackRock, 2019. www.blackrock.com/corporate /literature/publication/blk-profile-of-blackrock-investment-stewardship -team-work.pdf.

BlackRock Investment Stewardship: 2018 Annual Report. New York: BlackRock, 2018. www.blackrock.com/corporate/literature/publication /blk-annual-stewardship-report-2018.pdf.

Bloomberg. "Activist Hedge Fund Third Point Buys $3.5 Billion Stake in Nestle, Eyeing Opportunities in Europe." *Japan Times*, June 26, 2017. www.japan times.co.jp/news/2017/06/26/business/activist-hedge-fund-third-point-buys -3-5-billion-stake-nestle-eyeing-opportunities-europe/#:~:text=Business -,Activist%20hedge%20fund%20Third%20Point%20buys%20 %243.5%20billion,Nestle%2C%20eyeing%20opportunities%20 in%20Europe&text=NEW%20YORK%2FSAN%20FRANCISCO %20%E2%80%93%20Nestle,the%20world's%20biggest%20food%20 company.

Bloomberg. "Charting GE's Historic Rise and Tortured Downfall." January 31, 2019. www.bloomberg.com/graphics/2019-general-electric-rise-and-downfall/.

Bloomberg. "Chevron CEO Says Low-Cost Shale Has Forced Capital Discipline on Oil Industry." Institute for Energy Economics and Financial Analysis, February 14, 2019. https://ieefa.org/chevron-ceo-says-low-cost-shale-has -forced-capital-discipline-on-oil-industry/.

The Board Perspective. New York: McKinsey & Company, 2018. www .mckinsey.com/~/media/McKinsey/Featured%20Insights/Leadership /The%20board%20perspective/Issue%20Number%202/2018_Board%20 Perspective_Number_2.ashx.

Bohnet, Iris. "How to Take the Bias out of Interviews." *Harvard Business Review*, April 18, 2016. https://hbr.org/2016/04/how-to-take-the-bias-out -of-interviews.

———. *What Works*. Cambridge, MA: Harvard University Press, 2016.

Bolans, Vincent. "The Saga of Parmalat's Collapse." *Financial Times*, December 19, 2008. www.ft.com/content/c275dc7c-cd3a-11dd-9905-000077b07658.

Bowie, Carol. "ISS 2015 Equity Plan Scorecard FAQs." *Harvard Law School Forum on Corporate Governance*, February 2, 2015. https://corpgov.law .harvard.edu/2015/02/02/iss-2015-equity-plan-scorecard-faqs/.

Bristol-Myers Squibb. "Bristol-Myers Squibb Shareholders Approve Celgene Acquisition." News release, April 12, 2019. https://news.bms.com

/press-release/corporatefinancial-news/bristol-myers-squibb-shareholders
-approve-celgene-acquisition.

Brustein, Joshua, and Josh Eidelson. "Google Warns Staff About Protests
During Official Pride Events." Bloomberg, June 24, 2019. www.bloomberg
.com/news/articles/2019-06-25/google-warns-staff-about-protests-during
-official-pride-events.

The Budget and Economic Outlook: 2019 to 2029. Washington, DC: Congressional Budget Office, 2019. www.cbo.gov/publication/54918.

Buffett, Warren. *Warren Buffett on Business: Principles from the Sage of Omaha.*
Hoboken, NJ: John Wiley & Sons, 2009.

Burns, Judith. "Everything You Wanted to Know About Corporate Governance . . ." *Wall Street Journal*, October 27, 2003. www.wsj.com/articles
/SB106676280248746100.

Busby, Mattha. "Persimmon Launches Review in Drive to Rebuild Its Image."
The Guardian, April 6, 2019. www.theguardian.com/business/2019/apr/06
/persimmon-housebuilder-launches-review-drive-rebuild-image.

California S.B. 826 (2018). https://leginfo.legislature.ca.gov/faces/billText
Client.xhtml?bill_id=201720180SB826.

CalPERS. "Commitment to Diversity & Inclusion Report (2017–2018)." Last
modified February 12, 2020. www.calpers.ca.gov/page/forms-publications
/diversity-inclusion-report-2018-19.

Campell, David, David Edgar, and George Stonehouse. *Business Strategy: An
Introduction.* London: Red Globe Press, 2011.

Carney, Mark. "New Economy, New Finance, New Bank." Speech given at the
Mansion House, London, UK, June 21, 2018. www.bankofengland.co.uk
/-/media/boe/files/speech/2018/new-economy-new-finance-new-bank
-speech-by-mark-carney.pdf.

Catalyst. "About Us." www.catalyst.org/mission/.

———. "Women on Corporate Boards: Quick Take." March 13, 2020. www
.catalyst.org/research/women-on-corporate-boards/.

Cavale, Siddharth. "P&G Holds Peltz at Bay as Shareholders Back Company's
Board Picks." BNN Bloomberg, October 10, 2017. www.bnnbloomberg
.ca/p-g-holds-peltz-at-bay-as-shareholders-back-company-s-board-picks
-1.880445.

CB Insights. "How Blockchain Could Disrupt Banking." December 12, 2018.
www.cbinsights.com/research/blockchain-disrupting-banking/.

CEIC. "European Union Market Capitalization: % of GDP." Last modified July 2,
2020. www.ceicdata.com/en/indicator/european-union/market-capitalization
--nominal-gdp.

CEO Climate Dialogue. "Guiding Principles for Federal Action on Climate."
www.ceoclimatedialogue.org/guiding-principles.

CEOs' Curbed Confidence Spells Caution. New York: PwC, 2019. www.pwc .com/sg/en/publications/assets/global-ceo-survey-2019-asean.pdf.

Chandler, Simon. "In the Future We'll Be 'Data Trash Engineers' and 'Purpose Planners,' Says New Report." *The Sun*, November 2, 2018. www.thesun.co.uk /tech/7646173/in-the-future-well-be-data-trash-engineers-and-purpose -planners-says-new-report/.

Chapman, Ben. "PwC Partner Banned for 15 Years and Fined £500,000 over BHS Audit." *Independent*, June 13, 2018. www.independent.co.uk/news /business/news/pwc-partner-bhs-audit-banned-fined-financial-reporting -council-a8396666.html.

Chappatta, Brian. "Meredith Whitney Was Flat-Out Wrong About Municipal Bonds." Bloomberg, October 30, 2018. www.bloomberg.com/opinion /articles/2018-10-30/meredith-whitney-was-flat-out-wrong-about-municipal -bonds.

Chatzky, Andrew, and James McBride. "China's Massive Belt and Road Initiative." Council on Foreign Relations, May 21, 2019. www.cfr.org/back grounder/chinas-massive-belt-and-road-initiative.

Chen, Kuni. "How ESG Concerns Contributed to GE's Downfall." LinkedIn, April 30, 2018. www.linkedin.com/pulse/how-esg-concerns-contributed -ges-downfall-kuni-chen-cfa.

Cheng, Evelyn. "Wells Fargo Shares Dive After Fed Restricts Bank's Growth, Citing 'Consumer Abuses.'" CNBC, February 2, 2018. www.cnbc.com /2018/02/02/federal-reserve-orders-wells-fargo-to-replace-four-board -members-restricts-growth-because-consumer-abuses.html.

Chevron. "The Chevron Way." www.chevron.com/about/the-chevron-way.

———. "Corporate Governance." www.chevron.com/investors/%20corporate -governance.

Chick-fil-A. "Who We Are." www.chick-fil-a.com/about/who-we-are.

Christofferson, Scott A., Robert S. McNish, and Diane L. Sias. "Where Mergers Go Wrong." McKinsey & Company, May 1, 2004. www.mckinsey.com /business-functions/strategy-and-corporate-finance/our-insights/where -mergers-go-wrong.

Citizens United v. Federal Election Comm'n. 558 U.S. 310 (2010). https:// supreme.justia.com/cases/federal/us/558/08-205/index.pdf.

City of Boulder. "Sugar Sweetened Beverage Tax." https://bouldercolorado .gov/tax-license/finance-sugar-sweetened-beverage-tax.

City of Philadelphia. "Philadelphia Beverage Tax." Payments, Assistance, and Taxes. Last modified January 8, 2020. www.phila.gov/services/payments -assistance-taxes/business-taxes/philadelphia-beverage-tax/.

Climate Action 100+. "Global Investors Driving Business Transition." www .climateaction100.org.

Coase, R. H. "The Nature of the Firm." *Economica* 4, no. 16 (November 1937): 386–405. www.jstor.org/stable/2626876?seq=1#page_scan_tab_contents.

Cohan, Peter. "Delays in Boeing's 737 MAX and 777X Could Weigh on Stock." *Forbes*, June 6, 2019. www.forbes.com/sites/petercohan/2019/06/06/delays -in-boeings-737-max-and-777x-could-weigh-on-stock/#61de1af3e678.

Cohn, Yafit. "Independent Chair Proposals." *Harvard Law School Forum on Corporate Governance*, August 22, 2016. https://corpgov.law.harvard.edu /2016/08/22/independent-chair-proposals-2/.

Collins, Jim. *Good to Great*. New York: Harper Business, 2001.

Colvin, Geoff. "The Investor That Tripped on GE & P&G." *Fortune*, November 26, 2018. https://fortune.com/2018/11/26/nelson-peltz-ge-pg-stock/.

———. "What the Hell Happened at GE?" *Fortune*, May 24, 2018. https:// fortune.com/longform/ge-decline-what-the-hell-happened/.

Commonsense Corporate Governance Principles. "Open Letter: Commonsense Principles 2.0." www.governanceprinciples.org.

Conger, Kate, and Daisuke Wakabayashi. "Google Employees Say They Faced Retaliation After Organizing Walkout." *New York Times*, April 22, 2019. www.nytimes.com/2019/04/22/technology/google-walkout-employees -retaliation.html.

Congressional Budget Office. "Revenues in 2018: An Infographic." June 18, 2019. www.cbo.gov/publication/55345.

Connley, Courtney. "Google, Apple and 12 Other Companies That No Longer Require Employees to Have a College Degree." CNBC *Make It*, October 8, 2018. www.cnbc.com/2020/03/04/stop-wasting-money-on-these-7-useless -things-and-save-for-early-retirement.html.

Continued Listing Guide. New York: Nasdaq, 2020. https://listingcenter.nasdaq .com/assets/continuedguide.pdf.

Corporate Secretaries International Association. *Global Board Evaluation Practices and Trends*. London: Diligent, 2018. https://diligent.com /wp-content/uploads/sites/5/2018/07/Diligent-and-CSIA-Global-Board -Evaluations-Practices-and-Trends-Whitepaper.pdf.

Cox, Michael. *Understanding the Rise of Global Populism*. London: LSE IDEAS, 2018. www.lse.ac.uk/ideas/Assets/Documents/updates/LSE-IDEAS-Under standing-Global-Rise-of-Populism.pdf.

Crabtree, Steve. "Worldwide, 13% of Employees Are Engaged at Work." Gallup, October 8, 2013. https://news.gallup.com/poll/165269/worldwide -employees-engaged-work.aspx.

Creary, Stephanie J., Mary-Hunter "Mae" McDonnell, Sakshi Ghai, and Jared Scruggs. "When and Why Diversity Improves Your Board's Performance." *Harvard Business Review*, March 27, 2019. https://hbr.org/2019/03/when -and-why-diversity-improves-your-boards-performance.

Crooks, Ed. "GE Loses Crown as Biggest US Manufacturer by Market Cap." *Financial Times*, November 15, 2017. www.ft.com/content/43590368 -c99f-11e7-aa33-c63fdc9b8c6c.

Curran, Enda. "The AIIB China World Bank." Bloomberg, August 6, 2018. www.bloomberg.com/quicktake/chinas-world-bank.

Dalio, Ray. *Principles: Life and Work*. New York: Simon & Schuster, 2017.

Davenport, Coral, and Kendra Pierra-Louis. "U.S. Climate Report Warns of Damaged Environment and Shrinking Economy." *New York Times*, November 23, 2018. www.nytimes.com/2018/11/23/climate/us-climate -report.html.

A Decade After the Global Financial Crisis: Are We Safer? Washington, DC: International Monetary Fund, 2018.

Deep Focus. "Deep Focus' Cassandra Report: Gen Z Uncovers Massive Attitude Shifts Toward Money, Work and Communication Preferences." News release, March 30, 2015. www.globenewswire.com/news-release/2015/03 /30/1308741/0/en/Deep-Focus-Cassandra-Report-Gen-Z-Uncovers-Massive -Attitude-Shifts-Toward-Money-Work-and-Communication-Preferences .html.

Defond, Mark L., Rebecca N. Hann, and Xuesong Hu. "Does the Market Value Financial Expertise on Audit Committees of Boards of Directors?" *Journal of Accounting Research* 43 (2005): 153–193. https://doi.org /10.1111/j.1475-679x.2005.00166.x.

De La Merced, Michael J. "Eastman Kodak Files for Bankruptcy." *DealBook* (blog). *New York Times*, January 19, 2012. https://dealbook.nytimes .com/2012/01/19/eastman-kodak-files-for-bankruptcy/.

De Leon, Riley. "Beyond Meat and Impossible Foods Are in a Fast-Food Alternative-Meat Arms Race as Demand Swells." CNBC, June 24, 2019. www .cnbc.com/2019/06/24/beyond-meat-and-impossible-foods-in-an-alternative -meat-arms-race.html.

Deloitte. "Board Age Limits Continue Upward Trend." *Wall Street Journal*, January 26, 2016. https://deloitte.wsj.com/riskandcompliance/2016/01/26 /board-age-limits-continue-upward-trend-2/.

The Democratic Leadership Gap. Washington, DC: Freedom House, 2014. https://freedomhouse.org/sites/default/files/Overview%20Fact%20 Sheet.pdf.

Department for Business, Energy & Industrial Strategy. *Ethnicity Pay Reporting: Government Consultation*. London: The National Archives, 2018. https:// assets.publishing.service.gov.uk/government/uploads/system/uploads /attachment_data/file/747546/ethnicity-pay-reporting-consultation.pdf.

Department for Transport. *The Road to Zero*. London: HM Government, 2018. https://assets.publishing.service.gov.uk/government/uploads/system /uploads/attachment_data/file/739460/road-to-zero.pdf.

Dimon, Jamie. "Chairman & CEO Letter to Shareholders." JPMorgan Chase & Co., April 14, 2019. https://reports.jpmorganchase.com/investor-relations /2018/ar-ceo-letters.htm.

Disney, Abigail. "It's Time to Call Out Disney—and Anyone Else Rich off Their Workers' Backs." *Washington Post*, April 23, 2019. www.washingtonpost .com/opinions/its-time-to-call-out-my-familys-company—and-anyone-else -rich-off-their-workers-backs/2019/04/23/5d4e6838-65ef-11e9-82ba-fcfe ff232e8f_story.html.

Dodd-Frank Wall Street Reform and Consumer Protection Act. H.R. 4173. 111th Cong. (2009). www.congress.gov/bill/111th-congress/house-bill/4173/text.

Doige, Craig, Kathleen M. Kahle, G. Andrew Karolyi, and René M. Stulz. "Eclipse of the Public Corporation or Eclipse of the Public Markets?" Working Paper 24265, National Bureau of Economic Research, Cambridge, MA, January 2018. http://doi.org/10.3386/w24265.

D'Onfro, Jillian. "Google Employees Protest 'Anti-LGBTQ' Conservative's Appointment to AI Ethics Council." *Forbes*, April 1, 2019. www.forbes.com /sites/jilliandonfro/2019/04/01/google-employees-protest-anti-lgbtq -conservatives-appointment-to-its-ai-ethics-council/#192a5aab13e1.

Donnan, Shawn. "Globalisation in Retreat: Capital Flows Decline Since Crisis." *Financial Times*, August 21, 2017. www.ft.com/content/dade8ada8 -83f6-11e7-94e2-c5b903247afd.

D. S. "Unfree Exchange." *The Economist*, November 1, 2011. www.economist .com/blogs/americasview/2011/11/argentina's-currency-controls.

Dweck, Carol S. *Mindset: The New Psychology of Success*. New York: Random House, 2006.

Eavis, Peter. "It's Never Been Easier to Be a C.E.O., and the Pay Keeps Rising." *New York Times*, May 24, 2019. www.nytimes.com/2019/05/24/business /highest-paid-ceos-2018.html.

eBay. "Sukhinder Singh Cassidy Named President of StubHub." News release, April 5, 2018. www.ebayinc.com/stories/news/sukhinder-singh-cassidy -named-president-of-stubhub/.

Eccles, Robert G., and Svetlana Klimenko. "The Investor Revolution." *Harvard Business Review*, May–June 2019. https://hbr.org/2019/05/the -investor-revolution.

The Economist. "Chinese and US Tech Giants Go at It in Emerging Markets." July 7, 2018. www.economist.com/business/2018/07/07/chinese-and-us -tech-giants-go-at-it-in-emerging-markets.

The Economist. "Decades of Optimism About China's Rise Have Been Discarded." March 1, 2018. www.economist.com/briefing/2018/03/01/decades -of-optimism-about-chinas-rise-have-been-discarded.

The Economist. "How the West Got China Wrong." March 1, 2018. www .economist.com/leaders/2018/03/01/how-the-west-got-china-wrong.

The Economist. "Millennial Socialism." February 14, 2019. www.economist .com/leaders/2019/02/14/millennial-socialism.

The Economist. "Norway's Sovereign-Wealth Fund Passes the $1trn Mark." September 23, 2017. www.economist.com/finance-and-economics/2017/09 /23/norways-sovereign-wealth-fund-passes-the-1trn-mark.

The Economist. "Send in the Clouds." July 4, 2019. www.economist.com /business/2019/07/04/send-in-the-clouds.

Edgecliffe-Johnson, Andrew. "Activist Employees Pose New Labour Relations Threat to Bosses." *Financial Times*, July 3, 2019. www.ft.com/content /c1167d4a-9cb5-11e9-b8ce-8b459ed04726.

———. "Business Leaders Need to Speak Up Against Trump Trade Policy." *Financial Times*, August 22, 2018. www.ft.com/content/dfa62c66 -a48f-11e8-8ecf-a7ae1beff35b.

Egan, Matt. "America's Stock Market Is Shrinking." CNN Business, July 9, 2015. https://money.cnn.com/2015/07/09/investing/stock-market-shrinking/.

———. "The Two-Year Wells Fargo Horror Story Just Won't End." CNN Business, September 7, 2018. https://money.cnn.com/2018/09/07/news /companies/wells-fargo-scandal-two-years/index.html.

Elkins, Kathleen. "Most Young Americans Prefer Socialism to Capitalism, New Report Finds." CNBC *Make It*, August 14, 2018. www.cnbc.com /2018/08/14/fewer-than-half-of-young-americans-are-positive-about-capitalism .html.

Elson, Charles M. "What's Wrong with Executive Compensation?" *Harvard Business Review*, January 2003. https://hbr.org/2003/01/whats-wrong-with -executive-compensation.

Ely, Bert. "Savings and Loan Crisis." In *Concise Encyclopedia of Economics*. Library of Economics and Liberty, 2002. www.econlib.org/library/Enc1 /SavingsandLoanCrisis.html.

Embankment Project for Inclusive Capitalism. New York: Coalition for Inclusive Capitalism, 2018. www.epic-value.com/#report.

Enriquez, Edan. "When You Empower a Girl, You Empower a Community." Cisco, June 27, 2019. https://blogs.cisco.com/diversity/when-you-empower -a-girl-you-empower-a-community.

Equality Act. 2010. c. 15. www.legislation.gov.uk/ukpga/2010/15/contents.

Equality Trust. "The Scale of Economic Inequality in the UK." www.equalitytrust .org.uk/scale-economic-inequality-uk.

Espinoza, Javier, and Eric Platt. "Private Equity Races to Spend Record $2.5tn Cash Pile." *Financial Times*, June 27, 2019. www.ft.com/content /2f777656-9854-11e9-9573-ee5cbb98ed36.

Esterl, Mike. "Soda Taxes Approved in Four Cities, Vote Looms in Chicago's Cook County." *Wall Street Journal*, November 9, 2016. www.wsj.com /articles/soda-taxes-approved-in-four-cities-vote-looms-in-chicagos-cook -county-1478698979.

European Commission. "China." Last modified June 11, 2020. https://ec.europa .eu/trade/policy/countries-and-regions/countries/china/index_en.htm.

Evans, Rachel, Sabrina Willmer, Nick Baker, and Brandon Kochkodin. "With $20 Trillion Between Them, Blackrock and Vanguard Could Own Almost Everything by 2028." *Financial Post*, December 4, 2017. https://financialpost.com /investing/a-20-trillion-blackrock-vanguard-duopoly-is-investings-future.

Extractive Industries Transparency Initiative. "Who We Are." https://eiti.org /who-we-are.

EY Americas. "How Boards Are Governing Disruptive Technology." Ernst & Young, June 10, 2019. www.ey.com/en_us/board-matters/how-boards-are -governing-disruptive-technology.

Fair Pay Report 2018. London: Barclays, 2018. https://home.barclays/content /dam/home-barclays/documents/investor-relations/reports-and-events /annual-reports/2018/barclays-2018-fair-pay-report.pdf.

Fairchild, Caroline. "Women CEOs in the Fortune 1000: By the Numbers." *Fortune*, July 8, 2014. https://fortune.com/2014/07/08/women-ceos-fortune -500-1000/.

Fast Company. "The World's 50 Most Innovative Companies 2019." www.fast company.com/most-innovative-companies/2019.

Faulkner, Kristi. "Will Uber's Brand Refresh Convince Women to Forgive Them?" *Forbes*, September 14, 2018. www.forbes.com/sites/kristifaulkner /2018/09/14/will-ubers-brand-refresh-convince-women-to-forgive-them /#6a1a45ee1e4d.

Feeding America. "Hunger in America." www.feedingamerica.org/hunger-in -america/facts.

Financial Times. "Barrick Gold Corp." Accessed August 16, 2019. https:// markets.ft.com/data/equities/tearsheet/charts?s=ABX:TOR.

Fink, Larry. "Larry Fink's 2017 Letter to CEOs." BlackRock. www.blackrock .com/corporate/investor-relations/2017-larry-fink-ceo-letter.

———. "Larry Fink's 2016 Letter to CEOs." BlackRock. www.blackrock .com/corporate/investor-relations/2016-larry-fink-ceo-letter.

———. Letter to John L. Thornton, executive chairman of Barrick Gold Corp, January 12, 2018.

———. "Letter to Shareholders." In *BlackRock 2018 Annual Report*. New York: BlackRock, 2019. https://s24.q4cdn.com/856567660/files/oar/2018 /letter-to-shareholders.html.

———. "Purpose & Profit: Larry Fink's 2019 Letter to CEOs." BlackRock. www.blackrock.com/corporate/investor-relations/2019-larry-fink-ceo-letter.

———. "A Sense of Purpose: Larry Fink's 2018 Letter to CEOs." BlackRock. www.blackrock.com/corporate/investor-relations/2018-larry-fink-ceo-letter.

Finkelstein, Sydney. "Why Is Industry Related to CEO Compensation?: A Managerial Discretion Explanation." *Open Ethics Journal* 7, no. 3 (2009): 42–56. https://benthamopen.com/contents/pdf/TOJ/TOJ-3-42.pdf.

Flood, Chris. "Trillion-Dollar Asset Managers Hog Investor Inflows." *Financial Times*, November 19, 2018. www.ft.com/content/525dfeef-582f-357d-96d6-e6d56a4a19ef.

Food and Agriculture Organization of the United Nations. "Key Facts and Findings." www.fao.org/news/story/en/item/197623/icode/.

Foreign Corrupt Practices Act of 1977. Pub. L. No. 95-213. 91 Stat. 1495 (1977). www.govinfo.gov/content/pkg/STATUTE-91/pdf/STATUTE-91-Pg1494.pdf.

Forgey, Quint. "How Elizabeth Warren Would Reform Wall Street." *Politico*, July 18, 2019. www.politico.com/story/2019/07/18/elizabeth-warren-wall-street-2020-1421826.

Fortune. "Change the World." https://fortune.com/change-the-world/2019.

Fortune. "Fortune 500." https://fortune.com/fortune500/.

Fortune. "The Unicorn List." https://fortune.com/unicorns/.

Foster, Richard, and Sarah Kaplan. *Creative Destruction*. New York: Currency, 2001.

Fox, Justin. "Why German Corporate Boards Include Workers." Bloomberg, August 24, 2018. www.bloomberg.com/opinion/articles/2018-08-24/why-german-corporate-boards-include-workers-for-co-determination.

Fraser, Iain, and Laurence Smith. "Pareto Optimality." In *An Introduction to Environmental Economics & Economic Concepts*. London: SOAS University of London, 2014. www.soas.ac.uk/cedep-demos/000_P570_IEEP_K3736-Demo/unit1/page_26.htm.

Fried, Jesse M., and Charles C. Y. Wang. "Short-Termism and Capital Flows." *Review of Corporate Finance Studies* (forthcoming). Last modified November 25, 2018. https://papers.ssrn.com/sol3/papers.cfm?abstract_id=289516.

Friedman, Milton. "The Social Responsibility of Business Is to Increase Its Profits." *New York Times*, September 13, 1970.

Fromm, Jeff. "How Much Financial Influence Does Gen Z Have?" *Forbes*, January 10, 2018. www.forbes.com/sites/jefffromm/2018/01/10/what-you-need-to-know-about-the-financial-impact-of-gen-z-influence/#2f7ceaa856fc.

Fry, Richard. "Millennials Projected to Overtake Baby Boomers as America's Largest Generation." *Fact Tank* (blog). Pew Research Center, March 1, 2018. www.pewresearch.org/fact-tank/2018/03/01/millennials-overtake-baby-boomers/.

Gallup. "Tobacco and Smoking." https://news.gallup.com/poll/1717/tobacco-smoking.aspx.

Generation Investment Management. "Generation Philosophy." www.generationim.com/generation-philosophy/.

Gerdeman, Dina. "The Airbnb Effect: Cheaper Rooms for Travelers, Less Revenue for Hotels." *Forbes*, February 27, 2018. www.forbes.com/sites/hbsworkingknowledge/2018/02/27/the-airbnb-effect-cheaper-rooms-for-travelers-less-revenue-for-hotels/#18d69094d672.

Gertz, Geoffrey. "5 Things to Know About USMCA, the New NAFTA." Brookings Institution, October 2, 2018. www.brookings.edu/blog/up-front/2018/10/02/5-things-to-know-about-usmca-the-new-nafta/.

Gevurtz, Franklin A. "The Historical and Political Origins of the Corporate Board of Directors." *Hofstra Law Review* 33, no. 1 (2004). http://scholarlycommons.law.hofstra.edu/hlr/vol33/iss1/3.

Giammona, Craig. "Nelson Peltz, Who Mocked Company Name, Exits Mondelez Board." Bloomberg, February 13, 2018. www.bloomberg.com/news/articles/2018-02-13/nelson-peltz-who-mocked-company-s-name-departs-mondelez-board.

Gill, Indermit. "Joyless Growth in China, India, and the United States." Brookings Institution, January 22, 2019. www.brookings.edu/blog/future-development/2019/01/22/joyless-growth-in-china-india-and-the-united-states/.

Giugliano, Ferdinando. "BoE's Haldane Says Corporations Putting Shareholders Before Economy." *Financial Times*, July 25, 2015. www.ft.com/content/7d347016-32f4-11e5-b05b-b01debd57852.

Gius, Daniela, Jean-Christophe Mieszala, Ernestos Panayiotou, and Thomas Poppensieker. *Value and Resilience Through Better Risk Management.* New York: McKinsey & Company, 2018. www.mckinsey.com/~/media/McKinsey/Business%20Functions/Risk/Our%20Insights/Value%20and%20resilience%20through%20better%20risk%20management/Value-and-resilience-through-better-risk-management-final.ashx.

Glassdoor. "2019 Best Places to Work: Employee's Choice." www.glassdoor.com/Award/Best-Places-to-Work-2019-LST_KQ0,24.htm.

Global Warming of 1.5°C. Geneva, Switzerland: Intergovernmental Panel on Climate Change, 2018. https://report.ipcc.ch/sr15/pdf/sr15_spm_final.pdf.

Goldman Sachs. "Our Business Principles." In *Goldman Sachs 2001 Annual Report.* New York: Goldman Sachs Group, 2001. www.goldmansachs.com/our_firm/investor_relations/financial_reports/annual_reports/2001/html principles/index.html.

Gonzales, Richard. "McDonald's Facing New Charges of Sexual Harassment." NPR, May 21, 2019. www.npr.org/2019/05/21/725557211/mcdonalds-facing-new-charges-of-sexual-harassment.

Google.org. "Closing the Education Gap." www.google.org/closing-the-education-gap/.

Governance Insights Center. *How Might the Changing Face of Shareholder Activism Affect Your Company?* New York: PwC 2019. www.pwc.com/us/en/governance-insights-center/publications/assets/pwc-how-might-the-changing-face-of-shareholder-activism-impact-your-company.pdf.

Government Equalities Office. "100% of UK Employers Publish Gender Pay Gap Data." News release, August 1, 2018. www.gov.uk/government/news/100-of-uk-employers-publish-gender-pay-gap-data.

Green, Francis. "Occupational Pension Schemes and British Capitalism." *Cambridge Journal of Economics* 6, no. 3 (September 1982): 267–283. https://doi.org/10.1093/oxfordjournals.cje.a035513.

Green, Jeff. "#MeToo Snares More Than 400 High-Profile People." Bloomberg, June 25, 2018. www.bloomberg.com/news/articles/2018-06-25/-metoo-snares-more-than-400-high-profile-people-as-firings-rise.

GreenMatch. "4 Sustainable Behaviours of Gen Z's Shopping Habits." November 5, 2018. www.greenmatch.co.uk/blog/2018/09/gen-zs-sustainable-shopping-habits.

Griffith, Keith. "Staff at Online Furniture Retailer Wayfair Plan Mass Walkout over Claims the Firm Is Selling Beds to Migrant Detention Center on Border." *Daily Mail*, June 26, 2019. www.dailymail.co.uk/news/article-7181631/Wayfair-employee-walkout-called-alleged-furniture-sales-U-S-migrant-camp.html.

Grigoli, Francesco, Zsóka Kóczán, and Petia Topalova. "Labor Force Participation in Advanced Economies: Drivers and Prospects." In *World Economic Outlook: Cyclical Upswing, Structural Change*. Washington, DC: International Monetary Fund, 2018. www.elibrary.imf.org/view/IMF081/24892-9781484338278/24892-9781484338278/binaries/978148 4338278_Chapter_2-Labor_Force_Participation_in_Advanced_Economies-Drivers_and_Prospects.pdf.

Ground, Jessica, and Marc Hassler. "Corporate Governance: Thinking Fast and Slow." Schroders, May 8, 2019. www.schroders.com/en/us/insights/economic-views/corporate-governance-thinking-fast-and-slow/.

Guide to the General Data Protection Regulation (GDPR). Wilmslow, UK: Information Commissioner's Office, 2018. https://ico.org.uk/media/for-organisations/guide-to-the-general-data-protection-regulation-gdpr-1-0.pdf.

Guidelines: An Overview of the Glass Lewis Approach to Proxy Advice, United States. San Francisco: Glass Lewis, 2019. www.glasslewis.com/wp-content /uploads/2018/10/2019_GUIDELINES_UnitedStates.pdf.

Guillén, Mauro F. *The Global Economic & Financial Crisis: A Timeline.* Philadelphia: Lauder Institute, 2009. www-management.wharton.upenn.edu /guillen/2009_docs/crisis_financiera_formato_nuevo.pdf.

Hallett, Rachel. "These Countries Are Facing the Greatest Skills Shortages." World Economic Forum, July 5, 2016. www.weforum.org/agenda/2016/07 /countries-facing-greatest-skills-shortages/.

Hamilton, Isobel A. "Amazon Turned 25 Today, Which According to Jeff Bezos Means It Will Die in as Little as 5 Years Time." *Business Insider*, July 5, 2019. www.businessinsider.com/jeff-bezos-keeps-talking-about-amazons -inevitable-death-2018-12.

Hamlin, Katrina. "Hong Kong Death Offers Humbling Reminder to CEOs." *Canadian HR Reporter*, August 21, 2018. www.hrreporter.com/opinion/hr -guest-blog/hong-kong-death-offers-humbling-reminder-to-ceos/298697.

Harder, Amy. "The Big Corporate Shift on Climate Change." *Axios*, May 20, 2019. www.axios.com/the-big-corporate-shift-on-climate-change-1edea61e -ca43-4df9-a293-d42e00f08caa.html.

Harding, Sy. "Stock Market Becomes Short Attention Span Theater of Trading." *Forbes*, January 21, 2011. www.forbes.com/sites/greatspeculations /2011/01/21/stock-market-becomes-short-attention-span-theater-of-trading /#42a57b8f703e.

Harjoto, Maretno, Indrarini Laksmana, and Robert Lee. "Board Diversity and Corporate Social Responsibility." *Journal of Business Ethics* 132, no. 4 (2015): 641–660. https://doi.org/10.1007/s10551-014-2343-0.

Harrabin, Roger. "Climate Change: UK Government to Commit to 2050 Target." BBC News, June 12, 2019. www.bbc.co.uk/news/science-environment -48596775.

———. "Letter Makes Plea to Rich over Climate." BBC News, May 23, 2019. www.bbc.co.uk/news/science-environment-48357351.

Hart, Kim. "The New Job for CEOs: Building Trust." *Axios*, February 10, 2018. www.axios.com/new-job-for-ceos-building-trust-83df7db6-3c02-48c6 -bc43-e73d67c0057a.html.

Hartig, Hannah. "Stark Partisan Divisions in Americans' Views of 'Socialism,' 'Capitalism.'" *Fact Tank* (blog). Pew Research Center, June 25, 2019. www.pewresearch.org/fact-tank/2019/06/25/stark-partisan-divisions-in -americans-views-of-socialism-capitalism/.

Hastings, Reed. "Netflix Culture: Freedom and Responsibility." PowerPoint presentation, August 1, 2009. www.slideshare.net/reed2001/culture-1798664 /8-Actual_company_values_are_thebehaviors.

Hays, Constance L. "Kmart Reveals the Discovery of New Errors in Its Accounts." *New York Times*, December 10, 2002. www.nytimes.com /2002/12/10/business/kmart-reveals-the-discovery-of-new-errors-in-its -accounts.html.

Heilman, M. E., and T. G. Okimoto. "Motherhood: A Potential Source of Bias in Employment Decisions." *Journal of Applied Psychology* 93, no.1 (2008): 189–198. http://dx.doi.org/10.1037/0021-9010.93.1.189.

Heimans, Jeremy, and Henry Timms. *New Power: How Anyone Can Persuade, Mobilize, and Succeed in Our Chaotic, Connected Age.* New York: Anchor Books, 2019.

———. "Understanding 'New Power.'" *Harvard Business Review*, December 2014. https://hbr.org/2014/12/understanding-new-power.

Herbst-Bayliss, Svea. "Third Point Launches Proxy Fight for Full Campbell Board." Reuters, September 7, 2018. www.reuters.com/article/us-campbell -soup-thirdpoint/third-point-launches-proxy-fight-for-full-campbell-board- idUSKCN1LN1JI.

Hideg, Ivona, Anja Krstic, Raymond Trau, and Tanya Zarina. "Do Longer Maternity Leaves Hurt Women's Careers?" *Harvard Business Review*, September 14, 2018. https://hbr.org/2018/09/do-longer-maternity-leaves-hurt -womens-careers.

———. "The Unintended Consequences of Maternity Leaves: How Agency Interventions Mitigate the Negative Effects of Longer Legislated Maternity Leaves." *Journal of Applied Psychology* 103, no. 10 (2018): 1155–1164. http://dx.doi.org/10.1037/apl0000327.

Hill, Sam, and Hank Gilman. "Big Business Can Be Evil and Greedy, but Here's How Corporations Will Help Save Us from Ourselves." *Newsweek*, May 6, 2019. www.newsweek.com/business-evil-greedy-how-corporations -will-save-us-1415853.

Hinchliffe, Emma. "Female Employees Who Are the Only Woman at Work Are 50% More Likely to Consider Quitting." *Fortune*, October 23, 2018. https://fortune.com/2018/10/23/women-only-one-lean-in-survey/.

———. "Fortune 500 Boards, Taiwan Same-Sex Marriage, Nike Pregnancy: Broadsheet May 20." Yahoo Finance, May 20, 2019. https://finance.yahoo .com/news/fortune-500-boards-taiwan-same-110039840.html.

Holmberg, Susan R. *Fighting Short-Termism with Worker Power.* New York: Roosevelt Institute, 2017. https://rooseveltinstitute.org/wp-content/uploads /2020/07/RI-Fighting-Short-Termism-201710.pdf.

Hopgood, Suzanne. "Being a Woman on the Board." *Corporate Board*, November–December 2017. www.boardroomdiversity.org/wp-content/uploads /2017/11/1711Hopgood.pdf.

Horowitz, Ben. "Peacetime CEO/Wartime CEO." Andreessen Horowitz, April 14, 2011. https://a16z.com/2011/04/14/peacetime-ceowartime-ceo-2/.

Hosie, Rachel. "'Dumbphone' Sales Rise as People Seek to Disconnect and Become More Mindful." *Independent*, August 20, 2018. www.independent .co.uk/life-style/dumb-phones-sales-rise-disconnect-technology-mind fulness-social-media-a8499086.html.

How Can You Reshape Your Future Before It Reshapes You? Global Capital Confidence Barometer, 20th ed. London: Ernst & Young, 2019. https:// assets.ey.com/content/dam/ey-sites/ey-com/en_gl/topics/ey-capital -confidence-barometer/ccb20/pdf/ey-global-ccb-edition-20.pdf.

IDA. "Going Global: A Look at Public Company Listings." March 9, 2017. www.idawealth.com/going-global-a-look-at-public-company-listings/.

The Impact of the UK's Exit from the EU on the UK-based Financial Services Sector. New York: Oliver Wyman, 2016.

Intel. "Press Kit: STEM Education." Intel Newsroom, March 5, 2014. https:// newsroom.intel.com/press-kits/stem-education/#gs.zczt9c.

International Monetary Fund. "Consumer Price Index (CPI)." Accessed August 20, 2019. https://data.imf.org/?sk=4FFB52B2-3653-409A-B471-D 47B46D904B5.

International Renewable Energy Agency. "Falling Renewable Power Costs Open Door to Greater Climate Ambition." News release, May 29, 2019. www.irena.org/newsroom/pressreleases/2019/May/Falling-Renewable -Power-Costs-Open-Door-to-Greater-Climate-Ambition.

Intersoft Consulting. "General Data Protection Regulation: GDPR." https:// gdpr-info.eu.

Investor Stewardship Group. "About the Investor Stewardship Group and the Framework for U.S. Stewardship and Governance." https://isgframework .org.

Izadi, Elahe. "The Weinstein Co. Declares Bankruptcy. Here's What That Means and What Could Be Next." *Washington Post*, March 20, 2018. www.washingtonpost.com/news/arts-and-entertainment/wp/2018/03/20 /the-weinstein-company-declares-bankruptcy-heres-what-that-means-and -what-could-be-next/.

Jakab, Spencer. "McDonald's 300-Billionth Burger Delayed." *Wall Street Journal*, January 22, 2013. www.wsj.com/articles/SB100014241278873233 0110 4578258113829116672.

James, William, and Kate Holton. "Cameron Tells Pfizer Wants More Commitments for AstraZeneca Deal." Reuters, May 7, 2014. https://uk.reuters.com /article/uk-pfizer-astrazeneca-cameron/cameron-tells-pfizer-wants-more -commitments-for-astrazeneca-deal-idUKKBN0DN0S120140507.

Jessop, Simon, and Sinead Cruise. "Activist Investor Bramson May Get Bloody Nose at Barclays AGM." Reuters, April 26, 2019. https://uk.reuters.com /article/uk-barclays-agm-activist/activist-investor-bramson-may-get -bloody-nose-at-barclays-agm-idUKKCN1S21BZ.

Jiang, Bin, and Tim Koller. "Paying Back Your Shareholders." McKinsey & Company, May 1, 2011. www.mckinsey.com/business-functions/strategy -and-corporate-finance/our-insights/paying-back-your-shareholders.

Judd, Sheila. *Risk Governance: Evolution in Best Practices for Boards*. Toronto: Global Risk Institute, 2018. https://globalriskinstitute.org/publications risk-governance-evolution-best-practices-boards/.

Kantor, Jodi, and David Streitfeld. "Inside Amazon: Wrestling Big Ideas in a Bruising Workplace." *New York Times*, August 14, 2015. www.nytimes .com/2015/08/16/technology/inside-amazon-wrestling-big-ideas-in-a-bruising -workplace.html.

Kaplan, Robert S., and Anette Mikes. "Managing Risks: A New Framework." *Harvard Business Review*, June 2012. https://hbr.org/2012/06/managing -risks-a-new-framework.

Kark, Khalid, Tonie Leatherberry, and Debbie McCormack. "Technology and the Boardroom: A CIO's Guide to Engaging the Board." *Deloitte Insights*, February 22, 2019. www2.deloitte.com/insights/us/en/focus/cio-insider -business-insights/boards-technology-fluency-cio-guide.html.

Kawa, Luke. "Two Major Apple Shareholders Push for Study of iPhone Addiction in Children." Bloomberg, January 8, 2018. www.bloomberg .com/news/articles/2018-01-08/jana-calpers-push-apple-to-study-iphone -addiction-in-children.

Kay, Ira, and Blaine Martin. "CEO Pay Ratio and Income Inequality: Perspectives for Compensation Committees." *Harvard Law School Forum on Corporate Governance*, October 25, 2016. https://corpgov.law.harvard .edu/2016/10/25/ceo-pay-ratio-and-income-inequality-perspectives -for-compensation-committees/.

Khanna, Tarun, and Krishna G. Palepu. "Emerging Giants: Building World-Class Companies in Developing Countries." *Harvard Business Review*, October 2006. https://hbr.org/2006/10/emerging-giants-building-world-class-companies -in-developing-countries.

Kim, Eugene. "Jeff Bezos to Employees: 'One Day, Amazon Will Fail' but Our Job Is to Delay It as Long as Possible." CNBC, November 14, 2018. www .cnbc.com/2018/11/15/bezos-tells-employees-one-day-amazon-will-fail -and-to-stay-hungry.html.

King, Michelle. "Three Things You Need to Know About Marketing to Gen Z Women." *Forbes*, July 10, 2018. www.forbes.com/sites/michelleking

/2018/07/10/a-new-report-reveals-three-things-you-need-to-know-about
-marketing-to-gen-z-women/#597cb2ad6cc1.

King's Fund. "Communicable Diseases." www.kingsfund.org.uk/projects/time
-think-differently/trends-disease-and-disability-communicable-diseases.

Kiron, David, Nina Kruschwitz, Knut Haanaes, Martin Reeves, Sonja-Katrin Fuisz-Kehrbach, and George Kell. *Joining Forces: Collaboration and Leadership for Sustainability.* Cambridge, MA: MIT Sloan, 2015. www.unglobalcompact.org/docs/publications/Joining_Forces_MITSMR _BCG_UNGlobalCompact_Report.pdf.

Klingler-Vidra, Robyn. *Global Review of Diversity and Inclusion in Business Innovation.* London: LSE Consulting, 2018. https://assets.publishing .service.gov.uk/government/uploads/system/uploads/attachment_data/file /777640/Global_Review_LSE_Consulting_2019.pdf.

Kolakowski, Mark. "10 Banks with Soaring Dividend Payouts." *Investopedia*, June 25, 2019. www.investopedia.com/news/10-banks-soaring-dividend -payouts/.

Kolhatkar, Sheelah. "The P.G. & E. Bankruptcy and the Coming Climate-Related Business Failures." *New Yorker*, February 26, 2019. www.new yorker.com/business/currency/the-pg-and-e-bankruptcy-and-the-coming -climate-related-business-failures.

Koller, Tim, Mekala Krishnan, and Sree Ramaswamy. "Bracing for a New Era of Lower Investment Returns." McKinsey & Company, July 13, 2016. www.mckinsey.com/business-functions/strategy-and-corporate-finance /our-insights/bracing-for-a-new-era-of-lower-investment-returns.

Koller, Tim, James Manyika, and Sree Ramaswamy. "The Case Against Corporate Short Termism." McKinsey Global Institute, August 4, 2017. www.mckinsey .com/mgi/overview/in-the-news/the-case-against-corporate-short-termism.

Konrad, Alison M., Vicki Kramer, and Sumru Erkut. "Critical Mass: The Impact of Three or More Women on Corporate Boards." *Organizational Dynamics* 37, no. 2 (2008): 145–164. www.sciencedirect.com/science/article/pii /S0090261608000168.

Kottasová, Ivana, and Sara Ashley O'Brien. "Google Employees Are Staging Another Protest." CNN Business, May 1, 2019. https://edition.cnn .com/2019/05/01/tech/google-employees-protest-may-day/index.html.

Kowitt, Beth. "Inside Google's Civil War." *Fortune*, May 17, 2019. https:// fortune.com/longform/inside-googles-civil-war/.

Kramer, Jillian. "9 Incredible Companies for Working Women." Glassdoor, March 3, 2020. www.glassdoor.co.uk/blog/9-incredible-companies -for-working-women/.

Kutcher, Eric, Olivia Nottebohm, and Kara Sprague. "Grow Fast or Die Slow." McKinsey & Company, April 2, 2014. www.mckinsey.com/industries /high-tech/our-insights/grow-fast-or-die-slow.

Laboissiere, Martha, and Mona Mourshed. "Closing the Skills Gap: Creating Workforce-Development Programs That Work for Everyone." McKinsey & Company, February 13, 2017. www.mckinsey.com/industries/public -and-social-sector/our-insights/closing-the-skills-gap-creating-workforce -development-programs-that-work-for-everyone.

Lazard Shareholder Advisory Group. Memo to Lazard employees, July 8, 2019.

LEAD on Climate 2020. "2019 Participating Companies." www.leadoncarbon pricing.com/participating-companies/.

Leaf, Clifton. "The 2019 Fortune 500 List: The Prize of Size." *Fortune*, May 16, 2019. https://fortune.com/longform/fortune-500-2019-covers/.

Leiter, Michael E., Katie Clarke, and Joe Molosky. "US Finalizes CFIUS Reform: What It Means for Dealmakers and Foreign Investment." Skadden, Arps, Slate, Meagher & Flom LLP, August 6, 2018. www.skadden.com/insights /publications/2018/08/us-finalizes-cfius-reform.

Lerner, Diane. "Board of Directors Compensation: Past, Present and Future." *Harvard Law School Forum on Corporate Governance*, March 14, 2017. https://corpgov.law.harvard.edu/2017/03/14/board-of-directors-compensation -past-present-and-future/.

Levin, Sam. "Uber's Scandals, Blunders and PR Disasters: The Full List." *The Guardian*, June 28, 2017. www.theguardian.com/technology/2017/jun/18 /uber-travis-kalanick-scandal-pr-disaster-timeline.

Lewis, Leo, and Kana Inagaki. "Carlos Ghosn's Downfall Lays Bare Nissan's Board Problem." *Financial Times*, November 23, 2018. www.ft.com /content/f5bc49c0-ee47-11e8-89c8-d36339d835c0.

Li, Jun-Sheng. "How Amazon Took 50% of the E-commerce Market and What It Means for the Rest of Us." *Techcrunch*, February 27, 2019. https:// techcrunch.com/2019/02/27/how-amazon-took-50-of-the-e-commerce -market-and-what-it-means-for-the-rest-of-us/.

License and Tax Administration. "Sweetened Beverage Tax." Seattle.gov. www.seattle.gov/business-licensing-and-taxes/business-license-tax/other -seattle-taxes/sweetened-beverage-tax.

Lin, Jessica, and Ruqayyah Moyinhan. "Job Roles Are Dramatically Chang- ing Now Machines Are Here. These Are 21 Jobs Humans May Soon Be Doing Instead." *Business Insider*, October 27, 2018. www.businessinsider .com/here-are-the-21-jobs-you-may-be-doing-in-10-years-now-robots-are -here-2018-10.

Lipton, Martin. "Corporate Purpose: Stakeholders and Long-Term Growth." *Harvard Law School Forum on Corporate Governance*, May 29, 2019. https://corpgov.law.harvard.edu/2019/05/29/corporate-purpose-stakeholders -and-long-term-growth/.

———. "The New Paradigm and the EU Shareholder Rights Directive II." *Harvard Law School Forum on Corporate Governance*, May 11, 2019. https://corpgov

.law.harvard.edu/2019/05/11/the-new-paradigm-and-the-eu-shareholder-rights -directive-ii/.

———. "Some Thoughts for Boards of Directors in 2019." *Harvard Law School Forum on Corporate Governance*, December 14, 2018. https://corpgov.law .harvard.edu/2018/12/14/some-thoughts-for-boards-of-directors-in-2019/.

Lipton, Martin, and William Savitt. "Directors' Duties in an Evolving Risk and Governance Landscape." *Harvard Law School Forum on Corporate Governance*, September 19, 2019. https://corpgov.law.harvard.edu/2019/09/19 /directors-duties-in-an-evolving-risk-and-governance-landscape/.

———. "Stakeholder Governance—Some Legal Points." *Harvard Law School Forum on Corporate Governance*, September 20, 2019. https://corpgov.law .harvard.edu/2019/09/20/stakeholder-governance-some-legal-points/.

The Local. "France Telecom's Ex-Boss Faces Court over String of Staff Suicides." May 8, 2019. www.thelocal.fr/20190508/france-telecoms-ex-boss -faces-court-over-string-of-staff-suicides.

Magnusson, Niklas. "Ingvar Kamprad, Ikea's Swedish Billionaire Founder, Dies at 91." Bloomberg, January 28, 2018. www.bloomberg.com/news /articles/2018-01-28/ingvar-kamprad-ikea-s-swedish-billionaire-founder -has-died.

Mainwaring, Simon. "Purpose at Work: How Chobani Builds a Purposeful Culture Around Social Impact." *Forbes*, August 27, 2018. www.forbes.com /sites/simonmainwaring/2018/08/27/how-chobani-builds-a-purposeful -culture-around-social-impact/#42c6a14720f7.

Marcec, Dan. "CEO Tenure Rates." *Harvard Law School Forum on Corporate Governance*, February 12, 2018. https://corpgov.law.harvard.edu/2018 /02/12/ceo-tenure-rates/.

Massa, Annie. "Index Funds to Overtake Active in U.S. by 2021, Moody's Says." Bloomberg, March 14, 2019. www.bloomberg.com/news/articles/2019-03 -14/index-funds-to-pass-stock-pickers-in-u-s-by-2021-moody-s-says.

Matsui, Kathy, Hiromi Suzuki, Kazunori Tatebe, and Tsumugi Akiba. *Womenomics 4.0: Time to Walk the Talk*. New York: Goldman Sachs, 2014. www .goldmansachs.com/insights/pages/macroeconomic-insights-folder/women omics4-folder/womenomics4-time-to-walk-the-talk.pdf.

McCabe, Patrick. "The Shift from Active to Passive Investing: Potential Risks to Financial Stability?" *Harvard Law School Forum on Corporate Governance*, November 29, 2018. https://corpgov.law.harvard.edu/2018/11/29 /the-shift-from-active-to-passive-investing-potential-risks-to-financial -stability/.

McCarthy, Niall. "The Best and Worst Countries for Democracy [Infographic]." *Forbes*, February 1, 2018. www.forbes.com/sites/niallmccarthy/2018/02/01 /the-best-and-worst-countries-for-democracy-infographic/#605a21ac3fff.

McGeehan, Patrick, and Andrew Ross Sorkin. "Swiss Bank Is Acquiring PaineWebber." *New York Times*, July 12, 2000. www.nytimes.com/2000/07/12/business/swiss-bank-is-acquiring-painewebber.html.

McGovern, Patrick, Stephen Hill, Colin Mills, and Michael White. *Market, Class, and Employment*. New York: Oxford University Press, 2008.

McGrath, Maggie, ed. "The Just 100." *Forbes*, 2020. www.forbes.com/just-companies/#363c0e1a2bf0.

McGregor, Jena. "Corporate Boards Are Still Mostly White, Mostly Male—and Getting Even Older." *Washington Post*, April 24, 2018. www.washingtonpost.com/news/on-leadership/wp/2018/04/24/corporate-boards-are-still-mostly-white-mostly-male-and-getting-even-older/.

McKinsey & Company. "Working Across Many Cultures at Western Union." January 26, 2018. www.mckinsey.com/industries/financial-services/our-insights/working-across-many-cultures-at-western-union.

McKinsey Global Institute. *Globalization in Transition: The Future of Trade and Value Chains*. New York: McKinsey & Company, 2019.

McNabb, William F., III. "An Open Letter to Directors of Public Companies Worldwide." Vanguard, August 31, 2017. https://global.vanguard.com/documents/investment-stewardship-mcnabb-letter.pdf.

Meade, Amanda. "Coal Not So 'Amazing,' Public Say, as Mining Industry Advertising Backfires." *The Guardian*, November 6, 2015. www.theguardian.com/environment/2015/nov/06/coal-not-so-amazing-public-say-as-mining-industry-advertising-backfires.

Mejia, Zameena. "Just 24 Female CEOs Lead the Companies on the 2018 Fortune 500—Fewer Than Last Year." CNBC *Make It*, May 21, 2018. www.cnbc.com/2018/05/21/2018s-fortune-500-companies-have-just-24-female-ceos.html.

Merrick, Rob. "Philip Hammond Accused of Trying to Kill Off Landmark Action on Global Warming by Claiming Bill Will Top £1 Trillion." *Independent*, June 6, 2019. www.independent.co.uk/news/uk/politics/climate-change-global-warming-crisis-philip-hammond-uk-2050-a8947011.html.

Michaels, Ed, Helen Handfield-Jones, and Beth Axelrod. *The War for Talent*. Boston: Harvard Business School Publishing, 2001.

Microsoft. "TEALS Program." www.tealsk12.org.

Miller, Claire Cain. "How a Common Interview Question Hurts Women." *New York Times*, May 1, 2018. www.nytimes.com/2018/05/01/upshot/how-a-common-interview-question-fuels-the-gender-pay-gap-and-how-to-stop-it.html.

Milt, David Jinks. *2030: The Death of the High Street*. Brentford, UK: ParcelHero, 2017. www.parcelhero.com/content/downloads/pdfs/high-street/deathofthehighstreetreport.pdf.

Minghui, Ren. "Ending the Epidemics of High-Impact Communicable Diseases." World Health Organization, October 1, 2018. www.who.int/news-room/commentaries/detail/ending-the-epidemics-of-high-impact-communicable-diseases.

Mishel, Lawrence, and Jessica Schieder. "CEO Compensation Surged in 2017." Economic Policy Institute, August 16, 2018. www.epi.org/publication/ceo-compensation-surged-in-2017/.

Mole, Beth. "'Is Curing Patients a Sustainable Business Model?' Goldman Sachs Analysts Ask." *Ars Technica*, April 12, 2018. https://arstechnica.com/tech-policy/2018/04/curing-disease-not-a-sustainable-business-model-goldman-sachs-analysts-say/.

Moritz, Michael. "China Is Winning the Global Tech Race." *Financial Times*, June 17, 2018. www.ft.com/content/3530f178-6e50-11e8-8863-a9bb262c5f53.

———. "Silicon Valley Would Be Wise to Follow China's Lead." *Financial Times*, January 17, 2018. www.ft.com/content/42daca9e-facc-11e7-9bfc-052cbba03425.

Morrison, Nick. "Rapid Technological Change Is the Biggest Threat to Global Business." *Forbes*, February 9, 2017. www.forbes.com/sites/nickmorrison/2017/02/09/donald-trump-is-not-the-biggest-threat-to-global-business/#601e2b971b73.

Morse, Gardiner. "Designing a Bias-Free Organization." *Harvard Business Review*, July–August 2016. https://hbr.org/2016/07/designing-a-bias-free-organization.

Mortimer, Caroline. "Socialism 'More Popular' with British Public Than Capitalism, Survey Finds." *Independent*, February 24, 2016. www.independent.co.uk/news/uk/politics/socialism-is-more-popular-with-the-british-public-than-capitalism-survey-finds-a6892371.html.

Moskin, Julia, Brad Plumer, Rebecca Lieberman, and Eden Weingart. "Your Questions About Food and Climate Change, Answered." *New York Times*, April 30, 2019. www.nytimes.com/interactive/2019/04/30/dining/climate-change-food-eating-habits.html.

Moving Toward Gender Balance in Private Equity and Venture Capital. Washington, DC: International Finance Corporation, 2019. www.ifc.org/wps/wcm/connect/79e641c9-824f-4bd8-9f1c-00579862fed3/Moving+Toward+Gender+Balance+Final_3_22.pdf?MOD=AJPERES&CVID=mCBJFra.

Moyer, Liz. "Lazard Tightens the Reins on Pay." *Wall Street Journal*, March 15, 2013. www.wsj.com/articles/SB10001424127887324532004578362260143944882.

———. "Warren Buffett and Jamie Dimon Join Forces to Convince CEOs to End Quarterly Profit Forecasts." CNBC, June 6, 2018. www.cnbc.com/2018/06/06/warren-buffett-and-jamie-dimon-join-forces-to-convince-ceos-to-end-quarterly-profit-forecasts.html.

Moyo, Dambisa. "Does Your Board Need a Tech Expert?" *Harvard Business Review*, March 10, 2016. https://hbr.org/2016/03/does-your-board -need-a-tech-expert.

Murray, Alan. "Google and Huawei, Trump Allegations, Iran Threat: CEO Daily for May 20, 2019." Yahoo Finance, May 20, 2019. https://finance .yahoo.com/news/google-huawei-trump-allegations-iran-105513717.html.

Murray, Alan, and David Meyer. "Amazon HQ2, Iran Sanctions, Xi vs Trump: CEO Daily for November 5, 2018." *Fortune*, November 5, 2018. https://fortune.com/2018/11/05/amazon-hq2-iran-sanctions-xi-trump -ceo-daily-for-november-5-2018/.

———. "China Slumps, Pinterest Drops, Bitcoin Plunges: CEO Daily for May 17, 2019." *Fortune*, May 17, 2019. https://fortune.com/2019/05/17 /china-pinterest-bitcoin-ceo-daily-for-may-17-2019/.

———. "China Talks, Nuclear Deal, Boeing Safety: CEO Daily for May 9, 2019." *Fortune*, May 9, 2019. https://fortune.com/2019/05/09/china -talks-iran-nuclear-boeing-safety-ceo-daily-for-may-9-2019/.

———. "Huawei Order, Trump Pardon, PG&E Fire: CEO Daily for May 16, 2019." *Fortune*, May 16, 2019. https://fortune.com/2019/05/16 /huawei-order-trump-pge-fire-ceo-daily-for-may-16-2019/.

———. "The Limits of Employee Activism: CEO Daily." *Fortune*, June 27, 2019. https://fortune.com/2019/06/27/the-limits-of-employee-activism-ceo-daily/.

———. "Why We Need to Retrain the C-Suite: CEO Daily." *Fortune*, June 5, 2019. https://fortune.com/2019/06/05/why-we-need-to-retrain-the-c-suite-ceo -daily/.

Neate, Rupert, and Angela Monaghan. "Persimmon Boss Asked to Leave Amid Outrage over Bonus." *The Guardian*, November 7, 2018. www .theguardian.com/business/2018/nov/07/persimmon-boss-asked-to-leave -amid-ongoing-outrage-over-bonus.

New York Times. "The Dot-Com Bubble Bursts." December 24, 2000. www .nytimes.com/2000/12/24/opinion/the-dot-com-bubble-bursts.html.

New York Times. "Explaining Greece's Debt Crisis." June 17, 2016. www nytimes.com/interactive/2016/business/international/greece-debt-crisis -euro.html.

NFL. "NFL Expands Rooney Rule Requirements to Strengthen Diversity." December 12, 2018. www.nfl.com/news/story/0ap3000000999110/article/nfl -expands-rooney-rule-requirements-to-strengthen-diversity.

Noland, Marcus, and Tyler Moran. "Study: Firms with More Women in the C-Suite Are More Profitable." *Harvard Business Review*, February 8, 2016. https://hbr.org/2016/02/study-firms-with-more-women-in-the-c-suite-are -more-profitable.

Nzima, Simiso, Daniel Bienvenue, Beth Richtman, and Theodore Eliopoulos. "Corporate Board Diversity Update." Investment Committee. CalPERS, agenda item 9c, June 18, 2018. www.calpers.ca.gov/docs/board-agendas /201806/invest/item09c-00_a.pdf.

O'Brien, Sara Ashley. "WeWork Is Banning Meat." CNN Business, July 13, 2018. https://money.cnn.com/2018/07/13/technology/wework-meat-ban/index .html.

OECD. "Inflation (CPI)." OECD iLibrary. https://doi.org/10.1787/eee82e6e-en.

O'Kelley, Jack "Rusty," and Melissa Martin. "Global and Regional Trends in Corporate Governance for 2018." Russell Reynolds Associates, December 8, 2018. www.russellreynolds.com/insights/thought-leadership/global -and-regional-trends-in-corporate-governance-for-2018.

O'Kelley, Rusty, Anthony Goodman, and Melissa Martin. "2019 Global & Regional Trends in Corporate Governance." *Harvard Law School Forum on Corporate Governance*, December 30, 2018. https://corpgov.law.harvard .edu/2018/12/30/2019-global-regional-trends-in-corporate-governance/.

Olivetti, Claudia, and Barbara Petrongolo. "The Economic Consequences of Family Policies: Lessons from a Century of Legislation in High-Income Countries." *Journal of Economic Perspectives* 31, no. 1 (2017): 205–230. https://doi.org/10.1257/jep.31.1.205.

Olson, Nels, and Jane Stevenson. "Diverse Boards: Do They Deadlock More?" Korn Ferry, May 17, 2018. www.kornferry.com/institute/diverse-boards-do -they-deadlock-more.

Oppel, Richard A., Jr., and Andrew Ross Sorkin. "Enron's Collapse: The Overview; Enron Corp. Files Largest U.S. Claim for Bankruptcy." *New York Times*, December 3, 2001. www.nytimes.com/2001/12/03/business/enron-s -collapse-the-overview-enron-corp-files-largest-us-claim-for-bankruptcy .html.

Owles, Eric. "The Making of Martin Shkreli as 'Pharma Bro.'" *DealBook* (blog). *New York Times*, June 22, 2017. www.nytimes.com/2017/06/22/business /dealbook/martin-shkreli-pharma-bro-drug-prices.html.

Oxfam. "The Robin Hood Tax: The Time Is Now." News release, June 19, 2011. www.oxfam.de/sites/default/files/webfm/ftt_oxfam_media_brief_final _english_version_20110617.pdf.

Paradigm for Parity. "The 5-Point Action Plan." www.paradigm4parity.com /solution.

Parker, John. *Beyond One by '21: A Report into the Ethnic Diversity of UK Boards*. London: Parker Review Committee, 2017. https://assets.ey.com /content/dam/ey-sites/ey-com/en_uk/news/2020/02/ey-parker-review-2017 -report-final.pdf.

Parmelee, Michele. "The Workforce of the Future: The Skills Challenge Becomes More Apparent." *Forbes*, January 22, 2019. www.forbes.com/sites

/deloitte/2019/01/22/the-workforce-of-the-future-the-skills-challenge
-becomes-more-apparent/#63a44c761ea8.

Perry, Mark J. "Fortune 500 Firms 1955 v. 2017: Only 60 Remain, Thanks to the
Creative Destruction That Fuels Economic Prosperity." *Carpe Diem* (blog).
American Enterprise Institute, October 20, 2017. www.aei.org/publication
/fortune-500-firms-1955-v-2017-only-12-remain-thanks-to-the-creative
-destruction-that-fuels-economic-prosperity/.

Petroff, Alanna. "These Countries Want to Ban Gas and Diesel Cars." CNN
Business, September 11, 2017. https://money.cnn.com/2017/09/11/autos
/countries-banning-diesel-gas-cars/index.html.

Pichai, Sundar. "Google's Sundar Pichai: Privacy Should Not Be a Luxury Good."
New York Times, May 7, 2019. www.nytimes.com/2019/05/07/opinion
/google-sundar-pichai-privacy.html.

Plan Climat. Paris: Ministère de la transition écologique et solidaire, 2017.
www.ecologique-solidaire.gouv.fr/sites/default/files/2017.07.06%20-%20
Plan%20Climat_0.pdf.

Plat, Eric, and James Fontanella-Khan. "Bristol-Myers Squibb Defends Celgene
Takeover as 'Best Path.'" *Financial Times*, March 6, 2019. www.ft.com
/content/d6f391dc-401e-11e9-b896-fe36ec32aece.

Pledge to Fly Less. https://pledgetoflyless.co.uk.

Pollack, Andrew. "Theranos, Facing Criticism, Says It Has Changed Board Structure." *New York Times*, October 28, 2015. www.nytimes.com/2015/10/29
/business/theranos-facing-criticism-says-it-has-changed-board-structure
.html.

Poore, J., and T. Nemecek. "Reducing Food's Environmental Impacts Through
Producers and Consumers." *Science* 360, no. 6392 (2018): 987–992. https://
science.sciencemag.org/content/360/6392/987/tab-article-info.

Porter, Eduardo. "Japanese Cars, American Retirees." *New York Times*, May
19, 2006. www.nytimes.com/2006/05/19/automobiles/19auto.html.

Posner, Cydney. "The SEC's Current End Game on Proxy Advisory Firms." *Harvard Law School Forum on Corporate Governance*, April 26, 2019. https://
corpgov.law.harvard.edu/2019/04/26/the-secs-current-end-game-on-proxy
-advisory-firms/.

Powell, Andrew. "NEET: Young People Not in Education, Employment or Training." Briefing Paper SN 06705, House of Commons Library, London, UK,
August 24, 2018. http://researchbriefings.files.parliament.uk/documents/SN
06705/SN06705.pdf.

Pozen, Robert C. "What GE's Board Could Have Done Differently." *Harvard
Business Review*, July 17, 2018. https://hbr.org/2018/07/what-ges-board
-could-have-done-differently.

Pratley, Nils. "Theresa May's Plan to Put Workers in Boardrooms Is Extraordinary." *The Guardian*, July 11, 2016. www.theguardian.com/politics/nils -pratley-on-finance/2016/jul/11/theresa-may-plan-workers-boardroom -reform-extraordinary-tories.

Preparing for the 2019 Proxy Season: Practical Guidance for Directors and Board Committees. New York: Sullivan & Cromwell LLP, 2018. www .sullcrom.com/files/upload/SC-Publication-Practical-Guidance-for-the-2019 -Proxy-Season.pdf.

Pring, Ben, Robert H. Brown, Euan Davis, Manish Bahl, Michael Cook, Caroline Styr, and Desmond Dickerson. *21 More Jobs of the Future*. Teaneck, NJ: Cognizant, 2018. www.cognizant.com/whitepapers/21-more-jobs-of -the-future-a-guide-to-getting-and-staying-employed-through-2029 -codex3928.pdf.

Purpose & Progress: 2017 Environmental, Social, and Governance Report. New York: Goldman Sachs, 2017. www.goldmansachs.com/citizenship /sustainability-reporting/esg-content/esg-report-2017.pdf.

PwC Governance Insights Center and Spencer Stuart. *Getting Real Value from Board Assessments*. New York: PwC, 2017. www.pwc.com/us/en/governance -insights-center/publications/assets/pwc-getting-real-value-from-board -assessments.pdf.

Quance, Stephen. *Invesco Global Factor Investing Study 2018*. Atlanta, GA: Invesco, 2018. https://apinstitutional.invesco.com/dam/jcr:4526a7ee-2da9 -4f0f-a873-d96d13857d26/Factor-Investing_20181105_Invesco-Global-Factor -Investing-Study-2018.pdf.

Rajgopal, Shivaram. "Why Corporate Culture Is Hard." Columbia Business School, January 2, 2019. www8.gsb.columbia.edu/articles/ideas-work /why-corporate-culture-hard.

Rapp, Nicolas, and Brian O'Keefe. "See the Age of Every Company in the Fortune 500." *Fortune*, May 21, 2018. https://fortune.com/longform /fortune-500-through-the-ages/.

Raval, Anjli. "Shell Says Firm Carbon Emissions Targets Are 'Superfluous.'" *Financial Times*, July 5, 2018. www.ft.com/content/2851210a-8064-11e8 -bc55-50daf11b720d.

Recode. "Full Video and Transcript: Diversity in Tech Panel at Code 2018." June 11, 2018. www.vox.com/2018/6/9/17397178/full-transcript-diversity-women -tech-megan-smith-sukhinder-singh-cassidy-aileen-lee-panel-code-2018.

Reichheld, Frederick F. "The One Number You Need to Grow." *Harvard Business Review*, December 2003. https://hbr.org/2003/12/the-one-number -you-need-to-grow.

Reidmiller, D. R., C. W. Avery, D. R. Easterling, K. E. Kunkel, K. L. M. Lewis, T. K. Maycock, and B. C. Stewart, eds. *Fourth National Climate Assessment*.

Vol. 2. *Impacts, Risks, and Adaptation in the United States*. Washington, DC: US Global Change Research Program, 2018. https://nca2018.global change.gov.

Relihan, Tom. "4 Red Flags That Signaled Theranos' Downfall." MIT Management Sloan School, October 29, 2018. https://mitsloan.mit.edu/ideas -made-to-matter/4-red-flags-signaled-theranos-downfall.

Research in Motion. "Research in Motion Reports Year-End and Fourth Quarter Results for Fiscal 2012." News release, March 29, 2012. www.globenews wire.com/news-release/2012/03/29/1430818/0/en/Research-In-Motion-Reports -Year-End-and-Fourth-Quarter-Results-for-Fiscal-2012.html.

Reuters. "China Studying When to Ban Sales of Traditional Fuel Cars: Xinhua." September 10, 2017. www.reuters.com/article/us-china-autos/china-studying -when-to-ban-sales-of-traditional-fuel-cars-xinhua-idUSKCN1BL01U.

Reuters. "Government Says May Use Public Interest Test in Pfizer Bid for AstraZeneca." May 6, 2014. https://uk.reuters.com/article/uk-pfizerastra zeneca-cable/government-says-may-use-public-interest-test-in-pfizer -bid-for-astrazeneca-idUKKBN0DM17A20140506.

Reuters. "Trump Blocks Singapore-Based Broadcom's Takeover of Qualcomm, Citing National Security Concerns." *Straits Times*, March 13, 2018. www.straitstimes.com/business/trump-signs-order-prohibiting-broadcom -takeover-of-qualcomm.

Ries, Tonia E., David M. Bersoff, Sarah Adkins, Cody Armstrong, and Jamis Bruening. *2018 Edelman Trust Barometer: Global Report*. Chicago, IL: Edelman, 2018. www.edelman.com/sites/g/files/aatuss191/files/2018-10/2018 _Edelman_Trust_Barometer_Global_Report_FEB.pdf.

Riffkin, Rebecca. "For First Time, Majority in U.S. Oppose Nuclear Energy." Gallup, March 18, 2016. https://news.gallup.com/poll/190064/first-time -majority-oppose-nuclear-energy.aspx.

Ritchie, Hannah. "Number of People in the World Without Electricity Falls Below One Billion." *Our World in Data*, January 18, 2019. https://our worldindata.org/number-of-people-in-the-world-without-electricity-access -falls-below-one-billion#note-1.

Rosenblum, Steven A., Karessa L. Cain, and Sabastian V. Niles, eds. *NYSE: Corporate Governance Guide*. London: White Page Ltd., 2014. www.nyse .com/publicdocs/nyse/listing/NYSE_Corporate_Governance_Guide.pdf.

Rosner, Max. "Democracy." *Our World in Data*. Last modified June 2019. https://ourworldindata.org/democracy.

Roumeliotis, Greg. "U.S. Blocks MoneyGram Sale to China's Ant Financial on National Security Concerns." Reuters, January 4, 2018. https://uk.reuters.com /article/uk-moneygram-intl-m-a-ant-financial/u-s-blocks-moneygram-sale -to-chinas-ant-financial-on-national-security-concerns-idUKKBN1ET03A.

S&P Dow Jones Indices. "S&P 500 Foreign Sales for 2017 Total 43.6%." News release, August 16, 2018. https://us.spindices.com/documents/index-news-and-announcements/20180816-sp-500-global-sales-2017.pdf.

Saba, Jennifer. "Driving Change." *Breaking Views* (blog). Reuters, July 15, 2019. www.breakingviews.com/considered-view/uber-adds-useful-numbers-to-solve-gender-equation.

Saiz, Milagros Rivas. "More Than One Billion People Do Not Have Access to Electricity. What Will It Take to Get Them Connected?" World Economic Forum, August 14, 2018. www.weforum.org/agenda/2018/08/milagros-rivas-saiz-electricity-access-sdg7/.

Samuels, Simon. "Investors Must Allow Companies to Focus on the Long Term." *Financial Times*, July 8, 2018. www.ft.com/content/6105a8a0-8068-11e8-af48-190d103e32a4.

Sarbanes-Oxley Act of 2002. H.R. 3763. 107th Cong. (2002). www.govtrack.us/congress/bills/107/hr3763/text/ih.

Savitz, Eric. "CEO's 'Burning Platform' Memo Highlights Nokia's Woes." *Forbes*, February 9, 2011. www.forbes.com/sites/ericsavitz/2011/02/09/ceos-burning-platform-memo-highlights-nokias-woes/#571df23e8296.

Schroders. "Schroders Supports Embankment Project for Inclusive Capitalism's Sustainable Growth Drivers." News release, November 20, 2018. www.schroders.com/en/media-relations/newsroom/all_news_releases/schroders-supports-embankment-project-for-inclusive-capitalisms-sustainable-growth-drivers/.

Schulman, Dan. "Growth Headwinds." KPMG. https://home.kpmg/uk/en/home/insights/2018/05/uk-ceo-outlook-survey-2018/strategic-issues-facing-uk-ceos-in-2018.html.

Securities and Exchange Commission v. David P. Levine, Michael W. Spake, Barry S. Berlin, and Douglas J. Ely. (E.D. Mich., 2005). www.sec.gov/litigation/complaints/comp19353.pdf.

Seddon-Daines, Olivia, and Yasmine Chinwala. *Diversity from an Investor's Perspective*. London: New Financial, 2017. https://newfinancial.org/wp-content/uploads/2017/10/Diversity_from_investor_perspective_FINAL.pdf.

Shane, Daniel. "Trump Renews Attack on TPP: 'I Don't Like the Deal.'" CNN Business, April 18, 2018. https://money.cnn.com/2018/04/18/news/economy/trump-tpp-trade-deal-tweet/index.html.

Sheetz, Michael. "Star Analyst Is Getting Pushback from Clients on His Negative GE Takes, but He Doesn't Care." CNBC, June 24, 2019. www.cnbc.com/2019/06/24/jp-morgan-analyst-stephen-tusa-pushback-on-general-electric-skepticism.html.

Shi, Lin, Laurens Swinkels, and Fieke van der Lecq. "Board Diversity and Self-Regulation in Dutch Pension Funds." *Equality, Diversity, and Inclusion* (forthcoming). https://ssrn.com/abstract=2671534.

Silcoff, Sean, Jacquie McNish, and Steve Ladurantaye. "How BlackBerry Blew It: The Inside Story." *Globe and Mail*, September 27, 2013. www.the globeandmail.com/report-on-business/the-inside-story-of-why-blackberry -is-failing/article14563602/.

Sky News. "One Third of Brits Cutting Down on Meat, Waitrose Survey Finds." November 1, 2018. https://news.sky.com/story/one-third-of-brits -cutting-down-on-meat-waitrose-survey-finds-11541513.

Slater, Steve. "Activist Sherborne Snaps Up 5% of Barclays." Reuters, March 19, 2018. https://uk.reuters.com/article/activist-sherborne-snaps-up-5-of-barclay /activist-sherborne-snaps-up-5-of-barclays-idUKL8N1R12YQ.

Smith, Genevieve. *The Business Case for Gender Diversity*. Washington, DC: International Center for Research on Women, 2017. www.icrw.org/wp -content/uploads/2017/10/Advisors-The-Business-Case-for-Gender- Diversity.pdf.

Solheim, Erik. "Time to Retire Unsustainable Pensions." UN Environment Pro- gramme, June 25, 2018. www.unenvironment.org/news-and-stories/story /time-retire-unsustainable-pensions.

Solving the Talent Shortage. Milwaukee, WI: ManpowerGroup, 2018. https:// go.manpowergroup.com/hubfs/TalentShortage%202018%20(Global)%20 Assets/PDFs/MG_TalentShortage2018_lo%206_25_18_FINAL.pdf.

Somerville, Heather. "Chinese Tech Investors Flee Silicon Valley as Trump Tightens Scrutiny." Reuters, January 7, 2019. https://uk.reuters.com/article /uk-venture-china-regulation-insight/chinese-tech-investors-flee-silicon-valley -as-trump-tightens-scrutiny-idUKKCN1P10CA.

Sonnenfeld, Jeffery A. "What Makes Great Boards Great." *Harvard Busi- ness Review*, September 2002. https://hbr.org/2002/09/what-makes-great -boards-great.

Sorkin, Andrew Ross, and Floyd Norris. "Hewlett-Packard in Deal to Buy Compaq for $25 Billion in Stock." *New York Times*, September 4, 2001. www.nytimes.com/2001/09/04/business/hewlett-packard-in-deal-to-buy -compaq-for-25-billion-in-stock.html.

Souster, Robert. *Corporate Governance: The Board of Directors and Stand- ing Committees*. Glasgow, Scotland: ACCA, 2012. www.accaglobal.com /content/dam/acca/global/PDF-students/2012s/sa_oct12-f1fab_governance.pdf.

Stalter, Kate. "Why the Hot New ETF May Not Be a Great Idea." *Forbes*, August 29, 2018. www.forbes.com/sites/katestalter/2018/08/29/why-the-hot -new-etf-may-not-be-a-great-idea/#373a9c174753.

Stansbury, Anna, and Lawrence H. Summers. "What Marco Rubio Gets Right— and Wrong—About the Decline of American Investment." *Larry Summers* (blog), May 31, 2019. http://larrysummers.com/2019/05/31/what-marco -rubio-gets-right-and-wrong-about-the-decline-of-american-investment/.

Stary, Kate. "Gender Diversity Quotas on Australian Boards: Is It in the Best Interest of the Company?" Student research paper, University of Melbourne, 2015.

State of the Global Workplace. New York: Gallup, 2018. www.gallup.com /workplace/238079/state-global-workplace-2017.aspx#formheader.

Strauss, Karsten. "McDonald's Faces New Sexual Harassment Accusations." *Forbes*, May 22, 2019. www.forbes.com/sites/karstenstrauss/2019/05/22 /mcdonalds-faces-new-sexual-harassment-accusations/#6855c7707909.

———. "The Most Sustainable Companies in 2019." *Forbes*, January 22, 2019. www.forbes.com/sites/karstenstrauss/2019/01/22/the-most-sustainable -companies-in-2019/#7364287d6d7d.

Streitfeld, David, and Jodi Kantor. "Jeff Bezos and Amazon Employees Join Debate over Its Culture." *New York Times*, August 17, 2015. www.nytimes .com/2015/08/18/technology/amazon-bezos-workplace-management-practices. html.

Summers, Lawrence H. "Wells Fargo's Board Members Are Getting Off Too Easily." *Larry Summers* (blog), February 6, 2018. http://larrysummers.com /2018/02/06/wells-fargos-board-members-are-getting-off-too-easily/.

Sun, Mengqi. "More U.S. Companies Separating Chief Executive and Chairman Roles." *Wall Street Journal*, January 23, 2019. www.wsj.com/articles /more-u-s-companies-separating-chief-executive-and-chairman-roles -11548288502.

Taking the Right Approach to Ethnicity Pay Gap Reporting. New York: PwC, 2019. www.pwc.co.uk/human-resource-services/assets/pdfs/ethnicity-pay-gap -report.pdf.

Taraporevala, Cyrus. "2019 Proxy Letter—Aligning Corporate Culture with Long-Term Strategy." *Harvard Law School Forum on Corporate Governance*, January 15, 2019. https://corpgov.law.harvard.edu/2019/01/15/2019 -proxy-letter-aligning-corporate-culture-with-long-term-strategy/.

Tasfaye, Mekebeb. "IMF Head Christine Lagarde Warns of the Dangers of Big Tech's Push into Finance." *Business Insider*, June 11, 2019. www.business insider.com/imf-head-christine-lagarde-warns-big-tech-in-finance-2019-6.

Task Force on Climate-Related Financial Disclosures. "About the Task Force." www.fsb-tcfd.org/about/#.

Tax Policies for Inclusive Growth in a Changing World. Paris: OECD, 2018. www.oecd.org/g20/Tax-policies-for-inclusive-growth-in-a-changing-world -OECD.pdf.

Telford, Taylor, and Steven Mufson. "PG&E, the Nation's Biggest Utility Company, Files for Bankruptcy After California Wildfires." *Washington Post*, January 29, 2019. www.washingtonpost.com/business/2019/01/29/pge -nations-biggest-utility-company-files-bankruptcy-after-california-wildfires/.

Temin and Company. "Temin's #MeToo Research—In the Media This Week." In the News. www.teminandcompany.com/in-the-news/2536-temin-s-metoo -research-in-the-media-this-week.

30% Club. "United Kingdom." https://30percentclub.org/about/chapters/united -kingdom.

Thomas, Daniel. "European Financial Services Leads Charge on Women Directors." *Financial Times*, July 4, 2019. www.ft.com/content/ca623700 -9d95-11e9-9c06-a4640c9feebb.

Thomas, Jason M. "Where Have All the Public Companies Gone?" *Wall Street Journal*, November 16, 2017. www.wsj.com/articles/where-have-all -the-public-companies-gone-1510869125.

Thomas, Katie, and Reed Abelson. "Elizabeth Holmes, Theranos C.E.O. and Silicon Valley Star, Accused of Fraud." *New York Times*, March 14, 2018. www.nytimes.com/2018/03/14/health/theranos-elizabeth-holmes-fraud .html.

Thomas, Lauren. "These Are the Only Women CEOs Left Among S&P 500 Companies." CNBC, August 6, 2018. www.cnbc.com/2018/08/06/these-are -the-only-women-ceos-left-among-sp-500-companies.html.

Thomson Reuters. "Chairman Clayton: Companies Should Provide More Disclosure on Human Capital Management." May 6, 2019. https://tax .thomsonreuters.com/news/chairman-clayton-companies-should-provide -more-disclosure-on-human-capital-management/.

Thorndike, William, Jr. *The Outsiders: Eight Unconventional CEOs and Their Radically Rational Blueprint for Success.* Boston: Harvard Business School Publishing, 2012.

350.org. "About 350." https://350.org/about/.

Tibken, Shara. "Tim Cook Says Some Tech Regulation Likely Needs to Happen." *CNET*, October 2, 2018. www.cnet.com/news/tim-cook-talks -privacy-regulation-congress-alex-jones-china-during-interview/.

Tonello, Matteo. "Separation of Chair and CEO Roles." *Harvard Law School Forum on Corporate Governance*, September 1, 2001. https://corpgov .law.harvard.edu/2011/09/01/separation-of-chair-and-ceo-roles/.

Townsend, Solitaire. "88% of Consumers Want You to Help Them Make a Difference." *Forbes*, November 21, 2018. www.forbes.com/sites/solitaire townsend/2018/11/21/consumers-want-you-to-help-them-make-a-difference /#309b2d546954.

Tran, Mark. "WorldCom Accounting Scandal." *The Guardian*, August 9, 2002. www.theguardian.com/business/2002/aug/09/corporatefraud.worldcom2.

Treasurer and Tax Collector. "Sugary Drinks Tax." City and County of San Francisco. https://sftreasurer.org/sugary-drinks-tax.

Trichet, Jean-Claude. "The Financial Crisis and the Response of the ECB." Speech given at ceremony conferring the honorary title of doctor honoris causa, University of National and World Economy, Sofia, Bulgaria, June 12, 2009. www.ecb.europa.eu/press/key/date/2009/html/sp090612.en.html.

Trump, Donald (@realDonaldTrump). "In speaking with some of the world's top business leaders I asked what it is that would make business (jobs) even better in the U.S. 'Stop quarterly reporting & go to a six month system,' said one. That would allow greater flexibility & save money. I have asked the SEC to study!" Twitter, August 17, 2018. https://twitter.com/realdonaldtrump/status/1030416679069777921.

2018 United States Spencer Stuart Board Index. Chicago, IL: Spencer Stuart, 2018. www.spencerstuart.com/-/media/2019/july/ssbi_2018_new.pdf.

2019 Edelman Trust Barometer: Expectation for CEOs. Chicago, IL: Edelman, 2019. www.edelman.com/sites/g/files/aatuss191/files/2019-05/2019_Edelman_Trust_Barometer_CEO_Trust_Report.pdf.

UBS and PaineWebber. "UBS to Merge with PaineWebber." News release, July 12, 2000. www.sec.gov/Archives/edgar/data/75754/000095015700000328/0000950157-00-000328-0002.pdf.

The UK Corporate Governance Code. London: Financial Reporting Council Ltd., 2016. www.frc.org.uk/getattachment/ca7e94c4-b9a9-49e2-a824-ad76a322873c/UK-Corporate-Governance-Code-April-2016.pdf.

Ulukaya, Hamdi. "Chobani Founder: Higher Wages Important to Our Success." CNN Business, March 31, 2016. https://money.cnn.com/2016/03/31/news/economy/chobani-minimum-wage/index.html.

Umoh, Ruth. "Why Jeff Bezos Wants Amazon Employees to 'Wake Up Every Morning Terrified.'" CNBC *Make It*, August 28, 2018. www.cnbc.com/2018/08/28/why-jeff-bezos-wants-amazon-employees-to-wake-up-terrified.html.

UN Climate Change. "The Paris Agreement." https://unfccc.int/process-and-meetings/the-paris-agreement/the-paris-agreement.

UN Department of Economic and Social Affairs. "Growing at a Slower Pace, World Population Is Expected to Reach 9.7 Billion in 2050 and Could Peak at Nearly 11 Billion Around 2100." June 17, 2019. www.un.org/development/desa/en/news/population/world-population-prospects-2019.html.

UNESCO. "Women in Science." Fact Sheet No. 51, UNESCO Institute for Statistics, Montreal, Canada, June 2018. http://uis.unesco.org/sites/default/files/documents/fs51-women-in-science-2018-en.pdf.

UN Global Compact. "Global Compact Board Programme." www.unglobalcompact.org/take-action/action/gc-board-programme.

Union of Concerned Scientists. "Benefits of Renewable Energy Use." Last modified December 20, 2017. www.ucsusa.org/resources/benefits-renewable-energy-use.

United Nations. *The Corporate Responsibility to Respect Human Rights.* Geneva, Switzerland: UN Human Rights, 2012. www.ohchr.org/Documents /Publications/HR.PUB.12.2_En.pdf.

———. *Guiding Principles of Business and Human Rights.* Geneva, Switzerland: UN Human Rights, 2011. www.ohchr.org/Documents/Publications /GuidingPrinciplesBusinessHR_EN.pdf.

University of Hull. "How You Can Help Fight Modern-Day Slavery in the Food Industry." *Evening Standard*, December 7, 2018. www.standard.co.uk /lifestyle/how-you-can-help-fight-modernday-slavery-in-the-food-industry -a4010061.html.

US Census Bureau. "U.S. and World Population Clock." Accessed August 28, 2019. www.census.gov/popclock/.

US Securities and Exchange Commission. "Say-on-Pay Vote." Investor.gov. www.investor.gov/additional-resources/general-resources/glossary/say -pay-vote.

———. "SEC Charges Kmart's Former CEO and CFO with Financial Fraud." News release, August 23, 2005. www.sec.gov/news/press/2005-119.htm.

Valet, Vicky. "The World's Most Reputable CEOs 2019." *Forbes*, May 21, 2019. www.forbes.com/sites/vickyvalet/2019/05/21/the-worlds-most-reputable -ceos-2019/#790adf704e7a.

VandeHei, Jim, and Mike Allen. "United States of Corporate America." *Axios*, February 25, 2018. www.axios.com/united-states-of-corporate-america -1519568415-7abd95d5-ab22-43c1-a9f6-a5151c83b4fa.html.

Van Zadelhoff, Marc. "The Biggest Cybersecurity Threats Are Inside Your Company." *Harvard Business Review*, September 19, 2016. https://hbr .org/2016/09/the-biggest-cybersecurity-threats-are-inside-your-company.

Verily. "Privacy Policy." Last modified January 1, 2020. https://verily.com /privacy-policy/.

Verizon. "Verizon Innovative Learning." www.verizon.com/about/responsibility /verizon-innovative-learning.

Verret, J. W. "Providing Retail Investors a Voice in the Proxy Process." *Harvard Law School Forum on Corporate Governance*, April 25, 2019. https://corpgov.law.harvard.edu/2019/04/25/providing-retail-investors -a-voice-in-the-proxy-process/.

Vinnicombe, Susan, Doyin Atewologun, and Valentina Battista. *The Female FTSE Board Report 2019.* Cranfield, UK: Cranfield University, 2019.

Vlasic, Bill, and Nick Bunkley. "Hazardous Conditions for the Auto Industry." *New York Times*, October 1, 2008. www.nytimes.com/2008/10/02/business /02sales.html.

Waddell, Kaveh. "Why Google Quit China—and Why It's Heading Back." *The Atlantic*, January 19, 2016. www.theatlantic.com/technology/archive /2016/01/why-google-quit-china-and-why-its-heading-back/424482/.

Wakabayashi, Daisuke, and Scott Shane. "Google Will Not Renew Pentagon Contract That Upset Employees." *New York Times*, June 1, 2018. www .nytimes.com/2018/06/01/technology/google-pentagon-project-maven.html.

Walker, Owen. "Big Investors Demand Greater Non-financial Reporting Disclosure." *Financial Times*, November 16, 2018. www.ft.com/content/289f 7b1e-b004-3a97-85ce-8a695de4de92.

Walker, Steve. Letter to Dambisa Moyo on board effectiveness. May 9, 2018.

Walsh, Dominic. "Same Old Story from the Boardroom as Average Age of Directors Exceeds 60." *The Times*, December 19, 2017. www.thetimes.co.uk /article/same-old-story-from-the-boardroom-as-average-age-of-directors -exceeds-60-jb6s0x3dn.

Ward, Tom. "This Is the Most Efficient Solar Panel Ever Made." World Economic Forum, August 15, 2017. www.weforum.org/agenda/2017/08/this-is -the-most-efficient-solar-panel-ever-made.

Warren, Elizabeth. "Companies Shouldn't Be Accountable Only to Shareholders." *Wall Street Journal*, August 14, 2018. www.wsj.com/articles /companies-shouldnt-be-accountable-only-to-shareholders-1534287687.

Washington STEM. https://washingtonstem.org.

Watson, Richard. "Why Companies Die." LinkedIn, June 21, 2016. www.linkedin .com/pulse/why-companies-die-richard-watson.

Watt, Nicholas. "David Cameron in Contact with AstraZeneca over Pfizer Takeover Bid." *The Guardian*, May 2, 2014. www.theguardian.com/business /2014/may/02/david-cameron-contact-astrazeneca-pfizer-takeover-bid.

The Weight of America's Boards: Ranking America's Largest Corporations by the Governance Capacity of Their Boards. Chicago: James Drury Partners, 2018.

Weiner, Perrie M., and Robert D. Weber. "Shareholder Activism Is Good." *Financier Worldwide*, August 2015. www.financierworldwide.com/shareholder -activism-is-good#.XVxBCS2ZPOR.

What You Need to Know About the BRICS New Development Bank. Washington, DC: Coalition for Human Rights on Development, 2015. http://rights indevelopment.org/wp-content/uploads/2015/08/BRICS-NDB-Factsheet -Final-1.pdf.

Whieldon, Esther. "Moody's: PG&E Bankruptcy Comes with Broader ESG Implications." S&P Global Market Intelligence, March 1, 2019. www .spglobal.com/marketintelligence/en/news-insights/trending/KXP7vs7 tdacslfBBLenKpA2.

Wiggins, Rosalind Z., Thomas Piontek, and Andrew Metrick. "The Lehman Brothers Bankruptcy A: Overview." Yale Program on Financial Stability Case Study 2014-3A-V1, Yale School of Management, New Haven, CT,

October 2014. https://som.yale.edu/sites/default/files/files/001-2014-3A-V1
-LehmanBrothers-A-REVA.pdf.

Williamson, John. "The Washington Consensus as Policy Prescription for Development." Lecture delivered at the Institute for International Economics, World Bank, Washington, DC, January 13, 2004.

Wilshire. "Wilshire 5000 Total Market Index." December 31, 2016. https://wilshire.com/Portals/0/analytics/indexes/membership/wilshire-5000-index-membership.pdf.

Wolfers, Justin. "Fewer Women Run Big Companies Than Men Named John." *New York Times*, March 2, 2015. www.nytimes.com/2015/03/03/upshot/fewer-women-run-big-companies-than-men-named-john.html.

Women in the Workplace 2018. New York: McKinsey & Company and Lean In, 2018. https://wiw-report.s3.amazonaws.com/Women_in_the_Workplace_2018.pdf.

Wong, Julia Carrie. "Former Yahoo Employee Accuses Company of Gender Bias—Against Men." *The Guardian*, February 3, 2016. www.theguardian.com/technology/2016/feb/02/gender-discrimination-lawsuit-male-former-employee-yahoo-marissa-mayer.

———. "Google Staff Condemn Treatment of Temp Workers in 'Historic' Show of Solidarity." *The Guardian*, April 2, 2019. www.theguardian.com/technology/2019/apr/02/google-workers-sign-letter-temp-contractors-protest.

World Economic Forum (@worldeconomicforum). "Parental parity. #japan #korea #portugal #paternity #gender @unicef." Instagram, June 19, 2019. www.instagram.com/p/By4qwPHgr6b/?igshid=9qaoz90yfzuy.

World Health Organization. "Obesity and Overweight." February 16, 2018. www.who.int/news-room/fact-sheets/detail/obesity-and-overweight.

Worstall, Tim. "The Story of Henry Ford's $5 a Day Wages: It's Not What You Think." *Forbes*, March 4, 2012. www.forbes.com/sites/timworstall/2012/03/04/the-story-of-henry-fords-5-a-day-wages-its-not-what-you-think/#28025d8e766d.

Wu, Tim. "The Oligopoly Problem." *New Yorker*, April 15, 2013. www.newyorker.com/tech/annals-of-technology/the-oligopoly-problem.

Wursthorn, Michael, and Thomas Gryta. "GE Drops Out of the Dow After More Than a Century." *Wall Street Journal*, June 19, 2018. www.wsj.com/articles/walgreens-to-replace-ge-in-dow-industrials-1529443336.

Wursthorn, Michael, and Gregory Zuckerman. "Fewer Listed Companies: Is That Good or Bad for Stock Markets?" *Wall Street Journal*, January 4, 2018. www.wsj.com/articles/fewer-listed-companies-is-that-good-or-bad-for-stock-markets-1515100040.

Xinhua. "China Becomes World's Second-Largest Source of Outward FDI: Report." Xinhuanet, June 8, 2017. www.xinhuanet.com/english/2017-06/08/c_136350164.htm.

Zalis, Shelley. "Men Should Take Parental Leave—Here's Why." *Forbes*, May 3, 2018. www.forbes.com/sites/shelleyzalis/2018/05/03/why-mandatory-parental-leave-is-good-for-business/.

Ziegler, Chris. "Nokia CEO Stephen Elop Rallies Troops in Brutally Honest 'Burning Platform' Memo? (Update: It's Real!)" *Engadget*, February 8, 2011. www.engadget.com/2011/02/08/nokia-ceo-stephen-elop-rallies-troops-in-brutally-honest-burnin.

Zillman, Claire. "The EU Is Taking a Drastic Step to Put More Women on Corporate Boards." *Fortune*, November 20, 2017. https://fortune.com/2017/11/20/women-on-boards-eu-gender-quota/.

———. "These Are the 12 Fortune 500 Companies with Zero Women on Their Boards." *Fortune*, May 22, 2018. https://fortune.com/2018/05/22/fortune-500-companies-women-boards/.

———. "Why Female CEOs Are Outnumbered by Jeffreys: Broadsheet for June 28." *Fortune*, June 28, 2019. https://fortune.com/2019/06/28/female-ceos-outnumbered/.

Zillman, Claire, and Erika Fry. "HR Is Not Your Friend. Here's Why." *Fortune*, February 16, 2018. https://fortune.com/2018/02/16/microsoft-hr-problem-metoo/.

Zillman, Claire, and Emma Hinchliffe. "Google Forced Arbitration, RBG Hospitalized, Lucy McBath: Broadsheet November 9." *Fortune*, November 9, 2018. https://fortune.com/2018/11/09/google-forced-arbitration-rbg-hospitalized-lucy-mcbath-broadsheet-november-9/.

———. "Netflix Abortion Georgia, Angela Merkel, 2019 IPOs: Broadsheet May 29." *Fortune*, May 29, 2019. https://fortune.com/2019/05/29/netflix-abortion-georgia-angela-merkel-2019-ipos-broadsheet-may-29/.

———. "A VC Community Introduces a Gender Quota: The Broadsheet." *Fortune*, July 12, 2019. https://fortune.com/2019/07/12/a-vc-community-introduces-a-gender-quota-the-broadsheet/.

Zuboff, Shoshana. *The Age of Surveillance Capitalism: The Fight for a Human Future at the New Frontier of Power*. London: Profile Books, 2019.

Index

DAMBISA MOYO is a prize-winning economist. The author of the *New York Times* bestseller *Edge of Chaos: Why Democracy Is Failing to Deliver Economic Growth—and How to Fix It*, she was named one of the "100 Most Influential People in the World" by *Time* magazine. Moyo is a regular contributor to the *Wall Street Journal* and *Financial Times*. She lives in New York City and London.